THE KINGFISHER
Illustrated
Pocket
Thesaurus

GEORGE BEAL

D0003179

Kingfisher
NEW YORK

KINGFISHER
Larousse Kingfisher Chambers Inc.
95 Madison Avenue
New York, New York 10016

First edition in paperback 1996
4 6 8 10 9 7 5 3

LIBRARY OF CONGRESS CATALOGING-IN-PUBLICATION DATA
Beal, George,
The Kingfisher pocket thesaurus / George Beal.—1st ed.
p. cm.
Summary: An illustrated alphabetical thesaurus with a supplement
containing spelling tips and hints on word usage.
1. English language—Synonyms and antonyms.
[1. English language—Synonyms and antonyms.] I. Title.
PE1591.B39 1996
423'.—dc20 96-64 CIP AC

ISBN 1-85697-673-4

Editors: John Grisewood,
John Bollard

Illustrations: David Ashby (Garden Studio),
Julian Baker, Julie Banyard, Ian Howatson, Mark Iley,
Josephine Martin (Garden Studio),
John Marshall, Clive Spong (Linden Artists)

DTP operators: Tracey McNerney, Primrose Burton

Printed in Hong Kong

Introduction

This book is called a thesaurus, which is a Latin word of Greek origin, meaning "a treasury or storehouse of information," particularly when it deals with words and collections of words. If you examine what this book contains you will see that is exactly what it is: a collection of words. It is a kind of dictionary, with a list of words in alphabetical order.

Instead of simply giving the *meaning* of a word, it tells you of other words that have a *similar* meaning. Suppose you began a letter to a friend with the sentence *I hope you have a nice time on your vacation.* The word *nice* sounds dull in this case. If you look up the word *nice* in this thesaurus, you will find that it gives you a short list of words that you could use instead: *pleasant, agreeable, amiable, charming, delightful.* Such words are known as **synonyms**. The word *nice* also has another meaning, which is quite different: *precise, accurate, fine, subtle.*

To go back to our letter, you could now write *I hope you have a **pleasant** time on your vacation.* Your friend could write back to you and tell you that *I am having a **delightful** time on my vacation!* As you can see, the thesaurus helps you to write in a better style, and to use words other than the very ordinary, perhaps even boring ones.

In addition to giving these alternative words, this thesaurus also shows you *opposite* words. In the case of *nice*, you will find the opposite word *nasty*. These opposite words are called **antonyms**. In many cases, there are cross-references to other words of similar meaning which are found elsewhere in the book. Below is a key to show you how to find the various words and their meaning.

Parts of speech: *adj.* = adjective; *adv.* = adverb; *conj.* = conjunction; *n.* = noun; *prep.* = preposition; *v.* = verb

Opposite words: These are shown with a star (★) and in ★**bold type.**

Cross-reference to other meanings: If a word is shown with an arrow ▷ and in *italics*, it means that you can look up that word to find further, similar meanings. For example, if you look up the word *ruffian*, you find, at the end of the list, the word ▷ *rascal.* So, if you look under *rascal* you will find other, similar words.

A **homonym** is a word that sounds the same as another, but means something quite different.Such words are shown in small capitals, like this: HERE.

If a word has a number of different meanings, each different meaning is shown by a figure in a circle: ①, ②, ③.

George Beal

A a

abandon *v.* forsake, give up, leave in the lurch, surrender, sacrifice ▷ *leave, quit*

abate *v.* lessen, slacken, dwindle, fade

abbey *n.* monastery, priory, cloister, church

abbreviate *v.* shorten, cut, contract, reduce ▷ *abridge* ★**expand**

abdicate *v.* resign, retire, renounce ▷ *quit*

ability *n.* aptitude, knack, flair, talent, gift, skill ★**inability**

able *adj.* skillful, competent, talented, strong ▷ *clever* ★**incapable**

abnormal *adj.* unusual, exceptional, erratic ★**normal**

abode *n.* home, residence, haunt, dwelling, lodging

abolish *v.* destroy, cancel, do away with, exterminate ★**restore**

abominable *adj.* detestable, foul, hateful, horrible, loathsome, atrocious ▷ *awful* ★**desirable**

about *prep. & adv.* near, nearly, touching, concerning, around

above *prep. & adv.* over, beyond, exceeding, on high, aloft ★**below**

abridge *v.* condense, compact ▷ *abbreviate*

abroad *adv.* overseas, far, away, apart, adrift ★**home**

abrupt *adj.* ① sudden, curt, blunt, brusque ② steep, hilly ★**smooth**

absent *adj.* not present, away, elsewhere, missing ★**present**

absent-minded *adj.* distracted, heedless, forgetful ★**attentive**

absolute *adj.* perfect, complete, certain, positive ▷ *utter* ★**imperfect**

absorb *v.* take in, soak up, assimilate, devour, pull in, swallow, consume ★**emit**

absorbed *adj.* intent, rapt, engrossed, preoccupied

abstain *adj.* refuse, refrain, give up, keep from, avoid, forbear ★**indulge**

abstract ① *adj.* theoretical, intangible ② *v.* withdraw, steal, remove, take away

absurd *adj.* preposterous, nonsensical, foolish ▷ *silly* ★**sensible**

abundant *adj.* ample, profuse, rich, plentiful, overflowing ★**scarce**

abuse ① *v.* damage, injure, spoil, maltreat, hurt, misuse ★**protect** ② *n.* mistreatment, attack

accelerate *v.* speed up, hasten, quicken, urge ▷ *hurry* ★**delay**

accent *n.* ① stress, beat, rhythm, emphasis ② dialect, brogue *Eileen speaks with an Irish brogue,* drawl, pronunciation

accept *v.* receive, take, admit, adopt, take on ★**refuse**

accident *n.* chance, casualty, disaster, calamity, mishap ★**purpose**

acclaim *v.* applaud, praise, approve ★**denounce**

accommodate *v.* oblige, lodge, receive, admit, adapt ★**deprive**

accompany *v.* be with, go with, escort, attend, convoy ★**abandon**

accomplice *n.* ally, confederate, helper, partner, conspirator

accomplish *v.* perform, fulfill, finish, complete ▷ *achieve* ★**fail**

accord ① *v.* agree, consent, harmonize, allow ★ **differ** ② *n.* agreement, harmony

account *n.* ① bill, invoice, record, score ② tale, story *Mary told us the story of her trip to Washington,* narrative, history

accumulate *v.* collect, grow, gather, hoard, increase, amass ★**scatter**

accurate *adj.* careful, exact, faithful, precise ▷ *correct* ★**defective**

accuse *v.* charge, incriminate, taunt, denounce ★**defend**

accustom *v.* acclimatize, get used to, familiarize ★**estrange**

ache ① *n.* pain, twinge ② *v.* hurt, pain, sting, smart

achieve *v.* fulfill, accomplish, reach ▷ *attain* ★**fail**

achievement *n.* accomplishment, attainment, exploit, deed, completion ▷ *feat*

acid *adj.* sharp, vinegarish, acrid, sour, tart ★**sweet, mellow**

acknowledge *v.* admit, avow, recognize, own, accept, yield ★**disclaim**

acquaint *v.* inform, tell, teach, notify, advise ★ **deceive**

acquaintance *n.* ① friend, pal, associate ② knowledge *You will need some knowledge of Spanish if you visit Mexico,* familiarity, experience

acquainted *adj.* aware, familiar, informed

acquire *v.* gain, earn, obtain, get, capture ★**forfeit, lose**

acquit *v.* discharge, release, exonerate, dismiss, liberate ★**accuse**

acrid *adj.* bitter, harsh, sour ▷*acid* ★**mellow**

across *adj. & prep.* crosswise, athwart, slantingly, over against ★**along**

act ① *n.* deed, performance, action, step, presentation ② *v.* operate, work, function, perform *Our class will perform a play by Ibsen*

action *n.* operation, movement, feat, deed, exercise ★**rest**

actual *adj.* correct, true, positive, certain ★**possible**

acute *adj.* sharp, pointed, keen, penetrating, severe, distressing ★**blunt**

adapt *v.* fit, adjust, accommodate, suit, conform

adaptable *adj.* flexible, usable, adjustable

add *v.* ① total, combine, tote up ★**subtract** ② affix, annex, connect ★**detach**

address ① *n.* residence, place, home, domicile ② *v.* talk to, speak to, accost, call

adept *adj.* expert, adroit, handy, skillful ▷*clever* ★**clumsy**

adequate *adj.* ① sufficient, ample *The boat was small, but there was ample room for two,* plenty ② equal, able, qualified

adjacent *adj.* near, neighboring, next, bordering, touching ★**separate**

adjoin *v.* border, touch, verge, annex

adjust *v.* ① regulate, rectify, correct, amend, revise ② get used to *Our puppy quickly got used to her new home*

administer *v.* ① execute, perform, carry out, conduct, direct, manage ② give, dole out *The nurse doled out the pills each morning*

admirable *adj.* praiseworthy, commendable, excellent ★**despicable**

admiration *n.* adoration, affection, approval, delight, respect ★**contempt**

admire *v.* approve, esteem, appreciate ▷*respect* ★**despise**

admit *v.* ① pass, permit, grant, concede, allow, let in, acknowledge ② confess, own up ★**deny**

ado *n.* hubbub, commotion, fuss *Let's start the meeting without any more fuss,* excitement

adopt *v.* assume, select, choose, employ, apply, take over

adore *v.* worship, idolize, admire, revere, venerate ★**despise**

adorn *v.* beautify, decorate, embellish, deck, garnish ★**deface**

adrift *adv.* loose, afloat, floating, distracted

adroit *adj.* handy, skillful, dexterous, expert ▷*adept* ★**awkward**

adult *adj.* grown-up, mature, full-grown ★**immature**

advance *v.* ① progress, increase, further, go,

Adequate

The boat was small, but there was ample room for two.

go on, proceed ★**retreat** ② lend *Helen said she will lend me the money,* loan

advanced *adj.* beforehand, ahead, modern

advantage *n.* benefit, upper hand, opportunity, assistance, boon ★**hindrance**

adventure *n.* experience, escapade, venture, undertaking

adversary *n.* foe, opponent, antagonist, rival ▷*enemy* ★**ally**

adverse *adj.* unfavorable, hard, hostile, unfortunate ▷*unlucky* ★**fortunate**

advice *n.* counsel, suggestion, guidance

advise *v.* counsel, urge, suggest, prompt, inform, persuade ★**deter**

afar *adv.* far, far off, away, abroad ★**near**

affable *adj.* courteous, gracious, easy, frank, open ★**haughty**

affair *n.* ① matter, business, concern ② romance, liaison

affect *v.* ① assume, adopt, feign, sham, put on airs ② influence, change, sway *Your argument did not sway my opinion*

affection *n.* desire, fondness, feeling, kindness, liking ▷*love* ★**indifference**

affectionate *adj.* warmhearted, fond, loving ▷*tender* ★**indifferent**

affirm *v.* assert, state, declare, endorse, maintain ★**deny**

affix *v.* attach, fasten, unite, append ★**detach**

afflict *v.* trouble, ail, distress, upset

afford *v.* ① be wealthy, be rich ② produce, provide *The stream provided good, clean water,* yield, bear ★**deny**

afraid *adj.* timid, cautious, frightened, alarmed ▷*fearful* ★**fearless**

after *prep.* behind, later, following, succeeding ★**before**

again *adv.* ① frequently, repeatedly, anew, afresh ② furthermore, moreover

against *prep.* opposite, over, opposing, resisting ★**for**

age ① *n.* period, date, time ② *n.* old age, senility ★**youth** ③ *v.* grow old, mature

aged *adj.* ancient, antiquated ▷*old* ★**youthful**

agent *n.* doer, actor, performer, operator,

Aircraft

Hot air balloon

Microlight

Seaplane

worker, representative

aggravate *v.* ① increase, make worse, worsen ★**mitigate** ② irritate, annoy

aggressive *adj.* offensive, warlike, military, pushy ★**peaceful**

aghast *adj.* astonished, dumbfounded, bewildered ★**calm**

agile *adj.* nimble, active, fleet, brisk, alert ▷*lithe* ★**clumsy**

agitate *v.* disturb, trouble, excite, stir, fluster ★**smooth**

ago *adv.* past, gone, since ★**hence**

agony *n.* torture, torment, distress, pangs

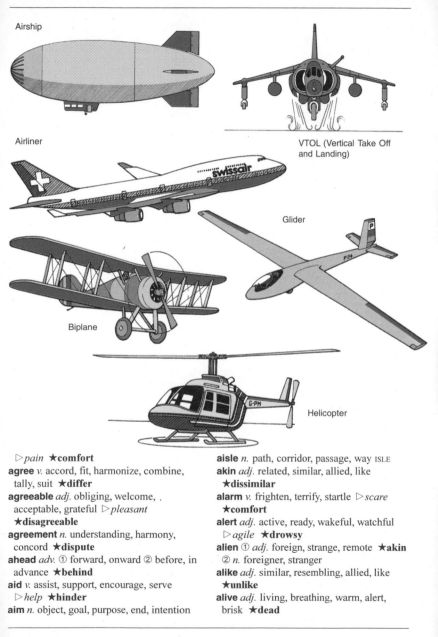

Airship

Airliner

VTOL (Vertical Take Off and Landing)

Glider

Biplane

Helicopter

▷ *pain* ★**comfort**

agree *v.* accord, fit, harmonize, combine, tally, suit ★**differ**

agreeable *adj.* obliging, welcome, acceptable, grateful ▷ *pleasant* ★**disagreeable**

agreement *n.* understanding, harmony, concord ★**dispute**

ahead *adv.* ① forward, onward ② before, in advance ★**behind**

aid *v.* assist, support, encourage, serve ▷ *help* ★**hinder**

aim *n.* object, goal, purpose, end, intention

aisle *n.* path, corridor, passage, way ISLE

akin *adj.* related, similar, allied, like ★**dissimilar**

alarm *v.* frighten, terrify, startle ▷ *scare* ★**comfort**

alert *adj.* active, ready, wakeful, watchful ▷ *agile* ★**drowsy**

alien ① *adj.* foreign, strange, remote ★**akin** ② *n.* foreigner, stranger

alike *adj.* similar, resembling, allied, like ★**unlike**

alive *adj.* living, breathing, warm, alert, brisk ★**dead**

all *adj.* whole, entire, complete, total ★**none**

allot *v.* apportion, give, allocate, dispense, grant ★**retain**

allow *v.* grant, permit, concede, owe, tolerate, entitle ★**forbid**

ally *n.* friend, companion, supporter, accomplice, colleague ★**foe**

almost *adj.* nearly, about, approximately, well-nigh

alone *adj.* lone, lonely, lonesome, forlorn ★**together**

aloud *adv.* loudly, noisily, clamorously, audibly ★**silently** ALLOWED

already *adv.* at this time, now, just now, previously

alter *v.* modify, vary, convert, transform ▷*change* ★**retain** ALTAR

altogether *adv.* completely, wholly, outright, totally ★**partially**

always *adv.* ever, forever, eternally ★**never**

amass *v.* collect, accumulate, heap, pile ★**scatter**

amaze *v.* astound, surprise, stun, dumbfound ▷*astonish*

ambition *n.* aspiration, desire, longing, zeal, aim ▷*goal*

amend *v.* revise, mend, correct, repair, improve ▷*alter*

amiable *adj.* affable, kindly, pleasant, amicable ▷*agreeable* ★**unfriendly**

amount *n.* figure, volume, sum, number, total

ample *adj.* bountiful, liberal, sufficient, plentiful ▷*abundant* ★**insufficient**

amplify *v.* increase, raise, enlarge, elaborate *Our teacher explained the problem and went on to elaborate on the details,* make louder ★**abbreviate**

amuse *v.* entertain, charm, beguile, please ★**bore**

ancestor *n.* forebear, parent, forefather, antecedent, predecessor

ancient *adj.* aged, antique, primeval, time-honored ▷*old* ★**modern**

anger *n.* wrath, ire, resentment, indignation, fury ▷*rage*

angry *adj.* wrathful, irate, resentful, furious, infuriated, indignant ★**good-tempered**

angle *n.* ① corner, bend, fork, branch ② aspect, phase, point of view *We quarreled at first, but then I saw Tom's point of view*

anguish *n.* torment, torture, pain ▷*agony* ★**ease**

announce *v.* broadcast, declare, propound,

Alphabets

Arabic

Hebrew

Cyrillic (Russian)

Thai

Egyptian hieroglyphs

Latin

Sanskrit

Japanese

Greek

Runes

reveal, herald ▷*proclaim* ★**conceal**

annoy *v.* tease, vex, irritate, disturb, harass ▷*upset* ★**soothe**

answer *n.* reply, response, solution *It was a difficult puzzle, but Emma came up with the solution* ★**question**

anticipate *v.* expect, prepare, hope for, foresee, predict

anxious *adj.* fearful, afraid, apprehensive, worried ★**carefree**

apart *adv.* away, separately, asunder, loosely ★**together**

aperture *n.* slit, hole, orifice, opening, cleft

apologize *v.* express regret, excuse, explain, plead, atone ★**insult**

apparel *n.* clothes, robes, vestments, raiment, trappings, attire

apparent *adj.* plain, conspicuous, unmistakable, clear ▷*obvious* ★**obscure**

appeal *v.* address, request, urge, entreat, invite, ask ▷*attract*

appear *v.* emerge, become visible, seem, look, come into view ★**disappear**

appearance *n.* aspect, look, shape, form, impression, likeness

appease *v.* pacify, moderate, satisfy, stay, soften ★**provoke**

appetite *n.* hunger, palate, relish, liking

applaud *v.* clap, cheer, praise, approve, encourage ★**denounce**

apply *v.* ① use, appropriate, employ ② devote, direct, dedicate *Sue was dedicated to her job and worked very hard*

appoint *v.* name, assign, nominate, engage

appreciate *v.* esteem, recognize, respect, value, enjoy

appropriate ① *v.* use, employ, adopt ② *adj.* fitting, proper *To do a job well, you should use the proper tools*, timely

approve *v.* acclaim, admire, appreciate, favor, agree ★**disapprove**

approximate *adj.* near, close, rough

apt *adj.* ① fit, clever, liable, likely ★**unfitted** ② liable, prone, inclined *Jack and Meg are both inclined to be late, so we'll wait a while*

ardent *adj.* passionate, warm, eager, fervent,

Apes

Gorilla

Gibbon

Orangutan

Chimpanzee

intense, dedicated ★**indifferent**

arduous *adj.* hard, laborious, tough, strenuous ▷*difficult* ★**easy**

area *n.* district, region, place, expanse, tract

argue *v.* ① discuss, debate, talk over ② quibble, quarrel, disagree

arid *adj.* parched, sterile ▷*dry* ★**moist**

arise *v.* ① awaken, get up ② begin, come into existence, originate, crop up, take place

army *n.* troops, legion, force, soldiery

around *adv.* about, encircling, on every side ★**within**

arouse *v.* awaken, excite, disturb, alarm ★**pacify**

arrange *v.* sort, order, dispose, deal, classify ★**confuse**

arrest *v.* seize, take prisoner, hold, detain, stop ★**release**

arrive *v.* reach, attain, land, get to, appear ★**depart**

arrogant *adj.* supercilious, proud, haughty, conceited, disdainful ★**modest**

art *n.* skill, artistry, cleverness, talent

artful *adj.* cunning, knowing, crafty, wily, sly ★**innocent**

article *n.* ① thing, object, substance ② essay, treatise, typescript

artificial *adj.* invented, fictitious, fabricated, synthetic ★**real**

ascend *v.* climb, rise, go up, get up, move up, scale, mount ★**descend**

ashamed *adj.* shamefaced, abashed, confused ★**proud**

ask *v.* demand, query, inquire, appeal ▷*request* ★**answer**

aspect *n.* front, face, side, appearance, presentation, look, expression

aspire *v.* wish, long, desire, aim, hope, crave

ass *n.* ① donkey, mule ② fool, dunce, idiot, jerk, dolt

assault *v.* attack, assail, set upon, charge, invade ★**defend**

assemble *v.* meet, gather, convene, come together, muster, collect ★**disperse**

assent *v.* agree, comply, accept, consent ★**dissent**

assert *v.* pronounce, maintain, state, aver ▷*declare* ★**deny**

assess *v.* estimate, evaluate, appraise

assign *v.* appoint, name, apportion, entrust

assist *v.* aid, support, protect, maintain, sustain ▷*help* ★**obstruct**

association *n.* union, connection, companionship, society, company, club

assortment *n.* variety, kind, sort, batch, parcel, collection

assume *v.* ① believe, accept, suppose, admit ② confiscate, take, possess oneself of

assure *v.* promise, guarantee, warrant, encourage ★**deter**

astonish *v.* startle, surprise, confound, alarm, scare ▷*amaze*

astound *v.* stagger, stupefy ▷*astonish*

astray *adj.* lost, gone, vanished, missing, loose ★**safe**

astute *adj.* shrewd, brainy, knowing, sharp, acute, crafty ★**simple**

atrocious *adj.* monstrous, enormous, shameful, cruel, abominable, vile

attach *v.* fasten, append, unite, tie ▷*connect* ★**unfasten**

attack *v.* assault, invade, set upon, pounce, descend upon ★**defend**

attain *v.* extend, master, obtain, acquire, grasp ▷*reach* ★**fail**

attempt *v.* endeavor, strive, seek, tackle ▷*try* ★**abandon**

attend *v.* ① listen, heed, notice, observe, follow ★**disregard** ② be present

attentive *adj.* mindful, particular, heedful, observant ★**careless**

attire *n.* costume, robes, clothes, garments ▷*apparel*

attitude *n.* disposition, bearing, outlook, posture, position, aspect

attract *v.* ① draw, influence, tempt, prompt, pull, drag ② fascinate, enchant, captivate ★**repel**

attractive *adj.* agreeable, beautiful, handsome, pretty, tempting ★**repellent**

avail *n.* benefit, advantage, use, help, profit

available *adj.* convenient, handy, ready, attainable, accessible

avenge *v.* retaliate, revenge, pay back ★**pardon**

average *adj.* usual, ordinary, mediocre, so-so, normal, standard ★**extreme**

avid *adj.* eager, greedy, grasping

avoid *v.* shun, elude, quit, keep clear of, evade ▷*dodge* ★**seek**

awake *v.* wake, rouse, arouse, awaken, stir

award *v.* reward, give, bestow, grant, donate ★**withdraw**

aware *adj.* conscious, sensible, informed, assured ★**unaware**

away *adv.* absent, not present, afar, elsewhere ★**near**

awe *n.* fear, dread, shock, consternation, wonder

awful *adj.* fearful, terrible, alarming, dreadful ★**commonplace** OFFAL

awkward *adj.* ungainly, unwieldy, uncouth, clownish, gawky ▷*clumsy* ★**dexterous**

awry *adj.* crooked, askew, amiss, twisted, wrong ★**straight**

B b

babble *v.* prattle, blab, cackle, chatter, gossip

baby *n.* babe, infant, child, toddler, tot

back ① *adj.* after, rear, hind, posterior ★**front** ② *v.* uphold, support *The party will support Tina Johnson at the next election,* endorse, be loyal to

backer *n.* supporter, ally, champion

backward *adj.* slow, shy, reluctant, unwilling, retarded ▷*dull* ★**forward**

bad *adj.* ① imperfect, dreadful, unsound, awful, atrocious ② naughty, wrong, wicked, ill-behaved ③ rotten *This barrel is full of rotten apples,* spoiled ★**good**

badge *n.* emblem, hallmark, symbol, crest

badger *v.* bother, annoy, nag ▷*pester*

bad-mannered *adj.* impolite, boorish, uncivil ▷*rude* ★**polite**

baffle *v.* puzzle, perplex, frustrate, bewilder, mystify ▷*puzzle*

bag *n.* net, sack, pouch, purse, backpack

bail *v.* scoop, ladle, dip

bait ① *v.* tease, bother, goad, rib, needle ▷*pester* ② *n.* decoy, lure, snare BATE

bake *v.* cook, roast, harden, fire

balance *v.* weigh, adjust, equalize, compare

bald *adj.* hairless, severe, stark, bare, unadorned

balk *v.* hinder, baffle, thwart, obstruct, foil ★**aid**

ball *n.* ① dance, masquerade ② globe, orb, sphere

ballad *n.* song, serenade, ditty

ballot *n.* vote, election, franchise, poll

ban *v.* prohibit, forbid, deny, stop

band *n.* ① stripe, strip, zone, belt ② orchestra, ensemble, group BANNED

bandit *n.* outlaw, robber, highwayman, thief, crook

bang *v.* crash, slam, smash, collide

banish *v.* expel, eject, exclude, exile, deport, cast out ▷*dismiss* ★**welcome**

bank *n.* ① shore, ledge, terrace, coast, embankment ② safe, vault, treasury

banner *n.* ensign, standard, streamer ▷*flag*

banquet *n.* meal, feast, repast

banter *v.* chaff, tease, ridicule, joke

bar *v.* ① obstruct, block, blockade, forbid, shut out ② fasten, bolt, lock, latch

bare *adj.* ① barren, empty, void ② naked, unclothed, severe, blunt *We expected a polite reply, but got a blunt refusal,* bald BEAR

barely *adv.* hardly, scarcely *The well had run dry, and there was scarcely enough water for all of us,* just, simply

bargain ① *n.* pact, deal ② *adj.* low-priced, cheap

bark *n.* ① rind, husk, peel ② yelp, growl, cry

barrel *n.* cask, keg, drum, tub, cylinder

barren *adj.* bare, unfertile, empty ▷*arid* ★**fertile** BARON

barrier *n.* obstruction, obstacle, block, fence

barter *v.* swap, exchange, trade

base ① *adj.* low, sordid, cheap, corrupt ② *adj.* dishonorable, vile ③ *adj.* humble, menial ④ *n.* bottom, foundation ⑤ *v.* found *The book* Robinson Crusoe *was founded on a true story* BASS

Band

Banned

bashful *adj.* shy, timid, modest, coy ★**bold**

basin *n.* bowl, pot, sink, tub

batch *n.* lot, amount, assortment, collection

batter *v.* beat, strike, shatter, break, smash

battle *v.* clash, combat, fight, struggle, wrestle

bawl *v.* shout, yell, roar, bellow ★**whisper**

bay ① *n.* inlet, gulf, basin, bight ② *v.* bark, yelp BEY

be *v.* exist, live, breathe

beach *n.* shore, sands, seaside, strand BEECH

beacon *n.* signal, lamp, light, guide

beak *n.* snout, bill, nose

beam *n.* ① ray, light, streak ② plank, joist, girder

bear *v.* ① tolerate, put up with, endure, suffer ★**protest** ② bring, fetch, carry BARE

bearing *n.* manner, behavior, appearance, attitude, posture *He was a tall man with a military bearing* BARING

bearings *n.* direction, whereabouts, location *In the storm we totally lost our bearings*

beat *v.* ① strike, pound, thrash ▷*batter* ② throb, flutter, thump *My heart thumped when I heard the sound of shouting in the street* BEET

beautiful *adj.* handsome, lovely, graceful, delicate, gorgeous ▷*pretty* ★**ugly**

beauty *n.* elegance, charm, loveliness, grace ★**ugliness**

because ① *conj.* for, owing to, by reason of, since *Since Tom and Jane are here, I will stay too,* as ② *adv.* consequently

beckon *v.* signal, call, nod, summon

becoming *adj.* graceful, suitable, comely, fitting, attractive

before ① *prep.* ahead, in front of, forward, preceding ② *adv.* earlier *Here is a pie that I baked earlier,* previously ★**after**

beg *v.* ask, request, entreat, beseech, plead, pray

begin *v.* commence, initiate, found, launch ▷*start* ★**end**

beginner *n.* novice, recruit, learner, pupil

beginning *n.* start, opening, origin, outset, foundation ★**end**

behavior *n.* conduct, demeanor, manners

Bell

Handbell

Belfry
Bell tower
Bicycle bell
Church bell
Doorbell
Gong

▷*bearing* ★**misbehavior**

behind ① *prep.* after, following *Bill arrived to meet us, with his dog following* ② *adv.* in the rear of, later, afterward ★**before**

being *n.* creature, animal

belief *n.* faith, confidence, opinion, trust ★**disbelief**

believe *v.* trust, assent, have faith in, think, suspect ★**disbelieve**

bellow *v.* roar, shout, cry ▷*bawl*

belong *v.* relate to, pertain, be owned by

below *adv.* under, beneath, underneath ★**above**

belt *n.* strap, sash, girdle, strip

bend *v.* curve, incline, turn, yield, relax ★**straighten**

benefit *n.* advantage, profit, good, favor, aid, blessing ★**disadvantage**

beside *adv.* alongside, side by side, next to, abreast, together ★**apart**

besides *adv.* in addition, furthermore, also, moreover

best *adj.* choice, prime, unequaled, finest ★**worst**

bestow *v.* award, donate, confer, present ★**deprive**

betray *v.* deceive, dupe, expose, unmask, inform on ★**protect**

better *adj.* superior, finer, preferable *I think it would be preferable to visit the museum this afternoon instead of this morning* ★**worse**

between *prep.* amid, among, betwixt

beware *v.* be careful, refrain from, heed,

avoid, mind

bewilder *v.* confound, dazzle, mystify, confuse ▷*astonish* ★**enlighten**

beyond *adv.* over, farther, past, more, after ★**near**

bicker *v.* quarrel, dispute, wrangle, argue ★**converse**

bid *v.* proffer, present, tender, request, propose

big *adj.* ① large, great, wide, huge, bulky, fat ② important ★**small**

bill *n.* ① statement *This is a statement of your investments with us,* account, invoice, check, chit, reckoning ② beak, mouth ③ poster, advertisement

bin *n.* box, can, case, chest, crate, tub

bind *v.* tie, fasten, secure, lace, swathe ★**untie**

birth *n.* origin, beginning, source, creation ★**death** BERTH

bit *n.* morsel, piece, fragment, part, crumb ★**whole**

bite *v.* gnaw, chew, rend, chomp BIGHT

bitter *adj.* ① harsh, sour, tart ▷*acid* ② severe, stern ▷*sarcastic* ★**mellow**

blame *v.* chide, rebuke, reproach, criticize, accuse, condemn ★**praise**

bland *adj.* soft, mild, gentle, soothing, tasteless

blank *adj.* empty, bare, void, bleak ★**full**

blare *v.* blast, boom, clang, roar, sound

blast *v.* explode, split, discharge, burst

blaze *v.* burn, flare, glare, flicker

bleak *adj.* bare, open, exposed, dismal, stormy, chilly, raw, desolate *The farm was a cold and desolate place in winter* ★**sheltered**

blemish *n.* spot, stain, mark, speck, flaw, blotch

blend *v.* mix, unite, harmonize, merge, fuse, combine ★**separate**

bless *v.* hallow, praise, exalt, endow, enrich, consecrate ★**curse**

blessing *n.* advantage, boon, approval, godsend ★**curse**

blight *n.* pest, plague, disease

blind *adj.* ① eyeless, sightless *These*

salamanders live in underground caves and are sightless, unsighted, unseeing ② ignorant, uninformed

blink *v.* wink, twinkle, glitter, gleam

bliss *n.* joy, ecstasy, rapture, blessedness, happiness ★**misery**

block ① *n.* lump, mass, chunk ② *v.* obstruct, bar, arrest BLOC

bloom ① *n.* flower, blossom, bud ② *v.* blossom, flourish, flower, thrive ★**decay**

blot *n.* stain, blotch ▷*blemish*

blow ① *v.* puff, gust, blast ② *n.* shock, stroke, impact, bang

blue *adj.* azure, turquoise, indigo, navy, ultramarine, cobalt BLEW

bluff ① *adj.* frank, brusque, abrupt, outspoken *Freda Jones will never be elected mayor; she's too outspoken* ② *v.* deceive, pretend *The lion closed its eyes, pretending it had not seen the antelope,* conceal

blunder ① *n.* mistake, error, slip, fault *It was my fault that the plates were broken,* oversight ② *v.* slip, err, bungle ★**correct**

blunt *adj.* ① plain, abrupt, curt ▷*bluff* ② dull, not sharp

blush *v.* redden, color, crimson, flush

The Body

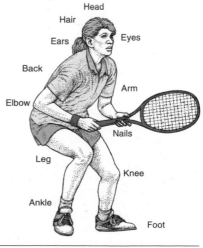

Head
Hair
Eyes
Ears
Back
Arm
Elbow
Nails
Leg
Knee
Ankle
Foot

board ① *n.* plank, table ② *n.* committee, council ③ *v.* live *The new teacher is going to live at our house,* lodge, accommodate BORED

boast *v.* swagger, swell, bluster ▷ *brag*

boat *n.* ship, vessel, craft, bark, barge

body *n.* ① corpse, trunk, carcass ② corporation, company, society

bog *n.* swamp, morass, marsh, quagmire

bogus *adj.* fake, false, spurious, sham, counterfeit ★**genuine**

boil *v.* cook, steam, poach, seethe, foam

boisterous *adj.* tempestuous, stormy, uncontrolled, loud, noisy ★**serene**

bold *adj.* fearless, courageous, adventurous, valiant, daring ▷ *brave* ★**fearful** BOWLED

bolt ① *v.* run away, take flight, flee *After the revolution, the queen had to flee the country* ② *v.* devour, gorge, eat ▷ *gulp* ③ *n.* lock, latch, fastening

bond *n.* tie, link, joint, band, fastening

bonny *adj.* fair, handsome, healthy, shapely, buxom ▷ *pretty* ★**plain**

bonus *n.* premium, benefit, award, prize

booby *n.* blockhead, sap, oaf, chump, nincompoop, dunce, fool, numbskull ★**oracle**

boom *n.* ① thunder, roar, rumble, blast ② prosperity *After the recession came years of prosperity*

boon *n.* blessing, windfall, advantage ▷ *benefit* ★**drawback**

boorish *adj.* unrefined, loutish, bad-mannered, rude, clumsy ★**refined**

boost *v.* strengthen, raise up, heighten

border *n.* fringe, edge, margin, frontier

bore *v.* ① tire, weary, fatigue *We were fatigued by the long bus ride home* ② drill, punch, perforate BOAR

bored *adj.* uninterested, tired, jaded, fed-up BOARD

borrow *v.* take, imitate, adopt, assume, raise money ★**lend**

boss *n.* ① stud, knob ② chief, manager *Helen is manager of the new beauty salon,* employer

bossy *adj.* domineering, tyrannical, overbearing ▷ *arrogant* ★**modest**

bother *v.* alarm, annoy, concern, distress ▷ *disturb*

bottom *n.* underside, deepest part, floor ▷ *base* ★**top**

bough *n.* branch, limb, shoot BOW

boulder *n.* rock, slab, stone

bounce *v.* leap, spring, bound, bump, jump

bound *v.* rebound, prance ▷ *bounce*

boundary *n.* bounds, limits, border, frontier ▷ *barrier*

bounty *n.* donation, gift, grant ▷ *bonus*

bow *v.* bend, nod, stoop, kneel, yield, submit BOUGH

bowl *n.* plate, basin, dish, vessel, casserole BOLL

box ① *n.* carton, case, chest, coffer *The town's coffers were empty, so they had to raise taxes,* pack ② *v.* fight, spar, punch

boy *n.* lad, youth, child, youngster

brag *v.* crow, swagger, gloat ▷ *boast*

braid *v.* entwine, weave, plait BRAYED

branch *n.* ① shoot, limb, twig ▷ *bough* ② department, office, division

brand *n.* ① trademark, emblem, label *This label shows that the cloth is of high quality* ② blot, stigma, stain

brandish *v.* flourish, parade, shake, swing, wave

brash *adj.* brazen, foolhardy, hasty, impetuous, impudent ▷ *rash*

brave ① *adj.* audacious, fearless, daring, dauntless, gallant, heroic ▷ *bold* ★**cowardly** ② *v.* dare, defy, endure

break *v.* batter, burst, crack, snap, fracture, shatter BRAKE

breathe *v.* draw in, gasp, inhale, sniff, gulp, wheeze, emit

breed *v.* reproduce, produce, cause, bear, rear, multiply, propagate

bribe *v.* corrupt, buy, grease the palm, fix

brief *adj.* short, little, concise, terse, crisp, curt ★**lengthy**

bright *adj.* ① clear, cloudless, fair, airy ② cheerful, genial *We were pleased to find so many genial members in the club* ③ clever, ingenious, acute ★**dull**

Bridges

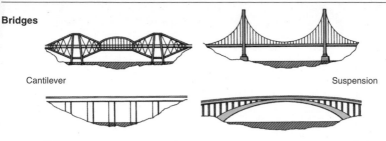

Cantilever

Suspension

Girder

Arch

Bascule bridge
Drawbridge
Footbridge

Rope bridge
Swing span bridge
Viaduct

brilliant *adj.* ① lustrous, shining, radiant, dazzling, luminous ② clever, intelligent ★**dull**

brim *n.* edge, brink, rim, fringe

bring *v.* bear, fetch, deliver, carry, convey

bring about *v.* bring off, accomplish, achieve, cause, make happen

bring up *v.* breed, develop, raise, educate, foster

brink *n.* margin, border, boundary, limit

brisk *adj.* agile, alert, busy, energetic, active, nimble, invigorating ★**sluggish**

brittle *adj.* breakable, fragile, delicate ▷*frail*

broad *adj.* wide, expansive, roomy, open, vast, large ★**narrow**

brood *v.* sigh, agonize, dwell upon *You must try to forget your disappointment and not dwell upon it,* languish BREWED

brook *n.* stream, creek, rivulet, watercourse

brow *n.* forehead, face, front, brink, edge, summit

bruise *v.* damage, discolor, blemish, injure, wound BREWS

brusque *adj.* abrupt, discourteous, gruff ▷*blunt* ★**polite**

brutal *adj.* cruel, inhumane, savage, barbarous, bloodthirsty ★**humane**

bubble *n.* drop, droplet, blob, bead

buckle *n.* catch, clasp, clip, fastening

bud *n.* sprout, germ, shoot

budge *v.* propel, push, roll, shift, slide

build *v.* make, form, assemble, construct, erect, put up ★**demolish** BILLED

bulge *n.* bump, swelling, lump, billow

bulky *adj.* big, huge, unwieldy, massive, cumbersome *I never liked that chair; it's too big and cumbersome to move*

bully ① *n.* ruffian, tease, bruiser, tyrant, tough ② *v.* tease, harass, oppress, terrorize

bump *v.* collide, hit, knock, strike, jab, jolt

bunch *n.* batch, bundle, cluster, collection, lot

bundle *n.* group, mass, heap, pack, parcel

bungle *v.* botch, blunder, mess up, ruin, fumble ★**succeed**

burden *n.* ① load, weight ② strain, hardship *We suffered great hardship during the war*

burly *adj.* beefy, big, hefty, brawny, muscular ★**frail**

burn *v.* blaze, flare, glow, singe, scorch, char, incinerate

burst *v.* break open, crack, explode, shatter, erupt

bury *v.* inter, conceal, cover up, hide, entomb, lay to rest BERRY

business *n.* ① occupation, career, profession ② company, enterprise, firm ③ problem, duty, affair

busy *adj.* active, brisk, industrious, lively, bustling ★**lazy**

buy *v.* acquire, get, purchase, procure *If I can procure a computer, I'll do the job for you* ★**sell** BY, BYE

C c

cab *n.* taxi, taxicab, hackney carriage

cabin *n.* ① hut, chalet, cottage, shack ② berth, compartment

cabinet *n.* ① cupboard, closet ② council, committee

cackle *v.* chuckle, giggle, snicker

café *n.* restaurant, coffee shop, snack bar

cage *v.* shut up, confine, imprison ★**free**

calamity *n.* catastrophe, disaster, misadventure ▷*mishap* ★**blessing**

calculate *v.* reckon, figure, estimate ▷*count*

call *v.* ① cry out, shout, hail ② name, designate ③ summon, telephone ④ visit *We will visit you next week,* drop in

calling *n.* occupation, job, profession

callous *adj.* unfeeling, harsh, hard-bitten ★**sensitive**

calm ① *v.* soothe, ease, pacify, comfort ② *adj.* easy, composed, mild ▷*peaceful* ★**excited**

can *n.* tin can, jar, container, canister

cancel *v.* abolish, erase, put off, obliterate ★**confirm**

candid *adj.* fair, honest, open, sincere, truthful ▷*frank* ★**devious**

capable *adj.* talented, able, competent, ▷*clever* ★**incompetent**

capacity *n.* ① space, volume, extent ② ability, aptitude *Jenny has an aptitude for learning languages,* intelligence

caper ① *v.* dance, gambol, frolic ② *n.* prank, joke, jest, lark

capital ① *n.* cash, assets, funds, finance ② *adj.* chief, excellent, important

captain *n.* chief, head, commander, master, skipper

capture *v.* seize, arrest, trap ▷*catch* ★**release**

car *n.* automobile, vehicle, conveyance, carriage, coach

carcass *n.* body, corpse, skeleton

care ① *v.* take care, beware, heed, mind ② *n.* attention, protection ★**carelessness**

careful *adj.* heedful, prudent, watchful ▷*cautious* ★**careless**

careless *adj.* neglectful, slack, casual, thoughtless ★**careful**

carelessness *n.* inaccuracy, negligence, slackness ★**care**

caress *v.* hug, stroke, cuddle, embrace, pet, pat

carriage *n.* car, coach, buggy, baby buggy

carry *v.* bring, convey, lift, support ▷*bear*

carry on *v.* continue, maintain, persist

carry out *v.* perform, achieve, fulfill, do

cart *n.* wagon, pushcart, buggy, wheelbarrow

carton *n.* bin, case, package, crate ▷*box*

carve *v.* sculpt, cut, chisel, fashion, whittle ▷*shape*

case *n.* chest, bin, carton ▷*box*

cash *n.* money, coins, bills, coinage CACHE

cask *n.* barrel, keg, drum

cast *v.* ① mold, form, shape ② fling, heave, sprinkle ▷*throw* CASTE

casual *adj.* accidental, chance, random ▷*occasional* ★**regular**

catch *v.* grasp, seize, arrest ▷*capture* ★**miss**

catching *adj.* infectious, contagious

cause ① *v.* bring about, create, provoke ② *n.* reason, source, origin CAWS

caution *n.* watchfulness, heed, vigilance, prudence ▷*care* ★**recklessness**

cautious *adj.* careful, discreet, prudent ▷*watchful* ★**heedless**

cavity *n.* dent, hole, gap, hollow

cease *v.* stop, conclude, end, refrain, terminate ★**begin**

celebrate *v.* commemorate, observe, honor, glorify, rejoice, praise

cell *n.* chamber, cavity, cubicle, compartment SELL

cellar *n.* basement, vault, crypt, cave SELLER

cement ① *v.* glue, stick, bind, gum, unite ② *n.* plaster, mortar, adhesive

censor *v.* cut, examine, take out CENSER

censure *v.* blame, rebuke, reprimand, chide ▷*scold* ★**praise**

center *n.* middle, core, heart, nucleus

ceremony *n.* ritual, custom, performance

certain *adj.* ① decided, definite, undoubted ▷ *sure* ★**dubious** ② particular *I had a particular reason for inviting you,* special

certainty *n.* confidence, assurance, trust, sureness ★**doubt**

certificate *n.* document, permit, deed, diploma, testimonial

chafe *v.* rub, rasp, grate, irritate

chain *v.* bind, fetter, shackle, tether, bond

challenge *v.* dare, demand, dispute, defy, object to

chamber *n.* room, apartment, bedroom, compartment, hollow

champion *n.* defender, victor, master, winner ★**loser**

chance *n.* ① fortune, hazard, luck, gamble, lottery, wager ② opportunity, occasion, risk ★**certainty**

change *v.* alter, vary, turn, shift, reform, transform ★**preserve**

chant *v.* intone, drone, croon, recite ▷ *sing*

chaos *n.* turmoil, confusion, disorder, pandemonium ★**order**

chapter *n.* clause, division, part, period *It was a period in my life that I will never forget,* phase

character *n.* ① letter, mark, emblem, device ② reputation *She had the reputation of being very generous,* temperament, qualities

charge *n.* ① attack, stampede, advance ② cost, amount, price ③ accusation, blame *The men were all guilty, but it was Harry Smith who took the blame,* indictment

charm *v.* please, delight, enchant, bewitch ▷ *attract* ★**irritate**

charming *adj.* delightful, appealing, lovely, pleasant ▷ *attractive* ★**disgusting**

chart *n.* map, sketch, diagram, plan

chase *v.* hunt, pursue, follow, run after, hurry

chaste *adj.* virgin, pure, virtuous, innocent ★**immodest** CHASED

chastise *v.* punish, whip, flog, beat, scold, tell off

chat *v.* converse, gossip ▷ *talk*

chatter *v.* babble, gossip ▷ *talk*

Chest

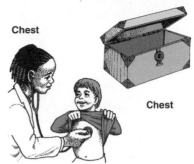

Chest

cheap *adj.* inexpensive, low-priced, bargain, reasonable, inferior ★**expensive**

cheat *v.* swindle, bilk, defraud, fleece ▷ *trick*

check ① *v.* inspect, compare, examine *The customs officer examined our luggage,* make sure ② *n.* bill, invoice, reckoning

cheek *n.* audacity, boldness, impertinence, insolence

cheer *v.* ① comfort, console, elate, buck up ② applaud *The audience applauded the leading soprano,* clap, hail

cheerful *adj.* lively, bright, happy, merry, joyful ▷ *happy* ★**sad**

cheery *adj.* blithe, breezy, bright, merry ★**downcast**

cherish *v.* caress, hold close, care for, shelter, treasure

chest *n.* ① case, coffer ▷ *box* ② bosom, torso

chew *v.* bite, gnaw, grind, munch ▷ *eat*

chide *v.* scold, criticize, blame, tell off

chief *adj.* main, principal, leading, foremost ★**minor**

child *n.* baby, infant, youth, juvenile

chilly *adj.* cool, crisp, brisk, cold, unfriendly ★**warm**

chip *v. & n.* crack, splinter, dent, flake

chirp *v. & n.* warble, trill, cheep, twitter

choice ① *n.* option *I had no option but to take the job,* preference, alternative ② *adj.* select, dainty, precious, cherished, special

choke *v.* throttle, suffocate, gag, strangle ▷ *stifle*

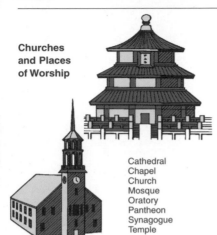

Churches and Places of Worship

Cathedral
Chapel
Church
Mosque
Oratory
Pantheon
Synagogue
Temple

choose *v.* pick, elect, decide, prefer ▷*select*
CHEWS

chop *v.* cut, hack, clip, cleave, sever, lop

chubby *adj.* plump, buxom, portly, round, stout ★**slim**

chum *n.* comrade, pal, friend, buddy, companion

chuck *v.* throw, toss, fling, heave, sling

chuckle *v.* cackle, chortle, snigger, giggle, ★**laugh**

chunk *n.* piece, lump, mass, portion, slab

churlish *adj.* brusque, harsh, impolite, morose *Dad had a headache and was in a morose mood* ▷*surly* ★**polite**

circle *n.* ① ring, band ② company, group, class

circular ① *adj.* round, disklike ② *n.* handbill, notice, poster

circulate *v.* broadcast, distribute, publicize

cistern *n.* tank, sink, basin, reservoir

cite *v.* mention, specify, name, quote
SIGHT, SITE

civil *adj.* polite, courteous, polished ▷*affable* ★**churlish**

claim *v.* demand, ask, require, insist, call for

clamor *n.* babel, blare, din, row, hubbub, racket ▷*noise* ★**silence**

clamp *v.* fasten, fix, hold, grasp

clap *v.* applaud, acclaim, cheer

clarify *v.* ① make clear, explain, simplify ② cleanse, purify

clash *v.* ① battle, conflict, quarrel ② bang, crash, clang, clatter

clasp ① *v.* grasp, grip, seize, hold, fasten ② *n.* buckle, catch, pin

class *n.* category, type, sort, grade, group, species

classical *adj.* pure, refined, scholarly, elegant, polished, well-proportioned

classify *v.* grade, sort, arrange, catalog

clean ① *adj.* pure, fresh, spotless, unsoiled ② *v.* cleanse, scrub ▷*wash* ★**dirty**

cleanse *v.* purify, scour ▷*clean* ★**defile**

clear *adj.* ① bright, fair, fine, light ★**dim** ② distinct, audible, lucid ★**vague** ③ free, open, empty

cleft *n.* crack, cranny, slit, split, aperture

clever *adj.* able, astute, apt, brainy, skillful, talented ▷*expert* ★**foolish**

cliff *n.* precipice, height, bluff, crag, overhang

climax *n.* crisis, head, summit, turning point

climb *v.* mount, scale, ascend, soar, go up

cling *v.* adhere, attach, embrace, grasp, hold

clip ① *n.* fastener, clasp ② *v.* trim, prune, snip, cut

clog *v.* block, dam up, hinder, jam, impede

close ① *v.* (kloz) shut, bolt, bar, obstruct *The drapes were thick and obstructed a lot of light,* end ② *adj.* (klos) near, neighboring, adjacent ★**far** ③ *adj.* heavy, stuffy, uncomfortable

closet *n.* cupboard, cabinet

clothing *n.* garments, dress, attire, raiment

cloud *n.* vapor, fog, billow, haze

clown *n.* buffoon, comedian, jester, joker

club *n.* ① cudgel, stick, truncheon ② company, group, society

clue *n.* evidence, inkling, lead, sign CLEW

clump *n.* cluster, group, bunch

clumsy *adj.* awkward, gawky, ungainly, blundering ★**graceful**

clutch *v.* snatch, clasp, grasp, seize, grip

clutter *n.* litter, muddle, mess

coach *n.* ① bus, car, carriage, vehicle ② trainer, tutor, instructor

Clothing

Dresses and pants
Bermuda shorts
cocktail dress
dress
evening gown
jeans
jodhpurs
kilt
miniskirt
petticoat
sari
sarong
skirt
slacks

Coats and jackets
blazer
parka
poncho
raincoat
suit
tuxedo

Headwear *see page 56*

Tops
blouse
pullover
sweater
sweatshirt
T-shirt

Foot and legwear
boots
galoshes
moccasins
shoes
sneakers
socks
stockings

---

coarse *adj.* ① rough, unrefined, unpolished ② brutish, rude, uncivil ★**refined** COURSE

coat *n.* ① jacket, blazer, windbreaker ② fleece, fur, skin, hide

coax *v.* cajole, wheedle, urge, persuade, beguile *We sat for hours as Aunt Anna beguiled us with stories* ★**dissuade** COKES

coddle *v.* pamper, spoil, indulge, baby, mollycoddle

coffer *n.* casket, case, chest, treasury

cog *n.* tooth, prong

coil *v.* twist, wind, loop

coincide *v.* match, agree, accord, synchronize, tally

cold *adj.* cool, chilly, frigid, freezing, frosty, frozen ★**hot**

collapse *v.* founder, topple, break down, crumple, fall down

collect *v.* accumulate, amass, assemble, save ▷*gather* ★**scatter**

collide *v.* crash, smash, hit, strike, meet

colossal *adj.* enormous, gigantic, immense, massive ▷*huge* ★**tiny**

column *n.* ① pillar, post, shaft ② file *The file of soldiers marched on parade,* line, procession

combat *v.* battle, contend, contest, oppose, defy ★**submit**

combine *v.* unite, join, link, fuse, merge, mix ★**separate**

come *v.* arrive, appear, enter, reach, advance ★**go**

come by *v.* get, procure, acquire *I acquired a new television set in the sale*

comfort *v.* cheer, hearten, calm, soothe, console ★**torment**

comfortable *adj.* restful, convenient, cozy, agreeable ★**uncomfortable**

comforting *adj.* cheering, encouraging, consoling

command *v.* ① order, dictate, direct ② rule, dominate

commence *v.* start, begin, initiate, originate ★**finish**

comment *v.* mention, remark, observe, point out

commiserate *v.* sympathize, show pity, be sorry for

commit *v.* carry out, do, enact, perform, promise, entrust

common *adj.* ① ordinary, vulgar, habitual, customary ② public, social, communal

commonplace *adj.* everyday, humdrum, ordinary, obvious ★**rare**

commotion *n.* excitement, flurry, stir, uproar ▷*fuss*

communicate *v.* tell, disclose, impart, reveal

community *n.* society, partnership, association ▷*group*

compact *adj.* dense, close, tight, firm, condensed, concise

companion *n.* comrade, friend, chum, colleague, comrade, escort ★**rival**

company *n.* association, league, alliance, business, firm

compare *v.* match, liken, equal, parallel

compartment *n.* cubicle, alcove, bay, cell, carriage

compassion *n.* kindness, mercy, sympathy, charity, understanding ▷*pity* ★**indifference**

compel *v.* make, coerce, drive, force *We could not understand the signs so we were forced to guess where to check in,* urge ★**coax**

compensate *v.* make good, refund, reimburse, repay, reward ★**injure**

compete *v.* contest, contend, rival, strive, oppose, challenge

competent *adj.* able, adapted, capable ▷*clever* ★**incompetent**

competition *n.* game, match, contest, tournament, rivalry, race

compile *v.* amass, put together, unite ▷*collect*

complacent *adj.* self-satisfied, contented ▷*smug* ★**diffident**

complain *v.* protest, gripe, grumble, grouse ▷*nag* ★**rejoice**

complement *v.* complete, round off, add to, supplement, match COMPLIMENT

complete ① *v.* finish, accomplish, achieve ② *adj.* finished, full, entire

complex *adj.* complicated, intricate, mixed, tangled ★**simple**

complicated *adj.* entangled, involved ▷*complex*

compliment *v.* flatter, admire, congratulate ▷*praise* ★**insult** COMPLEMENT

comply *v.* agree to, assent to, abide by, perform, yield ★**refuse**

compose ① *v.* make up, put together, form, construct, write ② calm, quell

composure *n.* assurance, calm, confidence ★**exuberance**

compound *n.* mixture, alloy, blend, combination

comprehend *v.* grasp, discern, take in ▷*understand* ★**misunderstand**

compress *v.* condense, contract, abbreviate ▷*squeeze* ★**expand**

comprise *v.* contain, consist of, include, embody, encompass

compromise *v.* ① meet halfway, strike a balance, adjust, agree ② imperil, weaken, jeopardize

compulsory *adj.* forced, necessary, obligatory *Everyone in the school has to go*

Compel

Gevonden voorwerpen →

Inlichtingen ↑

We could not understand the signs so we were forced to guess where to check in.

to the meeting; it's obligatory, required
★**voluntary**

compute *v.* calculate, figure, reckon, estimate

computer *n.* calculator, word processor

comrade *n.* companion, pal, chum, buddy ▷*friend* ★**enemy**

conceal *v.* bury, camouflage, cover ▷*hide* ★**reveal**

concede *v.* allow, admit, yield, acknowledge, surrender ★**dispute**

conceit *n.* vanity, self-importance, arrogance ▷*pride* ★**modesty**

conceited *adj.* proud, vain, arrogant ★**modest**

conceive *v.* create, design, devise *We devised a way to sharpen the scissors,* form, think up, develop

concentrate *v.* focus on, centralize, heed, pay attention

concept *n.* idea, thought, theory, view

concern ① *v.* affect, touch ② *n.* affair, matter, interest, business

concerning *prep.* as regards, respecting, about

concise *adj.* brief, condensed, short ▷*compact* ★**expansive**

conclude *v.* ① finish, terminate ▷*end* ② deduce, judge, reckon, presume

conclusion *n.* result, termination, end

concoct *v.* contrive, hatch, plan, devise, invent

concord *n.* agreement, understanding, good-will, harmony ★**discord**

concrete ① *adj.* actual, definite, real ② *n.* cement, mortar

concur *v.* approve, agree, coincide, consent ★**disagree**

condemn *v.* blame, denounce, reprove, sentence, disapprove ★**approve**

condense *v.* compress, concentrate, abridge, thicken ★**expand**

condition *n.* shape, way, state, position, plight, situation ▷*predicament*

condone *v.* overlook, disregard, forgive, excuse ★**censure**

conduct ① *n.* attitude, bearing, behavior

② *v.* guide, direct, lead, steer, pilot

confederate *n.* accomplice, ally, associate, partner

confer *v.* bestow, grant, award, give, present

conference *n.* discussion, meeting, forum

confess *v.* admit, acknowledge, own up, divulge ★**deny**

confide *v.* tell, divulge, reveal, whisper, entrust

confidence *n.* assurance, belief, boldness, firmness ★**doubt**

confident *adj.* certain, assured, poised, fearless ★**diffident**

confine *v.* restrict, limit, detain, imprison, constrain ★**free**

confirm *v.* verify, assure, approve, endorse, attest ★**deny**

confiscate *v.* seize, impound, commandeer *The house was commandeered by the army*

conform *v.* agree with, comply with, yield, adjust

confound *v.* perplex, mystify, puzzle, baffle, fluster ▷*bewilder* ★**enlighten**

confront *v.* challenge, defy, face, oppose, menace

confuse *v.* baffle, bemuse, mystify ▷*bewilder* ★**clarify**

congenial *adj.* companionable, natural, sympathetic, agreeable ▷*friendly* ★**disagreeable**

congested *adj.* jammed, crowded, clogged, packed, teeming ★**clear**

congratulate *v.* rejoice, compliment, praise, wish one joy ★**commiserate**

congregate *v.* assemble, meet, come together, converge ★**disperse**

congress *n.* meeting, assembly, council, convention

conjecture *v.* guess, surmise, suspect, imagine, assume

connect *v.* unite, join, combine, fasten, link ★**disconnect**

conquer *v.* beat, crush, overcome, overpower, triumph ▷*defeat* ★**surrender**

conscientious *adj.* moral, scrupulous, careful, diligent ▷*honest* ★**careless**

conscious *adj.* alert, alive, aware, sensible,

responsible ★**unconscious**

consecutive *adj.* chronological, in sequence, successive, continuous

consent *v.* assent, permit, concur, approve, comply ▷*agree* ★**oppose**

conserve *v.* keep, preserve, protect, save, store up, safeguard ★**waste**

consider *v.* discuss, examine, ponder, reflect *Alone on the island, I reflected on all that had happened,* take account of ★**ignore**

considerable *adj.* abundant, ample, great, large, noteworthy, important ★**insignificant**

consist of *v.* comprise, be composed of, contain, include

consistent *adj.* uniform, constant, regular, steady ★**inconsistent**

console *v.* comfort, cheer, sympathize, soothe, solace ★**upset**

conspicuous *adj.* noticeable, marked, apparent, obvious, prominent ★**inconspicuous**

conspire *v.* intrigue, scheme, plot *He was jailed for plotting against the government*

constant *adj.* ① regular, stable, uniform ▷*consistent* ② loyal, faithful, staunch, true ★**fickle**

consternation *n.* dismay, horror, fear, awe, stupefaction ▷*alarm* ★**composure**

constitute *v.* compose, comprise, set up, fix, form, establish ★**destroy**

constrict *v.* tighten, strain, tauten, draw together, choke, pinch ★**expand**

construct *v.* erect, compose, compound, assemble ▷*build* ★**demolish**

consult *v.* ask, seek advice, discuss, confer, debate

consume *v.* use up, absorb, eat up, devour

contact *n.* touch, connection, communication

contagious *adj.* catching, infectious

contain *v.* comprise, consist of, hold, accommodate, enclose

contaminate *v.* pollute, soil, stain, sully, taint, infect

contemplate *v.* think, reflect, deliberate, consider, ponder

contempt *v.* disdain, scorn, disregard, derision ★**admiration**

contend *v.* compete, contest, conflict, strive, struggle ★**concede**

content ① *adj.* (con-*tent*) satisfied, smug ② *v.* satisfy, delight, gratify ③ *n.* (*con*-tent) matter, text, subject

contest ① *n.* (*con*-test) competition, match, tournament ② *v.* (con-*test*) dispute, argue

continue *v.* go on, keep up, endure, last, persist ★**stop**

contract ① *v.* (con-*tract*) condense, lessen, shrink ② *n.* (*con*-tract) agreement, pact, understanding

contradict *v.* deny, dispute, challenge, oppose

contrary *adj.* opposed, adverse, counter, opposite ★**agreeable**

contrast ① *n.* (*con*-trast) difference, disparity, comparison ② *v.* (con-*trast*) compare, differ, oppose, distinguish

contribute *v.* donate, present, bestow, provide ★**withhold**

contrive *v.* form, fashion, construct, create, design, invent

control *v.* command, direct, dominate, lead, supervise

convene *v.* call together, rally, meet, muster *We mustered on the dock before boarding the ship,* assemble ★**dismiss**

convenient *adj.* handy, fit, helpful, suitable, accessible ★**awkward**

conversation *n.* talk, chat, communication, discussion

convert *v.* alter, change, transform, adapt

convey *v.* carry, transport, conduct, bear, transmit

convict ① *n.* (*con*-vict) prisoner, captive, criminal ② *v.* (con-*vict*) find guilty, condemn

convince *v.* assure, persuade, prove to, win over

cook *v.* boil, broil, heat, warm, steam, fry, stew, bake

cool *adj.* ① chilly, frigid ▷*cold* ② self-composed, calm, relaxed

cooperate *v.* collaborate, combine, aid,

assist, join forces

cope (with) *v.* deal, handle, struggle, grapple, manage

copy *v.* duplicate, reproduce, imitate, mimic, simulate

cord *n.* string, rope, twine, line CHORD

cordial *adj.* hearty, sincere, congenial, jovial, affable ★**hostile**

core *n.* heart, kernel, pith, crux *Now we're getting to the crux of the problem,* center CORPS

corner *n.* angle, bend, crook, cavity, cranny, niche, compartment

corpse *n.* body, carcass, remains

correct *adj.* true, actual, accurate, exact, precise ★**wrong**

correspond *v.* ① fit, harmonize, agree, coincide ② write letters

corridor *n.* hallway, passage, aisle

corroborate *v.* confirm, certify, endorse, establish ★**contradict**

corrode *v.* erode, waste, eat away, rust

corrupt ① *adj.* dishonest, fraudulent, rotten ② *v.* bribe, deprave, entice

cost *n.* ① charge, amount, price, outlay ② penalty, forfeit, sacrifice

costly *adj.* expensive, valuable, precious

costume *n.* suit, outfit, ensemble, attire, dress

cot *n.* bed, bunk, berth

cottage *n.* bungalow, cabin, chalet, shack, lodge

couch *n.* sofa, davenport, chaise longue

council *n.* assembly, committee, congress, convention COUNSEL

counsel ① *n.* lawyer, attorney, advocate ② *v.* advise, instruct, recommend COUNCIL

count *v.* add up, calculate, check, compute, reckon, tally

counter ① *n.* token, coin, disk ② *n.* bar, bench ③ *adj.* against, opposed

counterfeit *adj.* forged, fraudulent, fake, bogus *She entered the country on a bogus passport,* false

country ① *n.* nation, people, realm, state ② *adj.* rural, boondocks, sticks

Cooking utensils

Blender	Grill	Saucepan
Bottle	Jar	Saucer
Bowl	Juicer	Sieve
Casserole	Kettle	Skillet
Colander	Ladle	Spatula
Cup	Masher	Spoon
Cutting	Measuring	Tureen
board	cup	Urn
Dish	Pan	Waffle iron
Frying pan	Peeler	Whisk
Funnel	Plate	Wok
Grater	Pot	
Griddle	Ramekin	
	Rolling pin	

couple ① *n*. pair, brace, two ② *v*. link, yoke, unite, join, connect

courage *n*. bravery, valor, boldness, gallantry, daring, pluck ★**cowardice**

courageous *adj*. brave, bold, fearless, valiant ▷*plucky* ★**cowardly**

course *n*. ① route, channel, path, road, track, trail ② policy, plan, manner COARSE

court ① *n*. alley, courtyard, atrium, ② *n*. bar, law court, tribunal ③ *n*. palace, retinue ④ *v*. make love, woo, flatter

courteous *adj*. considerate, polite, refined, elegant ★**discourteous**

courtesy *n*. politeness, civility, manners, gentility, respect

cove *n*. inlet, bay, creek, firth

cover ① *v*. conceal, hide, secrete ② *v*. include, embody, incorporate ③ *n*. cap, case, lid, canopy

covet *v*. want, envy, fancy, hanker after, long for, crave

cow *v*. frighten, bully, terrorize, scare, subdue

coward *n*. weakling, craven, funk, sneak ★**hero** COWERED

cowardice *n*. fear, funk, faint-heartedness ★**courage**

cowardly *adj*. fearful, weak, scared,

Creature

It was a huge brute—the biggest crocodile I'd ever seen.

spineless, timid ★**courageous**

cower *v*. cringe, grovel, flinch, crouch

coy *adj*. demure, skittish, blushing, bashful, shy ★**forward**

crack ① *n*. slit, split, cleft, cranny, crevice, breach ② *v*. snap, split, splinter

craft *n*. ① cunning, deceit ② ability, cleverness, expertise ③ occupation, business ④ boat, ship, plane

crafty *adj*. cunning, artful, wily, shrewd

cram *v*. ram, stuff, squeeze, press

cramp *v*. restrict, obstruct, hinder, confine

crash *v*. bang, clash, clatter, break, fall, topple, collapse

crass *adj*. stupid, oafish, boorish, obtuse, gross, vulgar, coarse ★**sensitive**

crave *v*. long for, hanker after, need, yearn for, beg, plead

crawl *v*. creep, drag, slither, grovel

crazy *adj*. insane, mad, beserk, deranged, idiotic ★**sane**

creak *v*. grate, grind, rasp, groan CREEK

crease *n*. fold, pucker, ridge, tuck

create *v*. bring into being, compose, concoct, make, invent, devise

creation *n*. invention, handiwork, foundation, production ★**destruction**

creature *n*. animal, beast, being, brute *It was a huge brute—the biggest crocodile I'd ever seen,* person

credible *adj*. believable, likely, plausible ★**incredible**

credit *n*. ① acclaim, kudos, merit ② belief, faith, confidence

creek *n*. stream, brook, rivulet CREAK

creep *v*. crawl, slither, squirm, wriggle

crest *n*. top, crown, pinnacle

crestfallen *adj*. downcast, dejected, discouraged ★**elated**

crevice *n*. cleft, chink, crack, cranny, gap

crew *n*. team, company, party, gang

crime *n*. misdemeanor, offense, fault, felony

criminal ① *n*. culprit, convict, felon, crook ② *adj*. unlawful, wicked

cringe *v*. cower, flinch, duck, shrink, grovel

cripple *v*. disable, mutilate, paralyze, weaken, damage

Creek

Creak

crisis *n.* climax, turning point, catastrophe, disaster

crisp *adj.* brittle, crumbly, crunchy, firm, crusty

critical *adj.* crucial, all-important, acute, grave

criticize *v.* find fault with, disapprove of, condemn ★**praise**

crony *n.* accomplice, ally, confederate, comrade, chum ▷*friend*

crooked *adj.* ① bent, bowed, distorted, twisted ② dishonest, criminal

crop ① *n.* harvest, gathering, yield ② *v.* graze, shorten, browse

cross ① *adj.* angry, annoyed, crusty ② *v.* bridge, pass over ③ *n.* crucifix

crouch *v.* stoop, squat, bow, cringe

crow ① *v.* gloat, shout, brag, bluster ② *n.* blackbird, raven

crowd *n.* mob, multitude, flock, assembly, swarm, throng

crowded *adj.* jammed, packed, congested, cramped

crucial *adj.* decisive, critical, acute

crude *adj.* raw, unrefined, rustic, unpolished ▷*coarse* ★**refined**

cruel *adj.* unkind, brutal, inhuman, ruthless ▷*savage* ★**kind**

cruise *n.* voyage, trip, sail, crossing CREWS

crumb *n.* bit, morsel, seed, grain, scrap, shred

crumble *v.* decay, grind, powder, crunch

crumple *v.* crinkle, crush, wrinkle, pucker

crunch *v.* chew, grind, masticate, munch ▷*crush*

crush *v.* squash, mash, pound, compress

cry *v.* ① exclaim, call, shout, shriek ② weep, bawl, blubber, sob

cuddle *v.* hug, embrace, fondle, cosset, pet, snuggle

cue *n.* hint, key, nod, sign, signal QUEUE

cull *v.* choose, pick, thin out, amass, collect

culprit *n.* criminal, convict, felon, offender, malefactor

cultivated *adj.* refined, civilized, cultured, educated, trained ★**neglected**

cumbersome *adj.* bulky, awkward, clumsy, hefty ★**convenient**

cunning *adj.* artful, astute, crafty

curb *v.* check, tame, restrain

cure ① *n.* remedy, medicine, drug ② *v.* heal, remedy, treat, attend

curious *adj.* ① odd, peculiar, singular ② inquisitive, prying, nosy

curl *v.* coil, twist, curve, crimp

current ① *adj.* present, contemporary, topical, fashionable ② *n.* stream, course, flow, electrical flow CURRANT

curse ① *v.* swear, condemn, damn ② *n.* oath, denunciation

curt *adj.* brusque, blunt, churlish, crusty, gruff ▷*terse* ★**polite**

curtail *v.* trim, shorten, clip, truncate ▷*abbreviate* ★**lengthen**

curve *n.* loop, hook, curl, twist, wind, coil ▷*bend*

cushion *n.* pillow, bolster, pad, support

custom *n.* habit, usage, convention, rite ▷*fashion*

customer *n.* purchaser, buyer, client, patron

cut *v.* carve, whittle, chisel, cleave, sever, gash, slice

cut off *v.* disconnect, interrupt, stop

cute *adj.* charming, attractive, pretty, dainty

cutting *adj.* sharp, biting, bitter, sarcastic

D d

dab *v.* blot, swab, touch, pat

dabble *v.* toy, meddle, tinker, trifle, putter

daft *adj.* crazy, silly, innocent, idiotic, cracked, dopey ★**bright**

dagger *n.* knife, dirk, bayonet, stiletto

daily ① *adj.* everyday, normal, common *It is quite common to see squirrels in the woods* ② *n.* newspaper

dainty *adj.* delicate, charming, exquisite, choice, tasty

dally *v.* play, trifle, dawdle, linger, loiter

damage *n.* harm, sabotage, vandalism, injury, hurt

damn *v.* curse, swear, condemn, criticize ★**bless**

damp *adj.* humid, clammy, dank ▷*moist* ★**dry**

damsel *n.* girl, maiden, lady, woman

dance *v.* hop, skip, jump, prance, frolic, gambol

danger *n.* peril, hazard, risk, jeopardy, menace ★**safety**

dangerous *adj.* perilous, precarious, unsafe, risky, hazardous ★**safe**

dangle *v.* hang, swing, sway

dank *adj.* sticky, muggy, moist, soggy ▷*damp*

dapper *adj.* spruce, natty, neat, stylish, trim ▷*smart* ★**scruffy**

dare *v.* brave, face, risk, defy, challenge, venture

daring *adj.* adventurous, dashing, bold, fearless ▷*brave* ★**timid**

dark *adj.* dusky, swarthy, shady, dim, dingy, shadowy ★**light**

darling *n.* pet, love, dear, favorite, beloved, precious

darn *v.* mend, sew, patch, repair

dart ① *n.* arrow, missile ② *v.* dash, hurtle *The express train hurtled through the tunnel,* charge, gallop

dash *v.* rush, gallop, run, career, fly, hasten

date ① *n.* time, point ② *n.* appointment *I have an appointment to see the doctor,* engagement ③ *v.* become old, become dated

daub *v.* plaster, spread, smear, dab, paint

daunt *v.* intimidate, terrify, scare, confront

dauntless *adj.* fearless, gallant, courageous ▷*brave* ★**discouraged**

dawdle *v.* linger, loiter, lag, waste time

Dances

Ballet
Bolero
Bop
Cha-cha
Charleston
Conga
Country dance
Disco
Fandango
Flamenco
Fox-trot
Gavotte
Highland fling
Jitterbug
Jive
Mazurka
Minuet
Morris dance
Polka
Polonaise
Quadrille
Quickstep
Rumba
Samba
Square dance
Tango
Tarantella
Two-step
Twist
Waltz

▷*dally* ★**hurry**

dawn *n.* beginning, daybreak, daylight, morning, sunrise ★**dusk**

daze *v.* deaden, muddle, blind, dazzle ▷*bewilder* DAYS

dazzle *v.* blind, glare, confuse ▷*daze*

dead *adj.* deceased, departed, gone, lifeless, dull ★**alive**

deaden *v.* paralyze, blunt, muffle, drown

deadly *adj.* fatal, lethal, mortal, baleful, venomous

deaf *adj.* hard of hearing, unhearing, heedless

deal *v.* bargain, trade, market, communicate, traffic, give out

dealer *n.* merchant, trader, tradesman

dear ① *adj.* darling, beloved, loved, cherished *These old records are some of my cherished possessions* ② expensive, high-priced, costly DEER

death *n.* decease, end of life, mortality ★**life**

debate *v.* argue, discuss, dispute, question, contend

debris *n.* trash, junk ▷*garbage*

debt *n.* obligation, debit, dues, liability ★**credit**

decay *v.* ① decompose, rot *The potatoes had been left too long and had rotted,* spoil ② decline, sink, dwindle, waste

deceive *v.* dupe, hoax, trick, cheat, mislead ▷*betray* ★**enlighten**

decent *adj.* respectable, chaste, proper, fair, modest ★**indecent**

decide *v.* determine, rule, judge, resolve

declare *v.* avow, state, profess, proclaim, announce

decline ① *v.* descend, dwindle *The profits of the business had dwindled,* drop, fall ② *v.* refuse, say no ★**assent** ③ *n.* descent, slope, slant, dip, pitch

decorate *v.* embellish, adorn, ornament

decoy ① *v.* entice *We were enticed into the café by the smell of roasting coffee,* ensnare, mislead, tempt ② *n.* lure, bait

decrease *v.* diminish, lessen, wane, decline, reduce ★**increase**

decree *n.* law, edict, manifesto, rule, decision

decrepit *adj.* senile, infirm, crippled, feeble, frail ★**robust**

dedicate *v.* devote, apportion, assign, surrender, pledge

deduce *v.* draw, infer, conclude, glean, surmise, reason

deduct *v.* subtract, take from, remove, withdraw ★**add**

deed *n.* ① act, feat, stunt ② document, paper, contract *Michael was under contract to play ball for the team for three years*

deep *adj.* ① profound *The accident taught us a profound lesson about friendship,* bottomless, low ② learned, wise, sagacious

deface *v.* disfigure, deform, injure, mar, blemish ★**adorn**

defeat *v.* beat, conquer, overcome, vanquish ★**triumph**

defect *n.* flaw, fault, weak point, blemish, error

defective *adj.* imperfect, faulty, deficient, insufficient ★**perfect**

defend *v.* protect, guard, fortify, support, sustain, uphold ★**attack**

defer *v.* postpone, put off, adjourn, waive, yield ★**hasten**

defiant *adj.* mutinous, rebellious, resistant, aggressive ★**submissive**

deficient *adj.* wanting, imperfect, defective, faulty ★**superfluous**

defile *v.* taint, infect, pollute, sully, disgrace ★**cleanse**

define *v.* explain, interpret, designate, mark out, specify ★**obscure**

definite *adj.* clear, certain, clear-cut, distinct ▷*sure* ★**vague**

deform *adj.* misshape, distort, contort, twist, warp

defraud *v.* fleece, swindle, embezzle, diddle ▷*cheat*

defy *v.* resist, withstand, disregard, challenge, disobey ★**obey**

degrade *v.* humble, debase, corrupt, downgrade, cheapen ★**improve**

degree *n.* grade, step, measure, rate, scale

Our answers were scored on a scale from one to ten, class

dejected *adj.* depressed, downcast, crestfallen, disheartened ▷*gloomy* ★**elated**

delay *v.* postpone, put off, detain, halt, hinder, impede ★**hurry**

deliberate ① *adj.* willful, calculated, intentional, planned ★**unintentional** ② *v.* reflect, contemplate, discuss

delicate *adj.* dainty, refined, soft, luxurious, modest, fragile, tender ★**harsh**

delicious *adj.* palatable, luscious, mellow, savory, choice ▷*scrumptious* ★**unpleasant**

delight *n.* enjoyment, pleasure, rapture, bliss ▷*happiness* ★**displease**

delightful *adj.* enjoyable, cheery, enchanting, lovely ▷*agreeable* ★**horrible**

deliver ① *v.* transfer, hand over, bear *She came bearing gifts for the whole family,* carry, convey ② free, liberate, release

delude *v.* cheat, hoax, hoodwink, mislead ▷*deceive* ★**guide**

deluge *n.* inundation, swamp, spate ▷*flood*

demand *v.* ① request, ask, appeal, entreat ② badger, pester, nag *My sister has been nagging me to take her to the park*

demeanor *n.* bearing, manner, conduct, air

demented *adj.* distracted, foolish, insane ▷*mad* ★**sane**

demolish *v.* destroy, wreck, ruin, smash, overthrow, knock down ★**build**

demon *n.* fiend, imp, devil, evil spirit

demonstrate *v.* prove, exhibit, illustrate ▷*show*

demote *v.* degrade, downgrade, relegate ★**promote**

demur *v.* hesitate, object, protest, doubt, waver ★**consent**

demure *adj.* coy, sedate, staid, sober, prudish, discreet ★**indiscreet**

den *n.* ① nest, cave, haunt, lair ② hideaway, retreat *This little room is my retreat, where I can sit and think,* study

denote *v.* designate, indicate, mean, show, point out

denounce *v.* decry, defame, attack, brand ▷*accuse*

dense *adj.* ① thick, solid, stout, compact ★**sparse** ② stupid, thick, stolid, obtuse ★**smart** DENTS

dent *n.* notch, cavity, chip, dimple, hollow

deny *v.* ① refuse, reject, repudiate ② disagree with *I am afraid that I disagree with what you say,* oppose, contradict ★**admit**

depart *v.* quit, go, retire, withdraw, vanish ▷*leave* ★**arrive**

department *n.* section, division, office, branch, province

depend on *v.* lean on, rely upon, trust in

depict *v.* describe, sketch, portray, outline, draw

deplorable *adj.* distressing, disastrous, shameful, scandalous ★**excellent**

deplore *v.* regret, lament, mourn ★**celebrate**

deport *v.* banish, exile, expel, oust

deposit *v.* drop, lay, place, put, bank, entrust, save ★**withdraw**

depot *n.* ① warehouse, storehouse ② terminus, station

depraved *adj.* corrupted, immoral, evil, sinful, vile *After calling me vile names, he left* ★**upright**

depreciate *v.* ① devalue, lessen, lose value *From the moment it was bought the car began losing value,* reduce ② belittle, disparage, deride ★**appreciate**

depress ① *v.* dishearten, dispirit, cast down ★**cheer** ② flatten, push down

depressed *adj.* dispirited, disheartened, despondent, fed up

deprive *v.* take away, rob, starve, divest *The traitor had been divested of all her honors* ★**bestow**

depth *n.* pit, shaft, well, chasm, gulf, abyss

deputy *n.* agent, delegate, lieutenant, assistant, councillor

derelict *adj.* abandoned, deserted *The Mary Celeste sailing ship was found deserted in the Atlantic,* forlorn

deride *v.* laugh at, jeer at, ridicule ▷*mock*

derive *v.* develop *Many English words developed from Norman-French,* obtain, arise from, originate

descend *v.* fall, drop, lower, decline, collapse ▷*sink* ★**ascend**

describe *v.* depict, portray, detail, define, tell

desert ① *n.* (*dez*-ert) wasteland, wilderness ② *adj.* desolate, arid, barren ③ *v.* (dez-*ert*) forsake, leave ▷*abandon* DESSERT

deserve *v.* be worthy of, merit, warrant, be entitled to ★**forfeit**

design *n.* drawing, painting, plan, pattern, scheme

desirable *adj.* ① agreeable, pleasing, good ② attractive, alluring, adorable

desire *v.* ① wish, require, need, want, crave ② long for, yearn after, pine for *My sister lived abroad, but always pined for home* ★**detest**

desist *v.* abstain, avoid, break off, cease, end

desolate *adj.* lonely, forlorn, miserable, wretched, alone ★**cheerful**

despair *n.* depression, misery, hopelessness, sorrow ▷*gloom* ★**hope**

desperate *adj.* drastic, reckless, frantic, rash, wild ★**hopeful**

despicable *adj.* contemptible, low, detestable, degrading ★**noble**

despise *v.* abhor, detest, loathe, look down upon ▷*hate* ★**prize**

despite *prep.* in spite of, notwithstanding

despondent *adj.* depressed, dispirited, brokenhearted ▷*miserable* ★**cheerful**

destination *n.* goal, terminus, end, objective, journey's end

destiny *n.* fate, lot, fortune, future, prospect, doom

destitute *adj.* poor, needy, bankrupt, penniless, poverty-stricken ★**wealthy**

destroy *v.* ruin, demolish, spoil, smash, exterminate ▷*wreck* ★**create**

destruction *n.* desolation, downfall, ruin, defeat, havoc ★**creation**

detach *v.* separate, part, divide, loosen, undo ★**attach**

detail *n.* item, fact, circumstance, point

detain *v.* delay, retard, restrain, arrest, hold

Dessert

Desert

up, hinder, impede ★**release**

detect *v.* notice, discover, observe, scent, track down ★**miss**

deter *v.* prevent, hold back, check, stop ▷*detain* ★**encourage**

deteriorate *v.* become worse, worsen, corrode, decline, decompose ★**improve**

determine *v.* find out, decide, identify, choose, regulate

detest *v.* abhor *Lucy was a peaceful person and abhorred violence,* loathe, despise ▷*hate* ★**adore**

devastate *v.* lay waste, ravage, overwhelm ▷*destroy*

develop *v.* mature, ripen, grow up, evolve, extend ★**restrict**

deviate *v.* diverge, differ, vary, contrast, wander ★**conform**

device *n.* apparatus, contrivance, instrument, appliance

devil *n.* imp, evil spirit, demon, fiend, Satan

devious *adj.* tricky, sly, subtle, cunning, roundabout ★**forthright**

devise *v.* contrive, fashion, form, plan, conceive

devoid *adj.* barren, empty, free, without, lacking ★**endowed**

devote *v.* allocate, allot, give, assign, dedicate

devoted *adj.* dedicated, devout, loyal, caring, ardent ★**indifferent**

devour *v.* swallow, gulp, gorge, consume ▷*eat*

devout *adj.* pious, devoted, religious, faithful, passionate ★**insincere**

dexterous *adj.* able, active, deft, nimble ▷*skillful* ★**clumsy**

diagram *n.* outline, plan, sketch, draft, chart, drawing

dictate *v.* speak, utter, say, instruct, ordain, command

die *v.* expire, finish, end, pass away, perish, cease ★**live** DYE

differ *v.* ① vary, contrast, diverge *In this case, my views diverge strongly from yours* ② argue, conflict, clash

difference *n.* variance, distinctness, divergence, subtlety ★**agreement**

different *adj.* contrary, variant, distinct, original, unusual ★**same**

difficult *adj.* hard, puzzling, baffling, complex, laborious ★**easy**

difficulty *n.* trouble, bother, predicament ★**plight**

diffident *adj.* bashful, reserved, retiring, timid, unsure ▷*shy* ★**confident**

dig *v.* burrow, excavate, grub, delve, scoop

digest ① *v.* (di-*gest*) absorb, assimilate, dissolve ② *n.* (*di*-gest) abridgment, condensation, précis

digit *n.* ① number, figure, cipher ② finger, toe, thumb

dignified *adj.* grave, majestic, noble, lofty, grand ★**undignified**

dignity *n.* grandeur, merit, fame, gravity, nobility

dilapidated *adj.* neglected, unkempt, crumbling, decayed

dilemma *n.* quandary, plight, difficulty, predicament

dilute *v.* water down, weaken, reduce, thin

dim *adj.* dark, faint, pale, gloomy ▷*obscure* ★**bright**

diminish *v.* reduce, lessen, decrease, become smaller ★**enhance**

din *n.* uproar, racket, bable, commotion,

pandemonium ▷*noise* ★**quiet**

dingy *adj.* murky, dark, dreary, somber, gloomy ▷*dismal* ★**bright**

dip *v.* sink, subside, immerse, plunge

dire *adj.* alarming, appalling, awful, horrible ▷*terrible* DYER

direct ① *adj.* straight, even, blunt, candid ② *v.* aim, level, train, point

direction *n.* course, trend, way, track, route

dirt *n.* impurity, filth, grime, muck, soil

dirty *adj.* unclean, impure, filthy, sordid, squalid, nasty ★**clean**

disable *v.* cripple, lame, maim, disarm

disadvantage *n.* inconvenience, burden, damage, loss, obstacle ★**advantage**

disagree *v.* differ, revolt, decline, refuse, dissent, argue ★**agree**

disagreeable *adj.* unpleasant, obnoxious,

Dogs

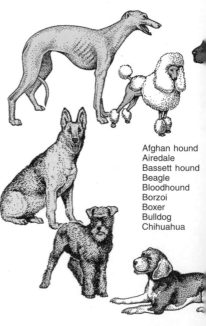

Afghan hound
Airedale
Bassett hound
Beagle
Bloodhound
Borzoi
Boxer
Bulldog
Chihuahua

unwelcome, offensive ★**agreeable**

disappear *v.* vanish, dissolve, fade, melt, depart, expire ★**appear**

disappoint *v.* frustrate, disillusion, let down, dismay, dissatisfy ★**please**

disapprove *v.* condemn, denounce, criticize, reproach ★**approve**

disaster *n.* calamity, catastrophe, accident, misfortune ★**triumph**

disbelief *n.* incredulity, distrust, doubt, suspicion ★**belief**

discard *v.* eliminate, get rid of, reject, scrap *Once we got a new car, I scrapped the old one,* throw away ★**adopt**

discern *v.* note, discover, distinguish

discharge *v.* ① dismiss, give notice to, expel ② detonate, emit, fire

disciple *n.* follower, learner, pupil, attendant

discipline *n.* correction, training, self-control, obedience

disclaim *v.* repudiate, disown, renounce, deny, reject ★**acknowledge**

disclose *v.* discover, show, reveal, expose, betray ▷ *divulge* ★**conceal**

disconcert *v.* abash, confuse, confound, upset, baffle ★**encourage**

disconnect *v.* separate, detach, cut off, sever, uncouple ★**connect**

disconsolate *adj.* distressed, sad, forlorn, melancholy, desolate ▷ *unhappy* ★**cheerful**

discontented *adj.* displeased, disgruntled, unsatisfied, reluctant ★**content**

discord *n.* disagreement, strife ★**concord**

discourage *v.* depress, dismay, dispirit, dishearten *I don't want to dishearten you, but our vacation is cancelled,* put off ★**encourage**

discouraged *adj.* crestfallen, daunted, depressed, downcast ★**encouraged**

discourteous *adj.* blunt, crude, churlish,

Chow chow	Great Dane	Pug
Collie	Greyhound	St. Bernard
Dachshund	Irish setter	Saluki
Dalmatian	Labrador	Spaniel
Doberman pinscher	Old English	Terrier
German shepherd	sheepdog	Whippet
Golden retriever	Pekingese	
	Pointer	
	Poodle	

outspoken, abrupt ★**courteous**

discover v. locate, surprise, unearth, uncover ▷*find* ★**conceal**

discreet adj. prudent, cautious, careful, tactful, sensible ★**indiscreet** DISCRETE

discriminate v. distinguish, penetrate, favor, judge, assess ★**confound**

discuss v. confer, consider, talk over, debate, argue

disdain n. ridicule, scorn, contempt, derision ★**admiration**

disease n. infection, contagion, illness, plague, ailment, sickness

disfigure v. blemish, deface, deform, mar, scar, spoil ★**adorn**

disgrace n. scandal, dishonor, shame, infamy, stigma ★**honor**

disguise v. conceal, mask, falsify, cloak, deceive, fake

disgust ① n. revulsion, loathing, distaste *The room was messy, and I entered it with distaste* ② v. repel, revolt, nauseate ★**admire**

dish n. plate, platter, bowl

dishearten v. depress, cast down, deter, deject ▷*discourage* ★**encourage**

dishonest adj. deceitful, unscrupulous, shady, crooked ★**honest**

disintegrate v. crumble, molder, decompose, rot, fall apart ★**unite**

dislike v. hate, loathe, detest, abhor, abominate ▷*despise* ★**like**

dismal adj. dreary, ominous, cheerless, depressing ▷*hopeless* ★**cheerful**

dismiss v. banish, discard, abandon, dispel, repudiate, release ★**appoint**

disobey v. rebel, transgress, resist, defy, ignore ★**obey**

disorder n. confusion, disarray, commotion, chaos ★**order**

dispel v. disperse, drive away, dismiss, allay, scatter ★**collect**

dispense v. distribute, arrange, allocate, supply, measure out ★**accept**

disperse v. scatter, separate, break up, spread abroad, distribute ★**gather**

display v. show, exhibit, unfold, expose,

flaunt *He flaunts his expensive clothes to his friends,* flourish ▷*reveal* ★**hide**

displease v. annoy, anger, irritate, upset, vex, offend, infuriate ★**please**

dispose v. arrange, place, position, regulate, order

dispose of v. discard, dump, destroy, eliminate, throw away ★**keep**

dispute ① n. conflict, quarrel, argument ② v. argue, refute, contend

disregard v. overlook, misjudge, despise, ignore, snub ★**heed**

disreputable adj. discreditable, dishonorable, disgraceful ▷*shameful* ★**honorable**

dissect v. examine, scrutinize, analyze, dismember

dissent n. disagreement, difference, repudiation, opposition ★**assent**

dissimilar adj. different, diverse, unlike, various ★**similar**

dissolve v. melt, thaw, break up, fade

dissuade v. deter, discourage, warn, put off ★**persuade**

distance n. extent, remoteness, range, reach, span, stretch

distinct adj. ① separate, independent, detached ② clear, conspicuous, lucid ★**hazy**

distinguish v. discern, discover, differentiate

distinguished adj. important, notable, great, famed, celebrated ★**ordinary**

distort v. deform, misshape, twist, bend, buckle

distract v. ① beguile, bewilder, disturb, confuse ② entertain

distress v. harass, embarrass, trouble, grieve ▷*worry* ★**soothe**

distribute v. give out, deliver, disperse, circulate ▷*dispense* ★**collect**

district n. area, community, locality *Pat and Mike have moved to a new locality,* neighborhood, region

distrust v. suspect, discredit, doubt, disbelieve ★**trust**

disturb v. annoy, bother, disquiet, unsettle, upset, confuse ★**calm**

Domesticated Animals

Camel
Canary
Cat
Cattle
Chicken
Dog
Donkey
Duck
Elephant

Goat
Goose
Horse
Parakeet
Parrot
Pig
Pigeon
Sheep

dither *v.* waver, hesitate, falter, oscillate

dive *v.* plunge, pitch, swoop, descend, drop

diverse *adj.* different, various, dissimilar, numerous, separate ★**identical**

divert *v.* ① alter, change, deflect ② entertain, gratify

divest *v.* disrobe, undress, strip

divide *v.* separate, dissect, part, divorce, distribute, apportion, split ★**join**

division *n.* portion, fragment, section, compartment, department

divorce *v.* annul, cancel, separate, divide, part, split up

divulge *v.* betray, disclose, tell, announce, broadcast, uncover

dizzy *adj.* giddy, confused, shaky, wobbling, muddled, staggering

do *v.* ① carry out, perform, act ② be adequate, suffice

do away with *v.* destroy, abolish, eliminate, kill

do up, *v.* fasten, tie, fix

docile *adj.* amenable, tame, meek, orderly, manageable ★**uncooperative**

doctrine *n.* article, belief, creed, dogma, teaching

document *n.* paper, deed, certificate, form

dodge *v.* avoid, parry, duck, elude, fend off

dogged *adj.* obstinate, morose, sullen, persistent, steadfast ★**docile**

doleful *adj.* dismal, woebegone, depressing, rueful, sad ▷ *gloomy* ★**merry**

domestic ① *adj.* homey, household *The children always help with the household chores,* family, internal ② domesticated, tame

dominant *adj.* masterful, superior, supreme, prevalent ★**subordinate**

dominate *v.* rule, control, direct, tyrannize, overbear ★**yield**

donation *n.* gift, present, contribution

doom *n.* judgment, fate, verdict, destiny, destruction

door *n.* entrance, doorway, gate, gateway, portal

dose *n.* draft, potion, quantity, amount

doubt *v.* hesitate, waver, demur, suspect, mistrust, be dubious ★**trust**

doubtful *adj.* suspicious, dubious, indefinite, uncertain, unclear ★**certain**

dour *adj.* austere, dreary, grim, hard, severe ★**cheery**

dowdy *adj.* dull, plain, dingy, frumpish ▷ *shabby* ★**elegant**

downcast *adj.* crestfallen, downhearted, dejected ▷ *miserable* ★**happy**

downfall *n.* ruin, overthrow, misfortune, disgrace, failure

downright *adj.* blunt, candid, absolute, forthright, straightforward

doze *v.* snooze, slumber, sleep, nod off, drowse

drab *adj.* colorless, cheerless, dull, gloomy, gray ▷*dreary* ★**bright**

draft *v.* sketch, outline, draw, design, plan

drag *v.* draw, pull, haul, tug, tow, lug

drain ① *v.* draw, strain, drip, percolate, empty, dry, drink up ② *n.* conduit, sewer, pipe

dramatic *adj.* theatrical, exciting, surprising, sensational ★**ordinary**

drape *v.* hang, suspend, droop, cover

drastic *adj.* extreme, dire, desperate, harsh, radical ★**mild**

draw *v.* ① pull, tug, drag, haul ② sketch, design, depict, portray

drawback *n.* weakness, shortcoming, failing, defect, handicap ★**advantage**

dread *n.* fear, terror, horror, alarm, awe, dismay ▷*fright* ★**confidence**

dreadful *adj.* fearful, terrible, horrible, alarming ▷*awful* ★**comforting**

dream *n.* trance, vision, fancy, reverie, fantasy, illusion

dreary *adj.* dingy, gloomy, somber, cheerless ▷*dismal* ★**bright**

drench *v.* saturate, soak, steep, flood

dress ① *n.* clothing, vestments, costume, garb, apparel, attire ② *v.* wear, put on, don

dress up *v.* playact, don costumes

drift *v.* float, flow, wander, stray, meander
The little stream meandered through lush countryside

drill ① *v.* teach, exercise, train, discipline ② bore, penetrate, pierce

drink *v.* imbibe, swallow, absorb, quaff, sip

drip *v.* drop, ooze, percolate, drizzle, trickle

drive *v.* ① make, compel, force, oblige, prod, goad ② propel, direct, operate, actuate

drivel *n.* nonsense, babble, twaddle, bunkum, gibberish

drizzle *v.* dribble, mizzle, shower, spit ▷*rain*

droll *adj.* whimsical, comical, comic ▷*funny*

droop *v.* flag, sink, decline, languish, drop, bend, wilt

drop ① *v.* fall, sink, dip, plunge, plummet ② *n.* droplet, globule, drip

drown *v.* sink, immerse, swamp, submerge, extinguish

drowsy *adj.* sleepy, somnolent, dazed, tired

drudge *v.* toil, labor, struggle, plod, slave

drug *v.* dope, deaden, sedate, stupefy, poison

dry *adj.* ① arid, parched, moistureless, dried up ★**wet** ② uninteresting, boring, tedious, prosaic, dull

dubious *adj.* suspicious, fishy, suspect, untrustworthy ▷*doubtful* ★**trustworthy**

duck ① *n.* waterfowl ② *v.* plunge, submerge, dip, dodge, lurch

due *adj.* ① owing, unpaid, payable ② just, fair, proper ③ scheduled, expected DEW, DO

duel *n.* combat, contest, battle, swordplay

duffer *n.* blunderer, bungler, booby, dolt

dull *adj.* ① stupid, stolid, obtuse, dim-witted ② blunt, not sharp ③ boring, uninteresting, tedious

dumb ① *adj.* silent, speechless, mute ② foolish, stupid ▷*dull* ★**intelligent**

dummy ① *n.* mannequin, puppet, doll ② *n.* blockhead, dimwit ③ *adj.* artificial, fake, false

dump *v.* deposit, ditch, empty, throw away

dunce *n.* dimwit, dolt, blockhead, duffer, ignoramus ★**genius**

dungeon *n.* cell, prison, jail, vault

dupe *v.* cheat, defraud, deceive, outwit

duplicate *n.* copy, facsimile, replica, reproduction

durable *adj.* lasting, enduring, permanent, stable, reliable ★**fragile**

dusk *n.* twilight, nightfall, evening, gloaming ★**dawn**

dusty *adj.* grimy, dirty, filthy, grubby ★**polished**

duty *n.* ① obligation, responsibility, allegiance, trust, task ② impost, tax, excise

dwell *v.* stop, stay, rest, linger, tarry, live, reside

dwell on *v.* emphasize, linger over, harp on

dwindle *v.* diminish, decrease, decline, waste, shrink, become smaller ★**increase**

dye *n.* pigment, coloring matter, color, stain, tint DIE

E e

eager *adj.* avid, enthusiastic, ambitious, ardent, zealous ▷*keen* ★**indifferent**

early *adj.* advanced, forward, soon ★**late**

earn *v.* make money, deserve, merit, rate, win, acquire ★**spend** URN

earnest *adj.* serious, sincere, determined, eager, zealous ★**flippant**

earth *n.* ① soil, dust, dry land ② world, globe, sphere

ease *n.* ① calm, repose, rest, quiet, peace ② dexterity, deftness ★**difficulty**

easy *adj.* effortless, smooth, simple, practicable ★**difficult**

eat *v.* consume, dine, chew, swallow, gorge

ebb *v.* flow back, fall back, recede, decline, wane ★**flow**

eccentric *adj.* queer, strange, odd, erratic, whimsical ▷*peculiar* ★**normal**

echo *v.* vibrate, reverberate, imitate

economical *adj.* moderate, reasonable, frugal ▷*thrifty* ★**expensive**

ecstasy *n.* joy, happiness, delight, elation ▷*bliss* ★**torment**

edge *n.* border, rim, brink, fringe, margin, tip ▷*end*

edible *adj.* eatable, comestible, safe, wholesome ★**inedible**

edit *v.* revise, correct, adapt, censor, publish

educate *v.* instruct, teach, tutor, coach, train

educated *adj.* learned, cultured, erudite, literate, well-bred ★**ignorant**

eerie *adj.* weird, unearthly, uncanny, awesome

effect ① *n.* outcome *What was the outcome of your interview?*, end, result ② *v.* cause, make, bring about, accomplish

effective *adj.* operative, serviceable, competent ★**useless**

efficient *adj.* competent, proficient, able ▷*effective* ★**inefficient**

effort *n.* exertion, toil, labor, accomplishment ▷*feat*

eject *v.* drive out, force out, expel, evict, oust, discharge

elaborate *adj.* complex, elegant, ornate, intricate ★**simple**

elated *adj.* excited, gleeful, joyous, overjoyed ▷*pleased* ★**downcast**

elderly *adj.* old, aged, ancient ★**youthful**

elect *v.* choose, determine, vote, select, pick

elegant *adj.* refined, luxurious, polished, classical ▷*graceful* ★**inelegant**

elementary *adj.* easy, effortless, basic, clear ▷*simple* ★**complex**

Eating verbs

bolt breakfast
chew chomp consume
devour dig in dine drink
eat eat up
feast feed finish off
gobble gorge gulp guzzle
imbibe
lap up lunch
masticate munch
nibble nosh
partake peck at pick at
quaff
relish
sample savor set to sip slurp
snack swallow sup swig swill
taste tuck in
wash down wine and dine
wolf down

elevate *v.* raise, erect, hoist, upraise ▷*lift* ★**lower**

eligible *adj.* qualified, suitable, acceptable, proper ▷*fit* ★**unfit**

eliminate *v.* do away with, abolish *The government has abolished many old laws,* exterminate, erase, delete ★**keep**

elude *v.* evade, avoid, depart, dodge, escape

embarrass *v.* abash, confuse, disconcert, fluster, shame

emblem *n.* badge, mark, brand, sign, crest, device

embrace *v.* ① hug, squeeze, cuddle, caress, hold ② include *The census figures include new arrivals this year,* encompass, enclose

emerge *v.* come out, exit, appear, arise, turn up ★**disappear**

emergency *n.* crisis, danger, extremity, predicament ▷*plight*

eminent *adj.* famous, noted, renowned, well-known, esteemed ▷*important* ★**unknown**

emit *v.* give off, belch, radiate, discharge, eject, vent ★**absorb**

emotion *n.* sentiment, feeling, fervor, passion

emotional *adj.* affected, sensitive, responsive, temperamental ★**cold**

emphasize *v.* accentuate, accent, intensify ▷*stress* ★**understate**

employ *v.* engage, hire, retain, apply, adopt ▷*use*

employee *n.* worker, workman, staff member, jobholder

empty ① *adj.* bare, barren, vacant *That house has been vacant for months,* hollow, unoccupied ★**full** ② *v.* discharge, drain, unload, pour out ★**fill**

enchant *v.* enthrall, bewitch, delight, gratify ▷*charm* ★**bore**

enclose *v.* surround, encircle, encompass, contain, include ★**open**

encounter *v.* come upon, meet, experience, face

encourage *v.* cheer, hearten, console, comfort, support ▷*urge* ★**dissuade**

encroach *v.* intrude, transgress, overstep, trespass, infringe

end ① *n.* conclusion, finish, limit, boundary *This river marks the boundary of the county* ② *v.* complete, close, terminate ▷*finish* ★**start**

endanger *v.* hazard, imperil, jeopardize ▷*risk* ★**protect**

endeavor *v.* aspire, aim, strive, struggle, try ▷*aim*

endless *adj.* ceaseless, continuous, everlasting, limitless

endorse *v.* undersign, uphold, support, guarantee, vouch for ★**disapprove**

endow *v.* settle upon, invest, award, bequeath, provide ▷*bestow* ★**divest**

endowed *adj.* talented, gifted, enhanced

endure *v.* bear, tolerate, suffer, go through, experience, cope with

enemy *n.* foe, adversary, rival, antagonist, opponent ★**friend**

energetic *adj.* dynamic, lively, vigorous, brisk ▷*active* ★**sluggish**

energy *n.* vigor, endurance, stamina, vitality, force, power

enforce *v.* apply, administer, carry out

engage *v.* ① employ, hire, charter, rent ② occupy *That new book has occupied my mind for weeks,* oblige, operate ③ pledge, betroth

engine *n.* machine, device, motor, turbine, appliance

engrave *v.* etch, stipple, incise, sculpture, carve, chisel

engrossed *adj.* absorbed, fascinated, enthralled ★**bored**

enhance *v.* intensify, strengthen, amplify, improve ★**decrease**

enigma *n.* riddle, puzzle, cryptogram, mystery, problem

enjoy *v.* like, be fond of, delight in, appreciate, savor ▷*relish* ★**detest**

enjoyable *adj.* likable, amusing, delicious ▷*agreeable* ★**disagreeable**

enlarge *v.* amplify, make bigger, expand, extend, magnify, increase, broaden ▷*swell* ★**shrink**

enlighten *v.* inform, teach, explain to,

Engines

Diesel engine
Internal combustion
 engine
Jet engine
Piston engine
Steam engine
Turbojet engine
Turboprop
 engine
Wankel engine

educate, instruct ★**confuse**

enlist v. conscript, employ, engage, muster, sign up, volunteer

enmity n. animosity, acrimony, bitterness, hostility, antagonism, antipathy ▷*hatred* ★**friendship**

enormous adj. immense, vast, tremendous, massive ▷*huge* ★**tiny**

enough adj. sufficient, adequate, ample, plenty ★**insufficient**

enrage v. aggravate, incite, incense, infuriate ▷*anger* ★**soothe**

enrich v. decorate, embellish, adorn, improve ★**impoverish**

enroll v. sign up, enlist, register, accept, admit ★**reject**

enslave v. bind, conquer, dominate, overpower, yoke ★**free**

ensue v. develop, follow, result, arise ▷*happen* ★**precede**

ensure v. confirm, guarantee, insure, protect, secure

entangle v. tangle, snarl, ensnare, complicate ▷*bewilder* ★**extricate**

enter v. go in, arrive, enroll, invade, commence, penetrate ★**leave**

enterprise n. endeavor, adventure, undertaking, concern, establishment

entertain v. amuse, charm, cheer, please, divert, beguile ★**bore**

enthrall v. captivate, charm, entrance, fascinate ★**bore**

enthusiasm n. fervor, ardor, interest, hobby, passion, eagerness

entice v. attract, beguile, coax, lead on, wheedle

entire adj. complete, intact, total, whole, full ★**partial**

entirely adj. absolutely, wholly, utterly *Our old dog came home, utterly tired and exhausted,* altogether ★**partially**

entitle v. ① allow, authorize, empower *As president, I am empowered to sign this document,* enable ② call, christen, term, name

entrance ① n. (*en*-trance) way in, access *There is an access to the garden on the far side,* doorway, gate, opening ② v. (en-*trance*) bewitch, captivate, charm ★**repel**

entreat v. beg, beseech, implore, ask

entry n. access, admission, admittance ▷*entrance* ★**exit**

envelop v. wrap, wind, roll, cloak, conceal, enfold

envious adj. jealous, grudging, covetous *Arlene cast a covetous eye at my new jacket,* resentful ★**content**

environment n. surroundings, neighborhood, vicinity, background

envy v. covet, grudge, desire, crave, resent

episode n. occasion, affair, circumstance, happening, installment

equal adj. ① matching, like, alike, same ★**different** ② fit *I'm not sure if Joe is really fit for this job*

equip v. furnish, provide, supply, fit out, rig

equipment n. stores, supplies, outfit, tackle *When we arrived at the lake, Sam found he'd left his fishing tackle behind,* gear

equivalent adj. equal, comparable, alike, similar, interchangeable ★**unlike**

era n. epoch, age, generation, period, time

eradicate v. uproot, weed out, remove, stamp out ▷*abolish*

erase v. cancel, rub out, obliterate, eliminate ▷*delete* ★**mark**

erect ① adj. upright, upstanding, rigid *The tent had a rigid metal frame* ★**relaxed** ② v. build, construct, put up ★**demolish**

err v. be mistaken, blunder, go astray,

mistake, misjudge, sin

errand *n.* mission, assignment, duty, job ▷ *task*

erratic *adj.* eccentric, irregular, unstable, unreliable ★**stable**

erroneous *adj.* untrue, false, faulty, inaccurate ▷ *wrong* ★**correct**

error *n.* mistake, fault, flaw, fallacy, untruth ▷ *blunder* ★**truth**

erupt *v.* blow up, explode, burst, vent ▷ *discharge*

escape *v.* break free, get away, dodge, elude, evade ▷ *flee* ★**capture**

escort ① *n.* (*es*-cort) guard, conductor, aide, attendant, procession ② *v.* (es-*cort*) accompany, conduct

especially *adv.* chiefly, principally, notably

essay *n.* ① effort, trial ② theme, manuscript, composition *Whoever writes the best composition gets a prize*

essence *n.* ① extract, juice, perfume ② substance *He spoke well, but there was no substance to his speech,* core, pith, character

essential *adj.* necessary, needed, vital, requisite ★**superfluous**

establish *v.* situate, place, station, found, organize, set up ★**upset**

estate *n.* property, land, fortune, inheritance

esteem *v.* honor, respect, admire ▷ *like* ★**dislike**

estimate *v.* consider, calculate, figure, assess, reckon

estrange *v.* alienate, antagonize, separate ★**unite**

eternal *adj.* endless, ceaseless, forever, immortal, undying ★**temporary**

evacuate *v.* leave, desert, quit ▷ *abandon* ★**occupy**

evade *v.* elude, avoid, get away from, escape from ★**face**

evaporate *v.* vanish, dissolve, disappear, condense, dry up

even *adj.* ① smooth, plane, flat, flush ② balanced, equal ★**uneven** ③ yet, still

evening *n.* eve, eventide, sunset ▷ *dusk* ★**morning**

event *n.* occurrence, incident, happening

ever *adv.* always, evermore, perpetually, forever ★**never**

everlasting *adj.* continual, endless, permanent, lasting ★**temporary**

everyday *adj.* common, frequent, daily, familiar ★**occasional**

everything *n.* all, the whole, the lot

evict *v.* expel, eject, cast out, remove, kick out

evidence *n.* appearance, proof, sign, token, testimony

evident *adj.* obvious, apparent, plain, visible, conspicuous ★**obscure**

evil *v.* wicked, sinister, wrong, bad, hurtful, sinful ★**good**

exact *adj.* accurate, precise, definite, correct ▷ *right* ★**inexact**

exaggerate *v.* magnify, overstate, overestimate, amplify ★**minimize**

examine *v.* check, inspect, scrutinize, test, quiz, question

example *n.* case, sample, specimen, pattern, model, illustration

exasperate *v.* provoke, anger, annoy, aggravate ★**soothe**

excavate *v.* mine, quarry, shovel, dig up, discover, unearth ★**bury**

exceed *v.* excel, surpass, better, beat, outstrip

excel *v.* outdo ▷ *exceed*

excellent *adj.* admirable, good, superb, exquisite ▷ *splendid* ★**inferior**

except *prep.* with the exception of, barring, save, saving, omitting

exceptional *adj.* unique, unusual, rare *Margaret has a rare gift for the piano,* uncommon ★**common**

excess *n.* too much, extreme, glut, extravagance, extreme ▷ *surplus* ★**scarcity**

exchange *v.* trade, barter, swap, convert, change

excite *v.* inflame, inspire, provoke, rouse, thrill ★**quell**

excited *adj.* ablaze, wild, ecstatic, frantic, thrilled ★**bored**

exclaim v. state, say, utter, ejaculate, declare, cry out

exclude v. bar, shut out, prevent, boycott, forbid, leave out ★**include**

exclusive adj. only, personal, choice, particular, special ★**inclusive**

excuse v. forgive, pardon, absolve, exempt, release ★**accuse**

execute v. ① accomplish, do, carry out *The work was carried out just as I had expected,* achieve ② put to death, hang

exempt v. excuse, release, discharge, relieve, exonerate

exercise ① n. performance, lesson, lecture, training ② v. apply, train, practice *We have been practicing our tennis for months*

exert v. apply, exercise, strain, struggle, toil

exhale v. breathe out, expel, expire ★**inhale**

exhaust ① v. use up *We have used up all our butter,* consume, deplete, empty ② overtire, fatigue, weaken

exhibition n. spectacle, show, fair, pageant, display

exhilarate v. invigorate, animate, stimulate, thrill ★**discourage**

exile v. deport, banish, relegate, transport, dismiss

exist v. be, live, breathe, subsist, stand

exit n. way out, outlet, egress, door

expand v. inflate, spread, dilate, extend, amplify ▷*swell* ★**contract**

expansive adj. affable, genial, friendly, open, comprehensive

expect v. look out for, anticipate, assume, foresee, contemplate

expedition n. ① outing, excursion, exploration, quest *As a child I spent long hours in the library in the quest for knowledge* ② speed, dispatch, alacrity

expel v. evict, eject, discharge, throw out ★**admit**

expend v. spend, lay out, waste, consume, use up ▷*exhaust* ★**save**

expensive adj. costly, high-priced, valuable, rich ★**cheap**

experience ① n. training, practice, wisdom, knowledge ② v. encounter, try, undergo, endure

experiment n. trial, test, check, venture

expert n. specialist, master, authority, professional ★**novice**

expire v. ① breathe out, exhale ② die, lapse *The lease on this house will lapse at the end of the year,* run out ★**begin**

explain v. elucidate, spell out, define, expound, teach ★**mystify**

explanation n. definition, outline, answer, meaning

explode v. detonate, blow up, go off, burst, discharge

exploit ① n. deed, feat, act, stunt ② v. take advantage of, profit by

export v. ship, send out, send abroad

expose v. show, reveal, exhibit, present, lay bare, betray ★**cover**

express ① v. phrase, voice, put into words, utter ② v. squeeze out ③ adj. speedy, fast

expression n. ① phrase, idiom, sentence, statement ② look, countenance, appearance

exquisite adj. dainty, subtle, fine, refined ▷*beautiful* ★**coarse**

extend v. stretch, reach, lengthen ▷*expand* ★**shorten**

extent n. breadth, expanse, width, bulk, mass, reach, duration

exterior ① n. outside, surface ② adj. external, outer, outdoor ★**interior**

extinct adj. defunct, dead, exterminated ★**living**

extinguish v. put out, blow out, abolish, destroy, quench ★**establish**

extract v. take out, select, remove, withdraw ★**insert**

extraordinary adj. unusual, incredible, strange, uncommon, marvelous ★**common**

extravagant adj. wasteful, reckless, prodigal, lavish ★**stingy**

extreme adj. ① excessive, outrageous, intense ★**moderate** ② farthest, final, remote

extricate v. loose, loosen, remove, retrieve, pull out

exultant adj. rejoicing, jubilant, joyous, triumphant ▷*elated* ★**depressed**

F f

fable *n.* myth, legend, story, fantasy ★**fact**

fabric *n.* cloth, textile, material

fabulous *adj.* imaginary, legendary *Many tales have been passed down about the legendary deeds of Robin Hood,* mythical, marvelous ▷*wonderful*

face ① *n.* countenance, visage ② *n.* front, frontage, facade *The original facade was kept when the building was renovated* ③ *v.* confront, be opposite

facetious *adj.* frivolous, jocular, humorous, witty, comical ▷*funny* ★**serious**

facility *n.* ease, readiness, quickness, adroitness, knack

facsimile *n.* replica, copy, repro, photocopy

fact *n.* truth, deed, occurrence, event, reality, actuality ★**fiction**

factory *n.* plant, mill, works, shop

factual *adj.* true, actual, accurate, correct ▷*real* ★**false**

fad *n.* craze, fashion, passion, desire, mania *My sister has a mania for teddy bears,* vogue

fade *v.* discolor, bleach, dwindle, dim

fail *v.* collapse, fall, miss, trip, lose, flop ★**succeed**

failing *n.* frailty, weakness, fault, flaw ▷*defect*

failure *n.* collapse, crash, fiasco, downfall ★**success**

faint ① *adj.* indistinct *The writing was so indistinct that we could hardly read it,* soft, low, dim, feeble ② *v.* swoon, pass out, collapse FEINT

fair *adj.* ① just, equal, reasonable ★**unfair** ② mediocre *He was not a good piano player, just mediocre,* average, moderate ③ blonde, light-skinned, beautiful

faith *n.* trust, confidence, belief, fidelity, creed

faithful *adj.* ① loyal, constant, staunch, true ★**faithless** ② accurate, dependable *My watch is very dependable; it keeps accurate time* ★**inaccurate**

faithless *adj.* false, unfaithful, untrue ★**faithful**

fake *adj.* false, fictitious, pretended ▷*bogus* ★**genuine**

fall *v.* ① fall down, stumble, drop ② decline, dwindle *My mother's shares had dwindled and were worth much less,* lower ★**rise**

fall down *v.* stumble, lose one's balance

fall through *v.* collapse, fail, founder *The family business had foundered during the recession*

fallacy *n.* flaw, fault, mistake, illusion, deception

false *adj.* ① untrue, counterfeit, fake, inaccurate ② dishonest, disloyal ★**reliable**

falsehood *n.* lie, fiction, fable, fabrication, untruth, fib ★**truth**

falter *v.* reel, totter, stumble, waver, tremble

fame *n.* glory, distinction, honor, eminence, renown

familiar ① *adj.* common, frequent, well-known ② intimate *Joe and Mary are intimate friends of mine,* close, dear

famine *n.* scarcity, hunger, shortage, starvation

famished *adj.* hungry, starving, ravenous

famous *adj.* famed, well-known, celebrated, legendary *My grandmother was very attractive; her beauty was legendary,* notorious ★**unknown**

fan *v.* ventilate, cool, blow, stimulate

fanatic *n.* enthusiast, zealot, follower, fan

fanciful *adj.* romantic, fantastic, imaginary, unreal ★**ordinary**

fancy ① *adj.* decorative, beautiful, ornamental ② *v.* desire, hanker after *I had been hankering after a sea cruise all year,* yearn

fantastic *adj.* strange, bizarre, unfamiliar, romantic ▷*fanciful* ★**ordinary**

far *adj.* distant, faraway, remote ★**near**

fare ① *v.* manage *I managed quite well while my parents were abroad,* get along, happen ② *n.* charge, cost, fee ③ *n.* food, meals, menu

farewell *interj.* good-bye, so long, adieu *We*

bade our hosts adieu as we drove off

farm ① *v.* cultivate, raise, grow ② *n.* farmstead, homestead, ranch, holding *We owned a small holding of land in the west*

fascinate *v.* bewitch, beguile, enthrall, engross ★**bore**

fashion ① *n.* style, fad, mode, manner ② *v.* form, carve, sculpt, devise

fast ① *adj.* rapid, quick, speedy, brisk ② *v.* starve, famish, go hungry

fasten *v.* fix, tie, attach, bind, hitch, truss ★**unfasten**

fat ① *adj.* stout, corpulent *Uncle Harry was a corpulent old man* ▷*plump* ★**thin** ② *n.* grease, oil, tallow, shortening

fatal *adj.* deadly, lethal, destructive, mortal ★**harmless**

fate *n.* fortune, destiny, future, lot, portion

fathom *v.* unravel, understand, follow, comprehend

fatigue ① *n.* tiredness, weariness ② *v.* tire, exhaust, languish *The survivors of the shipwreck languished in an open boat*

fault *n.* ① defect, flaw, imperfection ② blame, responsibility, error

faulty *adj.* imperfect, defective, unreliable, unsound, broken ★**perfect**

favor ① *n.* kindness, courtesy, benefit ② *v.* indulge, prefer, approve ★**disapprove**

favorite ① *n.* choice, darling, preference ② *v.* best-liked, chosen, preferred

fawn *v.* crouch, crawl, grovel FAUN

fear ① *n.* fright, alarm, terror, panic, shock ★**courage** ② *v.* dread, be afraid, doubt

fearful *adj.* timid, anxious, alarmed, worried ▷*afraid* ★**courageous**

fearless *adj.* gallant, courageous, daring, valiant *My ailing mother made a valiant effort to keep working* ▷*brave* ★**timid**

feast *n.* banquet, repast, dinner

feat *n.* deed, exploit, achievement, performance, stunt FEET

feature *n.* mark, peculiarity, distinction, characteristic

fee *n.* charge, commission, cost

feeble *adj.* frail, faint, flimsy, puny ▷*weak* ★**strong**

Feat

Feet

feed *v.* nourish, sustain, foster, nurture *These plants must be nurtured if they are to survive*

feel *v.* touch, handle, perceive, comprehend, know, suffer

feign *v.* fake, pretend, act, sham FAIN

feint *n.* bluff, pretense, dodge, deception FAINT

fellow *n.* companion, comrade, associate, colleague

female *adj.* feminine, womanly, girlish, maidenly ★**male**

fence ① *n.* barrier, paling, barricade ② *v.* dodge, evade, parry *The sudden attack was parried by the defenders,* duel

ferocious *adj.* fierce, savage, brutal, grim, vicious ★**gentle**

fertile *adj.* fruitful, productive, rich, abundant ★**barren**

fervent *adj.* warm, passionate, enthusiastic, zealous ▷ *ardent*

festival *n.* celebration, carnival, fête, jubilee

festive *adj.* convivial, jovial, sociable, gleeful, cordial ★**somber**

fetch *v.* bear, bring, carry, deliver, convey

fête *n.* bazaar, carnival, fair, festival

fetter *v.* manacle, handcuff, shackle, restrain

feud *n.* dispute, grudge, conflict, discord ★**harmony**

fever *n.* illness, infection, passion, excitement, heat, ecstasy

few *adj.* scant, scanty, meager, paltry, not many

fiasco *n.* washout, calamity, disaster, failure

fib *n.* lie, falsehood, untruth

fickle *adj.* unstable, changeable, faithless, disloyal ★**constant**

fiction *n.* stories, fable, myth, legend, invention ★**fact**

fidelity *n.* faithfulness, loyalty, allegiance *I owe allegiance to my family and my country* ★**treachery**

fidget *v.* be nervous, fret, fuss, jiggle, squirm

field *n.* farmland, grassland, green, verdure, meadow, prairie

fiend *n.* devil, demon, imp, beast, brute

fiendish *adj.* atrocious, cruel, devilish, diabolical

fierce *adj.* barbarous, cruel, brutal, merciless ▷ *savage* ★**gentle**

fiery *adj.* passionate, inflamed, excitable, flaming ★**impassive**

fight *n. & v.* conflict, argument, encounter, combat, contest, battle

figure ① *n.* symbol, character, numeral ② *n.* form, shape, model ③ *v.* calculate, reckon *Bella has reckoned the amount correctly*

filch *v.* steal, thieve, sneak, purloin *Someone has purloined the letters from our mailbox*

file ① *v.* scrape, grind, grate, rasp ② *n.* binder, case, folder

fill *v.* load, pack, cram, replenish, occupy ★**empty**

filter *v.* sieve, sift, refine, clarify, screen, percolate PHILTER

filth *n.* impurity, dirt, soil, slime, smut, grime, squalor, muck ★**purity**

filthy *adj.* unclean, impure, nasty, foul ▷ *dirty* ★**pure**

final *adj.* terminal, closing, ultimate, conclusive ▷ *last*

find *v.* discover, achieve, locate, obtain, perceive, meet with *Our plans met with the approval of the committee* ★**lose** FINED

fine ① *adj.* thin, minute, smooth, slender ② *adj.* excellent, sharp, keen, acute ③ *n.* forfeit, penalty

finesse *n.* skill, competence, deftness

finger ① *v.* feel, grope, handle, touch ② *n.* digit, thumb, pinkie

finish *v.* accomplish, complete, close, conclude ▷ *end* ★**begin**

fire ① *n.* blaze, conflagration, heat ② *v.* ignite, light, discharge, shoot

firm ① *adj.* stable, steady, solid, substantial ② *n.* company, business

first *adj.* beginning, earliest, initial, chief, principal

fishy *adj.* suspicious, dubious, doubtful ★**honest**

fissure *n.* breach, cleft, crack, cranny FISHER

fit *adj.* ① apt, suitable, fitting, able ② trim, hale, healthy, sturdy

fitting *adj.* proper, suitable, appropriate, correct ★**unsuitable**

fix ① *v.* repair, mend, attach, fasten ② *n.* predicament, jam, pickle, plight *After the earthquake, the town was in a desperate plight*

flabby *adj.* baggy, drooping, feeble, sagging, slack

flag ① *v.* droop, languish, dwindle, fail ② banner, ensign, colors *The regimental colors were flying at half-mast*

flagrant *adj.* blatant, bold, brazen, arrant ★**secret**

flair *n.* knack, talent, faculty, ability, gift FLARE

flame *n.* fire, blaze, radiance

flap *v.* agitate, flutter, wave, swing, dangle

flare ① *v.* blaze, burn, glare, flash, glow ② *n.* signal, beacon FLAIR

flash *v.* gleam, glimmer, sparkle, twinkle,

Flags

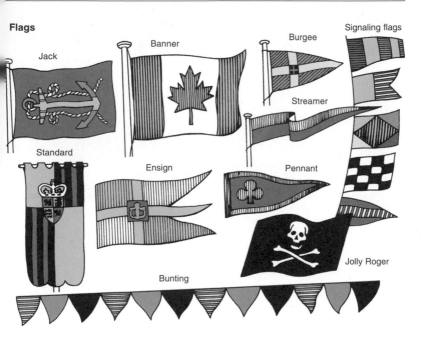

Jack

Banner

Burgee

Signaling flags

Streamer

Standard

Ensign

Pennant

Jolly Roger

Bunting

scintillate

flat ① *adj.* level, smooth, even, horizontal ② *n.* apartment, chambers

flatter *v.* blandish, toady, soft-soap, butter up, curry favor *He gives me presents, but only to curry favor with me* ★**criticize**

flavor *n.* taste, savor, tang, aroma, quality

flaw *n.* fault, defect, blemish, mark, weakness

flawless *adj.* perfect, immaculate, faultless, sound ★**imperfect**

flee *v.* escape, abscond, run away, bolt, vanish ★**stay** FLEA

fleet ① *adj.* rapid, speedy, quick, nimble ▷*swift* ★**slow** ② *n.* navy, armada, flotilla *A flotilla of yachts sailed up the river*

fleeting *adj.* passing, brief, momentary, temporary ★**lasting**

flexible *adj.* pliant, pliable, supple, elastic

flicker *v.* blaze, glitter, flare, burn, sparkle

flimsy *adj.* slight, meager, fragile, trivial, rickety, weak, feeble ★**sturdy**

flinch *v.* cower, cringe, shrink, wince *I had twisted my ankle, and winced with pain as I climbed the hill*

fling *v.* throw, pitch, cast, heave ▷*hurl*

flippant *adj.* saucy, pert, brash, impudent, glib ★**earnest**

float *v.* drift, glide, hover, sail, swim

flock *n.* herd, drove, crush, group

flog *v.* beat, chastise, flay, lash, spank

flood *v.* deluge, engulf, inundate *The town was inundated when the river overflowed*, drown, swamp

floor *n.* deck, base, bottom, platform, level, story

flop *v.* flap, fall, drop, droop, fall flat

florid *adj.* ruddy, flushed, red, ornate ★**pale**

flounce *v.* bounce, fling, jerk, spring, bob

flounder ① *v.* bungle, fail, falter, fumble ② *n.* flatfish

flour *n.* meal, bran, farina FLOWER

Flour

Flower

flourish *v.* ① shake, brandish, flaunt ② blossom, bloom, prosper ▷ *thrive*

flow *v.* run, stream, glide, sweep, swirl ▷ *gush* FLOE

flower *n.* & *v.* blossom, bloom, bud FLOUR

fluent *adj.* vocal, facile, articulate *Sally is very articulate and has a great command of language,* flowing, fluid

fluid *adj.* watery, flowing, liquid, runny ★**solid**

flummox *v.* baffle, confuse, fluster, confound ▷ *bewilder* ★**enlighten**

flush ① *v.* glow, bloom, blush ② *v.* douse, drench, rinse ③ *adj.* level, even

fluster *v.* bother, confuse, perturb ▷ *fuss* ★**calm**

flutter *v.* wave, flap, flop, flitter, hover, flit

fly ① *v.* take flight, glide, soar, float ② *v.* escape, hasten ③ *n.* winged insect

foam *n.* froth, scum, lather, suds, surf

foe *n.* enemy, opponent, rival, adversary ★**friend**

fog *n.* mist, vapor, haze, cloud

foil ① *v.* defeat, overcome, elude ② *n.* sheet metal, tinfoil, film, flake

fold *n.* & *v.* crease, hem, seam, crimp, pleat FOALED

follow *v.* ① pursue, succeed, come after ② understand, catch on to

folly *n.* silliness, foolishness, absurdity, craziness ▷ *nonsense* ★**wisdom**

fond *adj.* tender, loving, caring ▷ *affectionate* ★**hostile**

fondle *v.* pet, stroke, cuddle, caress, coddle

food *n.* nourishment, nutriment, provender, provisions, fare

fool ① *n.* idiot, dunce, clown, blockhead, simpleton ② *v.* deceive, trick, swindle

foolhardy *adj.* reckless, impetuous, madcap ▷ *rash* ★**cautious**

foolish *adj.* absurd, ridiculous, daft ▷ *silly* ★**wise**

for *prep.* on behalf of, toward, because of ★**against** fore, four

forbid *v.* bar, ban, prohibit, deter, hinder, prevent ★**allow**

force ① *n.* energy, strength, might, power ② *v.* make, compel, coerce *It's no use, you can't coerce me into flying home,* push

fore *adj.* first, front, leading FOR, FOUR

forecast *v.* foresee, predict, foretell, prophesy

foreign *adj.* alien, strange, remote, exotic, outlandish ★**domestic**

foremost *adj.* chief, leading, principal, uppermost

forfeit *v.* abandon, give up, lose, relinquish, sacrifice ★**reward**

forge *v.* ① counterfeit, falsify, copy, imitate ② construct, form, make, fashion

forgery *n.* fake, dud, counterfeit, imitation, phony

forget *v.* overlook, neglect, lose sight of ★**remember**

forgive *v.* pardon, absolve, reprieve, let off, overlook ★**blame**

forlorn *adj.* lonely, desolate, miserable, wretched ★**hopeful**

form ① *v.* make, fabricate, fashion, contrive, create ② *n.* manner, fashion, style ③ *n.* shape, figure *I made a clay figure of a pirate*

formal *adj.* stiff, solemn, ceremonial, ritualistic, aloof ★**informal**

former *adj.* earlier, previous, prior ★**later**

formidable *adj.* awful, terrible, alarming, terrifying, serious ★**trivial**

forsake *v.* abandon, give up, desert, discard, leave ▷*quit* ★**resume**

forth *adv.* ahead, forward, onward, outward

forthright *adj.* frank, candid, direct, bald, blunt ★**devious**

forthwith *adv.* immediately, directly, at once, instantly ★**soon**

fortify *v.* ① strengthen, confirm, corroborate, hearten ② garrison, protect, buttress *The old house was crumbling and the walls needed to be buttressed* ★**weaken**

fortitude *n.* courage, endurance, bravery, composure ▷*strength* ★**cowardice**

fortunate *adj.* happy, felicitous, auspicious, rosy ▷*lucky* ★**unfortunate**

fortune *n.* ① affluence, wealth, treasure ② chance, destiny, fate

forward ① *adv.* onward, forth, ahead, before ② *adj.* progressive, bold, audacious ★**modest** ③ *v.* advance, send, transmit

foster *v.* ① help, promote, aid ② care for, cherish, nurse

foul *adj.* mucky, nasty, filthy, dirty, murky ★**fair** FOWL

found *v.* create, build, erect, establish

foundation *n.* establishment, base, basis, groundwork *You will pick up Spanish easily, for you already have the groundwork*

fountain *n.* spring, well, reservoir, source

fowl *n.* bird, chicken, poultry FOUL

foxy *adj.* crafty, slick, cunning, tricky ▷*artful* ★**naive**

fraction *n.* portion, part, division ▷*fragment*

fracture *n.* break, cleft, crack, fissure, opening ▷*split*

fragile *adj.* brittle, frail, delicate, dainty ▷*flimsy* ★**robust**

fragment *n.* portion, bit, chip, morsel, piece ▷*fracture*

fragrance *n.* aroma, smell, odor ▷*scent*

frail *adj.* weak, feeble, infirm ▷*fragile*

frame *n.* framework, casing, shape, mount, chassis

frank *adj.* sincere, candid, open, honest, blunt ▷*truthful* ★**insincere**

frantic *adj.* excited, furious, distracted, wild, mad ▷*frenzied* ★**calm**

fraud *n.* deceit, fake, extortion, swindle ▷*forgery*

fraudulent *adj.* sham, fake, counterfeit ▷*bogus* ★**genuine**

fray *n.* combat, contest, battle, brawl ▷*rumpus*

freak *adj.* abnormal, bizarre *A snowstorm in the tropics would be bizarre,* odd, unusual ★**common**

free ① *adj.* unhindered, at liberty, liberated, unrestricted ② *adj.* gratuitous, gratis, without cost ③ *v.* let loose, unleash, release

freeze *n.* ice, frost, refrigerate FREES, FRIEZE

frenzied *adj.* agitated, excited, furious, hysterical *Lisa became hysterical when she saw the house on fire* ▷*frantic* ★**placid**

frequent *adj.* repeated, numerous, recurrent, common ▷*regular* ★**rare**

frequently *adv.* often, many times, commonly ★**rarely**

fresh *adj.* new, young, vigorous, blooming, recent, wholesome ★**stale**

fret *v.* worry, harass, irritate, torment ▷*vex* ★**calm**

friction *n.* ① rubbing, grating, contact, abrasion ② ill-feeling, discord, dispute

friend *n.* companion, associate, ally, crony *On Saturdays, my father plays golf with some of his cronies,* pal ▷*chum*

friendly *adj.* affable, amicable, kindly, cordial ▷*genial* ★**hostile**

friendship *n.* affection, fellowship, fondness, harmony ▷*concord* ★**enmity**

fright *n.* alarm, dread, dismay, terror ▷*fear* ★**calm**

frighten *v.* daunt, dismay, scare, alarm ▷*terrify* ★**reassure**

frightful *adj.* alarming, shocking, ghastly ▷*horrible* ★**pleasant**

frigid *adj.* cool, chilly, icy, frozen, wintry ★**warm**

fringe *n.* edge, border, limits, outskirts

frisky *adj.* lively, spirited, playful, active ★**quiet**

frivolous *adj.* frothy, facetious, flippant, foolish ▷*trivial* ★**serious**

frock *n.* robe, dress, gown, smock

frolic *v.* gambol, caper, frisk, sport

front *n.* fore, brow, forehead, face, facade, beginning ★**back**

frontier *n.* border, boundary, edge, limit

frosty *adj.* chilly, frigid, frozen, freezing ▷*cold* ★**warm**

froth *n.* scum, bubbles ▷*foam*

frown *v.* glower, grimace, glare ▷*scowl* ★**smile**

frugal *adj.* thrifty, economical, careful, sparing *We were poor in the old days and needed to be sparing with our money* ▷*meager* ★**wasteful**

fruitful *adj.* fertile, productive, flourishing

Futile

It was hopeless, the bear was too big for Zak to carry.

★**barren**

fruitless *adj.* unprofitable, sterile, barren, pointless ★**fruitful**

frustrate *v.* thwart, balk, foil, hinder, defeat ★**fulfill**

fugitive *n.* escapee, runaway, deserter

fulfill *v.* perform, render, please, accomplish, achieve ★**frustrate**

full *adj.* loaded, packed, laden, charged, abundant, complete ★**empty**

fumble *v.* grope, spoil, mismanage, flail ▷*bungle*

fun *n.* sport, frolic, gaiety, jollity, entertainment, amusement

function ① *n.* service, purpose, activity ② *n.* affair, party, gathering ③ *v.* act, operate, work

fund *n.* stock, supply, pool, store, treasury *The city treasury has a small surplus this year*, reserve

fundamental *adj.* basic, essential, primary, rudimentary ★**unimportant**

funny *adj.* comical, droll, amusing, ridiculous ▷*humorous* ★**solemn**

furious *adj.* agitated, angry, fierce, intense ▷*frantic* ★**calm**

furnish *v.* ① supply, provide, offer ② equip

furrow *n.* groove, channel, hollow, seam, rib

further ① *adj.* extra, more, other, supplementary, ② *v.* advanced, aid, hasten

furtive *adj.* secretive, sly, hidden ▷*stealthy* ★**open**

fury *n.* anger, frenzy, ferocity, passion ▷*rage* ★**calm**

fuse *v.* melt, smelt, combine, merge, solder, weld, integrate ▷*join*

fuss *n.* stir, excitement, tumult, bustle, bother, commotion ▷*ado* ★**calm**

fussy *adj.* busy, faddish, fastidious, finicky, exacting ★**plain**

futile *adj.* useless, in vain, hopeless *It was hopeless, the bear was too big for Zak to carry*, barren, forlorn, ineffective ★**effective**

future *adj.* forthcoming, coming, impending, eventual

fuzzy *adj.* murky, foggy, misty, unclear

G g

gain *v.* get, win, acquire, attain, profit

gale *n.* storm, wind, hurricane, tornado, cyclone

gallant *adj.* courageous, noble, chivalrous ▷*brave*

gallop *v.* dash, run, career, rush

gamble *v.* bet, risk, wager, chance GAMBOL

gambol *v.* prance, romp, frisk, frolic ▷*jump* GAMBLE

game *n.* ① sport, pastime, contest, competition ★**work** ② quarry, prey

gang *n.* crew, team, troop, crowd, cluster, party

gap *n.* space, blank, hole, break, cranny, chink, opening, crack, interval

gape *v.* yawn, stare, gaze, gawk ▷*look*

garbage, *n.* trash, rubbish, refuse, waste, slop

garden *n.* flower bed, vegetable patch, patio, park

garment *n.* clothes, dress, attire, robe, costume ▷*clothing*

garret *n.* attic, loft, cupola

gas *n.* vapor, fume, mist, smoke

gasp *v.* gulp, pant, choke ▷*breathe*

gate *n.* door, portal, gateway GAIT

gather *v.* ① collect, pick up, pick, draw, amass, assemble, flock, hoard, acquire ★**disperse** ② understand *I understand that you have been elected treasurer of the club,* assume, judge

gathering *n.* meeting, assembly, function, affair, company, collection

gaudy *adj.* flashy, cheap, tawdry, loud, showy

gaunt, *adj.* thin, lean, skinny, spare ▷*haggard* ★**robust**

gauge ① *n.* measure, meter, rule ② *v.* judge, measure, estimate *We must estimate the number of beans in the jar,* probe GAGE

gaze *v.* stare, look, regard, contemplate

gear *n.* tackle, array, accessories, machinery, harness, equipment

gem *n.* jewel, stone, treasure

general *adj.* normal, usual, habitual, customary, total, whole ★**local**

generous *adj.* free, liberal, kind ★**selfish**

genial *adj.* cheerful, cheery, sunny, hearty, cordial, pleasant ▷*jolly* ★**cold**

genius *n.* brilliance, prowess, talent, power, skill, cleverness, brains ★**stupidity**

genteel *adj.* refined, polished, civil, courteous, well-bred, polite, elegant ★**boorish**

gentle *adj.* ① easy, mild, soft, kind, moderate, tender, humane ② gradual, faint, feeble, slight *The field had a slight slope as it came down to the river*

genuine *adj.* ① real, authentic, true, sound ② sincere, honest, candid, frank ★**false**

germ *n.* microbe, seed, embryo, nucleus

gesture *n.* sign, signal, motion, nod, shrug, movement

get *v.* ① acquire, obtain, gain, win, receive, secure, achieve, inherit ★**forfeit** ② understand, catch on *It took Johnny quite a while to catch on to what I meant,* fathom, figure out, learn

get up *v.* arise, awake, awaken

get rid of *v.* discard, reject, throw away, scrap

ghastly *adj.* shocking, hideous, horrible, fearful, terrible, frightful

ghost *n.* spook, spirit, specter, banshee, phantom, apparition

ghostly *v.* uncanny, haunted, eerie, weird

giant *adj.* mammoth, huge, colossal, enormous, tremendous, immense ▷*big, gigantic* ★**tiny**

gibber *v.* gabble, prattle, jabber

gibberish *n.* nonsense, drivel, garbage

gibe *v.* jeer, sneer, scoff, deride ▷*taunt*

giddy *adj.* dizzy, whirling, reeling, unsteady, wild, reckless

gift *n.* ① present, donation, bounty, boon ② talent, skill *Her skill was so great that I knew she must have been born with it,* ability, power

gigantic *adj.* stupendous, titanic, colossal ▷*giant* ★**minute**

giggle *v.* chuckle, chortle, cackle, snicker
▷ *laugh*

gingerly *adv.* carefully, daintily, warily, cautiously

girder *n.* rafter, joist, beam

girl *n.* maid, maiden, miss, damsel, young woman, lass, wench

girlish *adj.* maidenly, dainty, feminine

girth *n.* circumference, perimeter, fatness, breadth

gist *n.* essence, substance, kernel, nub, pith, significance

give *v.* ① donate, grant, distribute, bestow ② bend, yield *The wooden footbridge suddenly yielded under his weight and crashed into the stream,* relax, recede ③ produce, yield ④ pronounce, utter, emit ★**take**

give back *v.* return, restore

give forth *v.* emit, send out, radiate

give in *v.* surrender, quit, yield

give off *v.* belch, emit, exude

give up *v.* surrender, give in, relinquish, hand over

giver *n.* donor, bestower, presenter

glad *adj.* joyful, joyous, delighted, pleased ▷ *happy* ★**sorry**

gladden *v.* make happy, gratify, delight, elate ▷ *please* ★**grieve**

gladly *adv.* freely, readily, cheerfully, willingly

glamour *n.* romance, interest, fascination, attraction, enchantment

glance ① *n.* look, glimpse, peep ② *v.* peer, notice ③ brush, shave, graze, *The bullet merely grazed his head*

glare ① *v.* blaze, glow, flare, sparkle, dazzle ② frown, glower, stare

glaring *adj.* ① sparkling, dazzling ② blatant, notorious, conspicuous

glass *n.* tumbler, goblet, beaker, mirror, looking glass

glaze *v.* polish, gloss, burnish, varnish

gleam *v.* sparkle, glitter, flash, glisten, twinkle

glee *n.* jollity, gaiety, elation, triumph ▷ *happiness*

glib *adj.* fluent, slick, smooth, slippery, facile, talkative

glide *v.* slide, slither, slip, soar, sail, skate, skim

glimmer *v.* sparkle, scintillate, flicker, glow, gleam

glimpse *v.* spy, spot, glance, view

glisten *v.* shine, glitter, glow, gleam

glitter *v.* gleam, sparkle, flash, glint, glisten, scintillate

gloat *v.* whoop, exult, crow, revel, triumph

globe *n.* ball, sphere, planet, earth, world

gloom *n.* darkness, gloaming, dusk, shadow, dimness, bleakness ★**light**

gloomy *adj.* cheerless, black, dark, bleak, cloudy, overcast, dismal, dour, glum, melancholy ▷ *dreary* ★**happy**

glorious *adj.* brilliant, lustrous, noble, exalted, renowned ▷ *splendid*

glory *n.* brilliance, radiance, pride ▷ *splendor*

gloss *n.* luster, sheen, shimmer, polish ▷ *glaze*

glossy *adj.* shiny, burnished, sleek, slick, polished

glow *n. & v.* glare, glitter, bloom, blush, flush, shine, gleam, twinkle

glower *v.* frown, stare, scowl, glare

glue ① *n.* paste, gum, cement, mucilage, adhesive, rubber cement ② *v.* stick, fasten

glum *adj.* sullen, sulky, morose, miserable, dejected, downcast ▷ *gloomy*

glut *n.* abundance, plenty, too much, surplus

glutton *n.* gorger, stuffer, crammer, pig, gormandizer, gourmand

gnash *v.* grind, chomp, bite, crunch

gnaw *v.* chew, nibble, bite, champ, consume

go *v.* ① walk, pass, move, travel, depart, proceed ② stretch, reach, extend *The prairie extended as far as the mountain range*

go after *v.* pursue, chase, follow

go ahead *v.* progress, proceed, continue

go away *v.* leave, depart, vanish, disappear

go back *v.* return, resume, withdraw

go by *v.* pass, elapse, vanish

go in *v.* enter, advance, invade, penetrate

go in for *v.* enter, take part, participate, compete

go off *v.* explode, blow up, depart

go on *v.* continue, advance, proceed, move ahead, keep up

go up *v.* climb, mount, rise ▷*ascend*

goad *v.* prod, incite, impel, drive, urge, sting, worry

goal *n.* target, ambition, aim, object, destination

gobble *v.* devour, gorge, swallow, gulp, bolt

goblin *n.* sprite, demon, gnome, elf

God *n.* the Creator, the Father, the Almighty, Jehovah, the Divinity, the Holy Spirit, King of Kings, the Supreme Being

godless *adj.* unholy, unclean, wicked, savage, profane ★**righteous**

golden *adj.* excellent, precious, brilliant, bright

good *adj.* ① excellent, admirable, fine ② favorable, *The calm weather provides favorable conditions for waterskiing,* advantageous, profitable ③ righteous, moral, true *A true friend can forgive your mistakes* ④ clever, skillful, expert ⑤ fit, proper, suited ★**bad**

goodness *n.* excellence, merit, worth, honesty, kindness ▷*virtue* ★**evil**

goods *n.* wares, commodities, cargo, load, material, belongings

gorge ① *v.* swallow, gulp, devour ▷*eat* ② *n.* canyon, glen, valley

gorgeous *adj.* beautiful, ravishing, stunning, superb, magnificent

gossip *v.* chat, chatter, prattle, tittle-tattle

gouge *v.* excavate, groove, dig out

govern *v.* rule, reign, manage, direct, guide, control, conduct, command

government *n.* rule, administration, supervision, parliament

governor *n.* director, manager, leader, chief, overseer, head of state

gown *n.* robe, dress, frock

grace *n.* elegance, refinement, polish, symmetry ▷*beauty*

graceful *adj.* beautiful, lovely, shapely, refined ▷*elegant*

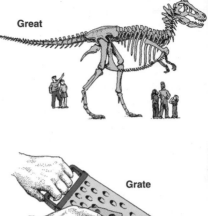

Great

Grate

gracious *adj.* amiable, kind, suave, urbane, affable, elegant ★**churlish**

grade *n.* ① class, rank, degree ② slope, gradient, incline, slant

gradual *adj.* by degrees, step-by-step, continuous, little by little ★**sudden**

graft ① *v.* splice, insert, bud, plant ② *n.* bribery, corruption

grain *n.* fiber, crumb, seed, particle, atom, bit, drop

grand *adj.* splendid, impressive, stately, magnificent, wonderful, superb

grandeur *n.* magnificence, splendor, majesty, lordliness

grant ① *n.* bounty, award, subsidy ② *v.* bestow, donate *We all donated some money to help the earthquake victims,* confer, give

grapple *v.* struggle, tussle, wrestle, seize, grasp, clutch

grasp *v.* ① grip, seize, take, grab, hold ② understand, comprehend

grasping *adj.* greedy, avaricious, covetous, miserly ★**generous**

grate ① *v.* rasp, file, jar, clash, rub, grind ②

annoy, irritate, vex ③ *n.* fireplace GREAT

grateful *adj.* thankful, appreciative, obliged, indebted

gratify *v.* delight, satisfy, please, content, enchant, indulge, favor ★**displease**

gratitude *n.* thankfulness, appreciation, obligation

grave ① *adj.* solemn, sober, momentous, dignified, majestic ② essential, important *I have important news to tell* ③ *n.* tomb, vault, shrine

gravity *n.* ① seriousness, solemnity, importance, significance ② force, gravitation, weight

graze *v.* ① scrape, brush, shave, glance ② browse, crop, bite GRAYS

grease *n.* fat, suet, tallow, oil

great *adj.* ① large, considerable, bulky, huge, ample ② important, elevated, noted *Here is a list of noted citizens of this town* ③ main, chief, principal GRATE

greedy *adj.* gluttonish, voracious, grasping, selfish, acquisitive ★**unselfish**

green *adj.* ① emerald, jade, turquoise ② ungrown, immature, raw *During the war, many raw recruits were drafted into the army,* untrained ★**expert**

greet *v.* welcome, accost, hail, salute, salaam, address

grief *n.* woe, sadness, regret, distress, anguish ▷*sorrow* ★**joy**

grievance *n.* injury, hardship, complaint, wrong, trial ★**boon**

grieve *v.* lament, deplore, mourn, sorrow, be sad, afflict, hurt ★**rejoice**

grievous *adj.* lamentable, deplorable, grave, critical, severe, mortal

grill ① *v.* fry, broil ② *n.* grating, grid

grim *adj.* ① serious, stern, harsh, solemn, dour, forbidding ② horrid, dreadful, terrible ▷*somber* ★**mild**

grime *n.* filth, soil, dust, soot ▷*dirt*

grin *n. & v.* smile, beam, smirk, simper

grind *v.* ① scrape, file, crush, powder ② sharpen, whet, grate

grip *v.* grasp, grab, snatch, clasp, seize ▷*hold* ★**loosen**

Groups of Animals

a drove of cattle
a flock of birds
a herd of elephants
a mob of kangaroos
a pack of wolves
a pride of lions
a school of porpoises
a sloth of bears
a swarm of bees
a troop of monkeys
a colony of seals
a cete of badgers
a skulk of foxes

grisly *adj.* horrid, horrible, dreadful, ghastly ▷*grim*

grit *n.* ① powder, dust, sand, gravel ② nerve, mettle, pluck ▷*courage*

groan *v.* moan, complain, grumble, creak GROWN

groom ① *n.* husband, bridegroom ② *n.* stable boy, servant, hostler ③ *v.* spruce, tidy, preen

groove *n.* furrow, ridge, corrugation, channel, rut, score

grope *v.* feel, handle, finger, manipulate, touch, pick

gross *adj.* ① large, bulky, unwieldy, massive ② coarse, vulgar, crude ③ outrageous,

Growls, grunts, and other animal noises

Bees buzz	Lions roar
Cats meow	Mice squeak
Cows moo	Owls hoot
Dogs bark	Pigs grunt
Dogs also growl	Roosters crow
Ducks quack	Snakes hiss
Horses neigh	Wolves howl

glaring, flagrant *The driver was arrested for a flagrant disregard of the speed limit*

grotesque *adj.* deformed, malformed, misshapen, freakish, abnormal, bizarre

ground *n.* ① dry land, soil, earth, dust ② bottom, base, foundation

grounds *n.* ① foundation, cause, basis, excuse ② dregs, sediment, silt ③ gardens, parkland, estate

group *n.* ① division, section, branch ② gang, throng, cluster, bunch, class, set

grovel *v.* fawn, crouch, crawl, toady, cringe, wallow, cower

grow *v.* ① increase, advance, expand, extend, develop, raise ② sprout, germinate, shoot

growl *v.* snarl, snap, threaten, thunder

growth *n.* expansion, development, advance ▷*increase*

grow up *v.* mature, develop, ripen

grubby *adj.* messy, dirty, mucky

grudge *n.* & *v.* hate, envy, dislike, spite

gruesome *adj.* frightful, hideous, ghastly ▷*grisly*

gruff *adj.* husky, throaty, croaky, blunt, churlish, crusty, curt ★**affable**

grumble *v.* complain, snivel, murmur, growl, protest

grumpy *adj.* disgruntled, dissatisfied, surly, sour, irritable, sullen ★**affable**

grunt *n.* & *v.* snort, groan ★**growl**

guarantee *n.* warranty, assurance, security, pledge

guard ① *n.* protector, sentry, guardian, watchman ② *v.* protect, defend, watch over, shelter, shield

guess *v.* surmise, conjecture, judge, think, suspect, suppose

guest *n.* visitor, caller GUESSED

guide ① *n.* pilot, director, leader, controller ② *v.* steer, navigate, lead, direct, manage, conduct *Our teacher conducted us to the bus and we all climbed aboard*

guild *n.* club, trade union, association, federation, fellowship, band, society

guile *n.* knavery, foul play, trickery, deceit, cunning, fraud ★**honesty**

guilty *adj.* blameworthy, sinful, wicked, wrong ★**innocent**

guise *n.* garb, pose, posture, role, aspect *The motel manager's aspect was a little too friendly; we did not trust him,* appearance GUYS

gulch *n.* valley, gully, ravine

gulf *n.* ① bay, basin, inlet ② chasm, opening, abyss, depths

gullible *adj.* credulous, innocent, naive, trusting

gully *n.* trench, ditch, channel, ravine

gulp *v.* swallow, consume, guzzle, devour

gun *n.* rifle, cannon, revolver, pistol, automatic, shotgun

gurgle *v.* ripple, murmur, purl, babble

gush *v.* stream, spurt, spout, flow, run, pour out

gust *n.* blast, blow, squall, wind

gusto *n.* relish, zest, eagerness, zeal, pleasure

gutter *n.* moat, ditch, dike, drain, gully, channel, groove

guzzle *v.* gulp, imbibe, drink, swill, quaff

H h

habit *n.* ① custom, practice, routine, way, rule ② mannerism *One of his annoying mannerisms is drumming his fingers on the table,* addiction, trait

hack *v.* chop, mangle, gash, slash

hackneyed *adj.* stale, trite, commonplace, tired ★**new**

hag *n.* crone, harridan, witch, virago *I know I have a temper, but Julia is a real virago*

haggard *adj.* drawn, wan, pinched, thin ▷*gaunt* ★**hale**

haggle *v.* bargain, barter, bicker, dispute ★**yield**

hail ① *v.* salute, call to, accost, welcome, greet ② *n.* sleet, frozen rain, ice storm HALE

hair *n.* locks, mane, tresses, strand

hale *adj.* hearty, robust, sound, fit ▷*healthy* ★**ill** HAIL

half *n.* division, fraction, segment

hall *n.* entrance, foyer, corridor, lobby, vestibule *There is a coat rack and an umbrella stand in the vestibule of her house* HAUL

hallow *v.* sanctify, consecrate, bless, dedicate, make holy

hallucination *n.* illusion, fantasy, delusion, mirage, dream ★**reality**

halt *v.* end, pause, rest, cease ▷*stop* ★**start**

halting *adj.* faltering, hestitating, wavering, awkward ★**fluent**

hammer ① *v.* beat, pound, bang ② *n.* mallet, gavel *The leader banged his gavel on the desk and called for order*

hamper ① *v.* hinder, interfere, impede, curb ★**aid** ② *n.* basket, creel *The fisherman carried a creel to put his catch in,* crate

hand ① *v.* give, pass, present, yield ② *n.* fist, palm

handicap *n.* defect, disability, drawback, restriction ★**advantage**

handicraft *n.* skill, hobby, art, workmanship, craft, occupation

handle ① *n.* shaft, holder, grip ② *v.* feel,

Habitations

Apartment	Igloo
Bungalow	Lodge
Cabin	Mansion
Castle	Palace
Chalet	Ranch
Chateau	Shack
Cottage	Shanty
Duplex	Villa
Estate	
Flat	
Hacienda	
Hut	

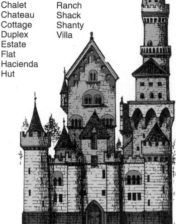

touch, finger, work, wield

handsome *adj.* ① good-looking, graceful, attractive ② generous, lavish *Aunt Betsy is always lavish with presents for the children* HANSOM

handy *adj.* ready, convenient, deft, skilled ★**clumsy**

hang *v.* dangle, suspend, sag, droop, swing

hanker for *v.* long for, yearn for, crave, desire ★**dislike**

haphazard *adj.* accidental, random, aimless, casual ▷*chance* ★**deliberate**

hapless *adj.* ill-fated, luckless, unlucky ▷*miserable* ★**lucky**

happen *v.* occur, take place, come about, result

happening *n.* event, incident, occurrence, occasion

happiness *n.* delight, ecstasy, gaiety, joy, enjoyment ▷*bliss* ★**unhappiness**

happy *adj.* cheerful, blithe, content, joyous, jubilant ▷*merry* ★**unhappy**

harass *v.* beset, annoy, upset, bother

▷ *distress* ★**assist**

harbor ① *n.* port, anchorage, mooring ② *n.* refuge, shelter, safety *At last we were back in the safety of our home* ③ *v.* give shelter to

hard *adj.* ① firm, stony, rocky, solid ★**soft** ② difficult, tough *I had a very tough problem to solve,* perplexing ★**easy** ③ stern, severe, callous, ruthless

hardly *adv.* seldom, rarely, scarcely, slightly

hardship *n.* trouble, suffering, want ▷ *difficulty* ★**ease**

hardy *adj.* rugged, sturdy, tough, healthy, stout, sound ▷ *robust* ★**weak**

hark *v.* listen, hear ▷ *listen*

harm ① *n.* damage, mischief, ruin, wrong, abuse, sin ② *v.* abuse, blemish, hurt *I'm sorry, I didn't mean to hurt you,* injure ★**benefit**

harmful *adj.* injurious, evil, wicked, damaging ★**harmless**

harmless *adj.* safe, gentle, innocuous, innocent ★**harmful**

harmony *n.* agreement, conformity, accord, unity, goodwill ★**discord**

harp ① *n.* lyre, stringed instrument ② *v.* harp on, dwell on *I tried to forget our quarrel, but Carol continued to dwell on it,* allude to

harrow *v.* agonize, taunt, distress, torture, harry ▷ *harass* ★**hearten**

harsh *adj.* ① jarring, coarse, rough ② severe, strict, ruthless ★**mild**

harvest *v.* plow, harrow, reap, pluck

hash *n.* ① mess, confusion, muddle ② stew, goulash, meat loaf

hassle *n.* argument, bother, difficulty, squabble, struggle

haste *n.* rush, bustle, dispatch, urgency, swiftness ▷ *hurry* ★**delay**

hasten *v.* hurry, hustle, quicken, accelerate, speed up ★**dawdle**

hasty *adj.* hurried, rushed, abrupt, indiscreet ★**deliberate**

hate *v.* abhor, detest, loathe ▷ *despise* ★**love**

hateful *adj.* abominable, loathsome, odious, despicable ★**pleasing**

haughty *adj.* arrogant, disdainful, scornful, snobbish ★**humble**

haul *v.* pull, draw, tug, drag, heave HALL

have *v.* possess, occupy, own, receive, take in

haven *n.* harbor, port, refuge, retreat, sanctum, shelter

havoc *n.* wreckage, ruin, destruction, disorder, mayhem

hay *n.* pasture, silage, grass, straw HEY

haze *n.* cloud, vapor, fog, mist HAYS

hazy *adj.* foggy, misty, murky, vague, uncertain ★**clear**

head ① *n.* visage, skull, cranium, pate ② *adj.* chief, main, principal

heading *n.* caption, headline, title, inscription

headlong *adj.* rough, dangerous, reckless ▷ *rash*

heal *v.* soothe, treat, cure, mend, restore HEEL, HE'LL

healthy *adj.* fine, fit, hearty, sound, vigorous ▷ *hale* ★**sick**

heap *n.* pile, mass, mound, collection

hear *v.* listen to, hearken, overhear HERE

hearten *v.* assure, encourage, embolden, inspire ★**dishearten**

heartless *adj.* brutal, callous, cold ▷ *unkind* ★**kind**

hearty *adj.* cordial, sincere, earnest, honest, jovial ★**cold**

heat *n.* ① warmth, temperature ② passion, ardor, fervor *She spoke with great fervor about what she believed*

heave *v.* fling, cast, hurl, hoist, pull, tug

heavenly *adj.* beautiful, blessed, divine, lovely ★**hellish**

heavy *adj.* weighty, hefty, ponderous, loaded ★**light**

hectic *adj.* excited, fast, frenzied, wild ▷ *frantic* ★**leisurely**

heed *v.* listen, pay attention, follow, respect, obey ★**ignore**

heedless *adj.* thoughtless, reckless, unwary, rash ▷ *careless*

height *n.* ① altitude, stature ② top, apex, peak, zenith ★**depth**

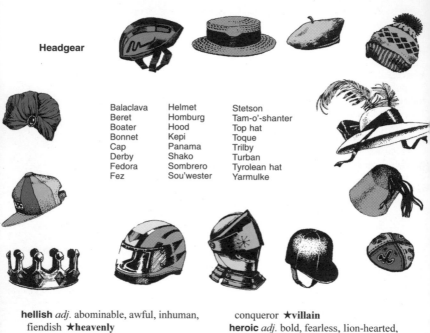

Headgear

Balaclava
Beret
Boater
Bonnet
Cap
Derby
Fedora
Fez

Helmet
Homburg
Hood
Kepi
Panama
Shako
Sombrero
Sou'wester

Stetson
Tam-o'-shanter
Top hat
Toque
Trilby
Turban
Tyrolean hat
Yarmulke

hellish *adj.* abominable, awful, inhuman, fiendish ★**heavenly**

help ① *n.* aid, support, assistance ② *v.* lend a hand *We all lent a hand in building the hut,* aid, assist ★**hinder**

helpful *adj.* caring, considerate ▷*useful* ★**useless**

helping *n.* ration, portion, piece, serving, helping *Mike would like a second helping. He's still hungry,* share

helpless *adj.* incapable, powerless, unfit, forlorn ▷*weak* ★**strong**

hem *n.* edge, border, fringe, margin

hence *adv.* accordingly, thus, therefore, henceforward

herd *n.* crowd, crush, flock, group, mass, mob, horde HEARD

here *adv.* present, attending, hereabouts, in this place HEAR

heritage *n.* inheritance, legacy, birthright, tradition

hermit *n.* recluse, solitary, monk

hero *n.* champion, daredevil, star, idol, conqueror ★**villain**

heroic *adj.* bold, fearless, lion-hearted, gallant ▷*brave* ★**cowardly**

heroine *n.* celebrity, goddess *Marilyn Monroe was a goddess of the silver screen,* idol, star, lead

hesitate *v.* falter, dither, doubt, wait

hew *v.* chop, cut, fashion, carve, sculpt HUE

hidden *adj.* concealed, covered, veiled, unseen ★**open**

hide *v.* conceal, cover, obscure, bury, cloak ★**reveal** HIED

hideous *adj.* repulsive, unsightly, gruesome, horrible ▷*ugly* ★**beautiful**

hiding *n.* beating, thrashing, caning

high ① *adj.* tall, towering, lofty, elevated ② shrill *The referee blew a shrill blast on his whistle,* treble, strident ③ expensive, costly ★**low**

highbrow *adj.* brainy, educated, intellectual

hijack *v.* raid, kidnap, seize, snatch, steal

hike *v.* walk, ramble, tramp

hilarious *adj.* amusing, gleeful, jocular,

entertaining ▷*funny* ★**serious**

hill *n.* hummock, rise, climb, height, elevation, slope

hinder *v.* hamper, impede, obstruct, retard, frustrate ▷*handicap* ★**help**

hindrance *n.* impediment, obstruction, check, barrier ★**aid**

hint *n.* clue, inkling *We had just an inkling of what was in store,* whisper, tip, suggestion

hire *v.* charter, rent, lease, retain, engage ★**dismiss** HIGHER

hiss *v.* boo, hoot, jeer, deride, whistle ▷*ridicule* ★**applaud**

history *n.* narration, account, saga, story, chronicle *The new book is a chronicle of the progress of equal rights*

hit ① *v.* strike, slap, beat, batter, whack ② *v.* collide, strike, clash ★**miss** ③ *n.* stroke, collision, blow, success, triumph

hitch ① *v.* attach, connect, fasten ② *n.* delay, holdup, problem, snag *The work went smoothly for hours, until we hit a snag*

hoard *v.* accumulate, save, collect, treasure ★**squander** HORDE

hoarse *adj.* raucous, croaky, husky, throaty ★**mellow** HORSE

hoax *n.* trick, deception, fraud, joke, spoof, lie

hobble *v.* dodder, falter, shuffle, stagger

hobby *n.* pastime, amusement, recreation, interest

hoist *v.* lift, raise, erect, heave

hold ① *v.* have, possess, own, retain, keep, grasp ② *v.* contain, accommodate *This cabin can accommodate four people* ③ *v.* stop, arrest ④ *n.* fortress, keep, storeplace HOLED

hole *n.* aperture, slot, perforation, opening, cavity WHOLE

hollow ① *adj.* concave, empty, vacant ② *adj.* insincere, artificial ③ *n.* basin, depression *Water had accumulated in a small depression,* crater, channel

holy *adj.* sacred, pure, consecrated, blessed, hallowed ★**wicked** WHOLLY

home *n.* house, dwelling, homestead

homely *adj.* ① humble, unpretentious, comfortable, modest ② ordinary, plain, simple ③ unattractive, plain

honest *adj.* upright, fair, sincere, honorable ★**devious**

honesty *n.* integrity, honor, sincerity, morality ★**dishonesty**

honor *n.* morality, honesty, reputation, integrity, uprightness ★**disgrace**

honorable *adj.* honest, respectable, highminded, virtuous ★**dishonest**

hook *n.* clasp, link, catch, fastener, barb *The fishhook ended in a number of small barbs*

hoop *n.* loop, ring, band, circle

hoot *v.* call, cry, howl, shout, shriek, yell

hop *v.* jump, leap, skip, spring, vault, caper

hope *v.* anticipate, envision, envisage, desire, expect, foresee ★**despair**

hopeful *adj.* expectant, confident, optimistic ★**pessimistic**

hopeless *adj.* despairing, desperate, downhearted, unattainable ★**hopeful**

horde *n.* crowd, gang, band, throng, swarm *We were suddenly attacked by a swarm of hornets,* HOARD

horrible *adj.* awful, atrocious, frightful, ghastly ▷*horrid* ★**agreeable**

horrid *adj.* beastly, bloodcurdling, dreadful, frightening ▷*horrible* ★**pleasant**

horror *n.* dread, fear, fright, outrage, panic, loathing ★**attraction**

horse *n.* mount, charger, hack, stallion, mare, filly, colt, foal HOARSE

hose *n.* ① tubing, pipe ② socks, stockings HOES

hospitable *adj.* sociable, neighborly, charitable, welcoming ★**hostile**

host *n.* ① entertainer, master-of-ceremonies, sponsor ② army, band, legion, horde

hostile *adj.* unfriendly, antagonistic, alien, malevolent ★**friendly**

hot ① *adj.* warm, fiery, scalding, roasting, heated ★**cold** ② pungent, peppery, sharp

hotel *n.* inn, hostelry *The stagecoach pulled in to a local hostelry for refreshment,* tavern, motel, resort

house *n.* home, residence, dwelling, abode

Hue

A hue is a tint or variety of a color.
Blue: aquamarine beryl turquoise indigo azure sapphire ultramarine
Brown: amber chocolate dun fawn beige khaki auburn chestnut
Green: apple emerald jade moss olive pea sea
Purple: violet lilac heliotrope amethyst mauve magenta
Orange: carrot tangerine sandy saffron citron canary lemon
Red: crimson scarlet cherry cerise terracotta salmon pink cardinal
Yellow: sulfur primrose apricot saffron citron canary lemon

hovel *n.* cabin, shed, den, shack, shanty

hover *v.* fly, float, hang, dally, linger

howl *v.* hoot, cry, bellow, shriek ▷*scream*

hub *n.* center, axis, focal point, pivot

hubbub *n.* babel, bedlam, chaos, clamor, uproar ▷*row* ★**calm**

huddle *v.* cluster, flock, gather, herd, nestle ★**separate**

hue *n.* color, dye, shade, tinge, tint HEW

huff *n.* anger, passion, mood, pique *My cousin stormed off in a fit of pique* ▷*sulk*

hug *v.* clasp, embrace, enfold ▷*cuddle*

huge *adj.* enormous, monstrous, colossal, immense ▷*vast* ★**tiny**

hum *v.* drone, croon, buzz, pulsate, throb

human *adj.* reasonable, understandable, mortal ▷*humane* ★**inhuman**

humane *adj.* benign, forgiving, gentle, lenient, kind ★**inhumane**

humble *adj.* low, lowly, meek, unassuming ▷*modest* ★**arrogant**

humbug *n.* bluff, bunkum, claptrap *The salesman's goods were cheap and he talked a lot of claptrap about them,* quackery, trickery

humdrum *adj.* monotonous, commonplace, everyday, boring ▷*dreary* ★**exceptional**

humid *adj.* clammy, damp, moist, wet, vaporous ★**dry**

humiliate *v.* embarrass, humble, abash, degrade, deflate ★**boost**

humor ① *n.* comedy, fun, banter, whimsy ② *v.* flatter, coax, pamper, spoil

humorous *adj.* amusing, droll, comical, whimsical ▷*funny* ★**serious** HUMERUS

hunch ① *n.* feeling, guess, idea, inkling ② *v.* crouch, curl up, squat *We squatted in the long grass, where we were out of sight*

hunger ① *n.* craving, desire, starvation ② *v.* crave, desire, hanker

hungry *adj.* famished, starving, voracious

hunt *v.* chase, seek, scour, search, stalk, trail

hurdle *n.* barrier, fence, hedge, obstruction

hurl *v.* cast, fling, heave, pitch, throw, propel, toss

hurry *v.* dash, hustle, quicken, accelerate ▷*hasten* ★**dally**

hurt ① *v.* harm, wound, pain, sting, suffer ② *v.* upset, annoy, distress ③ *adj.* rueful, sad, offended

hurtful *adj.* cutting, cruel, distressing, wounding ★**kind**

hurtle *v.* chase, charge, dash, rush, speed, tear

hush *v.* calm, quiet down, soothe ★**disturb**

husky *adj.* croaking, gruff, harsh ▷*hoarse*

hustle *v.* bustle, speed, hasten ▷*hurry*

hut *n.* cabin, shelter, shanty, shack

hymn *n.* anthem, chant, carol, psalm HIM

hypnotize *v.* mesmerize, fascinate, spellbind *We stood spellbound as we watched the trapeze artist,* bewitch

hypocrite *n.* fraud, deceiver, impostor, mountebank

hysterical *adj.* ① distraught, mad, delirious, beside oneself ② comical, hilarious, farcical ★**calm**

I i

icy *adj.* freezing, frozen, cold, frigid, frosty

idea *n.* notion, thought, belief, fancy, impression, image

ideal *adj.* perfect, absolute, supreme, best, model, complete

identical *adj.* same, alike, twin, duplicate, equal ★**different**

identify *v.* detect, recognize, know, distinguish, spot

identity *n.* existence, self, singularity, individuality

idiot *n.* imbecile, moron, fool, dimwit, dolt

idiotic *adj.* crazy, stupid, simple, fatuous ▷*foolish* ★**sane**

idle *adj.* ① unoccupied, unemployed, unused ② lazy, frivolous, sluggish ★**active** IDOL

idol *n.* ① image, icon, god, fetish ② hero, favorite, star *Buster Keaton was a star of the silent movies* IDLE

ignite *v.* kindle, set light to, spark off, catch fire

ignorant *adj.* unknowing, ill-informed, unread, stupid, dumb ★**wise**

ignore *v.* disregard, neglect, omit, overlook, pass over ★**note**

ill *adj.* ① ailing, diseased, frail, infirm, sick, poorly ★**well** ② hostile, malicious *Cinderella's sisters were cruel and malicious,* evil, harmful

ill-mannered *adj.* coarse, crude, boorish, uncivil ▷*rude* ★**polite**

ill-tempered *adj.* bad-tempered, curt, irritable ★**good-tempered**

ill-treat *v.* abuse, harm, injure, neglect, oppress ★**care for**

ill will *n.* animosity, hard feelings, dislike, hatred, hostility ▷*malice* ★**good will**

illegal *adj.* unlawful, wrong, villainous, illicit, contraband ★**legal**

illegible *adj.* unreadable, indecipherable, obscure, indistinct ★**legible**

illegitimate *adj.* illegal, unlawful, improper, wrong ★**legitimate**

illiterate *adj.* uneducated, unlearned, unlettered, unread, untaught ★**literate**

illness *n.* ailment, attack, complaint, disease, disorder

illuminate *v.* brighten, clarify, enlighten, light up ★**darken**

illusion *n.* apparition, fancy, fantasy, mirage, deception ★**reality**

illustration *n.* picture, drawing, explanation, sketch

image *n.* likeness, effigy, portrait, replica, reflection, double

imaginary *adj.* unreal, fanciful, fictitious, visionary ★**real**

imagination *n.* idea, notion, thought, illusion, conception, fancy, vision, impression ★**reality**

imagine *v.* assume, believe, invent, pretend, think up ▷*visualize*

imbecile *n.* blockhead, fool, idiot, bungler, dolt

imitate *v.* emulate, follow, reproduce, simulate, mock ▷*copy*

immaculate *adj.* clean, spotless, faultless, stainless ▷*pure* ★**soiled**

immature *adj.* callow, raw, crude, childish, unripe ★**mature**

immediate *adj.* ① instant, instantaneous, prompt ② nearest, next, neighboring *As children, my mother and father lived in neighboring houses* ★**distant**

immediately *adv.* at once, directly, without delay, forthwith

immense *adj.* tremendous, enormous, vast ▷*huge* ★**tiny**

immerse *v.* plunge, dip, douse, submerge ▷*sink*

imminent *adj.* impending, approaching, looming, close

immobile *adj.* at rest, at a standstill, motionless ★**moving**

immodest *adj.* shameless, barefaced, indelicate, improper ★**modest**

immoral *adj.* evil, unscrupulous, vicious, vile, depraved ▷*wicked* ★**moral**

immortal *adj.* undying, eternal, everlasting, constant ★**mortal**

immune *adj.* exempt, resistant, safe, protected ★**susceptible**

imp *n.* rascal, urchin, elf

impact *n.* blow, shock, stroke, collision, crash, knock

impair *v.* damage, spoil, devalue, cheapen, harm ▷*hinder* ★**enhance**

impart *v.* communicate, render, bestow, disclose *I am unable to disclose where I heard that story* ▷*tell*

impartial *adj.* unbiased, candid, fair-minded, impersonal ★**biased**

impatient *adj.* intolerant, irritable, hasty, curt ★**patient**

impede *v.* hamper, interfere with, obstruct ▷*hinder* ★**aid**

impel *v.* goad, incite, urge, actuate, push ▷*drive* ★**dissuade**

impending *adj.* approaching, coming, forthcoming, looming ★**remote**

imperfect *adj.* defective, unsound, blemished, flawed ▷*faulty* ★**perfect**

imperial *adj.* august, majestic, lofty, regal, royal, grand

imperious *adj.* arrogant, domineering, overbearing ★**humble**

impersonal *adj.* aloof, detached, remote, neutral, cold ★**friendly**

impersonate *v.* imitate, mimic, masquerade as, pose as, portray

impertinent *adj.* insolent, impudent, discourteous ▷*saucy* ★**polite**

impetuous *adj.* sudden, unexpected, impulsive, spontaneous ▷*hasty* ★**careful**

implement ① *v.* accomplish, bring about, fulfill *I was able to fulfill my dream of going to Japan* ② *n.* instrument, tool, gadget

implicate *v.* connect, entangle, involve, throw suspicion on ★**absolve**

implicit *adj.* implied, indicated, understood, tacit

implore *v.* beseech, entreat, beg, crave, plead

imply *v.* hint at, intimate, insinuate ▷*suggest* ★**declare**

impolite *adj.* discourteous, ill-mannered ▷*rude* ★**polite**

import ① *v.* bring in, carry in ② *n.* meaning, purport *When I grew old enough I realized the purport of my mother's advice,* sense

important *adj.* significant, essential, serious, substantial ▷*great* ★**trivial**

imposing *adj.* impressive, massive, magnificent ▷*stately* ★**modest**

impossible *adj.* hopeless, not possible, unworkable, unacceptable ★**possible**

impostor *n.* impersonator, masquerader, deceiver, fraud, pretender, quack

impoverish *v.* bankrupt, diminish, weaken, ruin, beggar ★**enrich**

impractical *adj.* impossible, unworkable, idealistic, unusable ★**practical**

impress *v.* ① influence, affect, sway, inspire ② emboss *She wore a crown of gold embossed with diamonds,* engrave, indent

impression *n.* ① belief, concept, fancy, effect ② dent, imprint, stamp, printing *The book had sold 5,000 copies, and a new printing was planned*

imprison *v.* jail, lock up, confine, ★**free**

improbable *adj.* doubtful, unlikely, implausible ▷*dubious* ★**probable**

impromptu *adj.* improvised, spontaneous, ad lib, unrehearsed ★**planned**

improper *adj.* ① erroneous, false, unsuitable ② immoral *My parents always taught me that lying and cheating were immoral,* indecent ▷*wrong* ★**proper**

improve *v.* make better, repair, restore, improve upon, refine ★**diminish**

impudent *adj.* impertinent, audacious, brazen, disrespectful ▷*rude* ★**polite**

impulse *n.* motive, drive, force, inclination, urge, wish

impulsive *adj.* sudden, unexpected, reckless ▷*impetuous* ★**cautious**

impure *adj.* contaminated, corrupted, foul, corrupt ★**pure**

inaccessible *adj.* remote, isolated, unattainable ★**accessible**

inaccurate *adj.* erroneous, incorrect, imprecise ▷*faulty* ★**accurate**

inactive *adj.* inert, static, dormant, quiet, unoccupied ★**active**

inadequate *adj.* deficient, unequal, incapable ▷*unfit* ★**adequate**

inane *adj.* absurd, ridiculous, stupid, senseless ▷*silly* ★**sensible**

inappropriate *adj.* improper, wrong, incorrect, unsuitable, unfitting ★**appropriate**

inattentive *adj.* unheeding, indifferent, careless, neglectful ★**attentive**

incapable *adj.* helpless, inadequate, unable, unfit, weak ★**capable**

incense ① *v.* (in-*cense*) enrage, infuriate, annoy ② *n.* (*in*-cense) fragrance *We walked through fields where the fragrance of wild flowers was wonderful,* aroma, perfume

incentive *n.* motive, impulse, drive, spur, lure

incident *n.* event, happening, episode, circumstance, occurrence

incidental *adj.* casual, chance, accidental, random, minor

incite *v.* encourage, urge, drive, goad, impel, provoke ▷*prompt* ★**restrain**

incline ① *n.* (*in*-cline) slant, slope, grade, gradient ② *v.* (in-*cline*) tend, verge, lean to, bias, favor

inclined *adj.* liable, prone, disposed, favorable

include *v.* contain, cover, incorporate, embody, comprise ★**exclude**

inclusive *adj.* comprehensive, all-embracing ★**exclusive**

income *n.* earnings, royalty, revenue, receipts, profits ★**expenses**

incomparable *adj.* brilliant, first-class, superb ▷*unrivaled* ★**ordinary**

incompetent *adj.* incapable, inadequate, inept, helpless ▷*clumsy* ★**competent**

incomplete *adj.* unfinished, partial, imperfect, wanting ★**complete**

incomprehensible *adj.* unintelligible, perplexing, puzzling ★**comprehensible**

inconceivable *adj.* incredible, unlikely, strange ▷*extraordinary* ★**comprehensible**

inconsiderate *adj.* tactless, careless, insensitive ▷*thoughtless* ★**considerate**

inconsistent *adj.* incongruous, unstable, unpredictable ★**consistent**

inconspicuous *adj.* indistinct, faint, hidden, ordinary ★**conspicuous**

inconvenient *adj.* annoying, awkward, difficult, troublesome ★**convenient**

incorrect *adj.* erroneous, imprecise, mistaken ▷*wrong* ★**correct**

increase ① *v.* add to, boost, magnify, heighten ② *n.* addition *We heard the news today that Emily has had an addition to her family,* rise, enhancement ★**decrease**

incredible *adj.* unbelievable, amazing, farfetched, wonderful ★**ordinary**

incriminate *v.* implicate, accuse, indict ▷*blame* ★**acquit**

indecent *adj.* immodest, improper, impure, coarse ★**decent**

indeed *adv.* actually, truly, really, very much, positively

indefinite *adj.* uncertain, unsure, unreliable, dubious ▷*vague* ★**certain**

indelicate *adj.* coarse, immodest, indecent ▷*unseemly* ★**delicate**

independent *adj.* free, self-reliant, separate, self-governing ★**dependent**

indicate *v.* show, point out, denote, suggest, symbolize, flag, signal

indifference *n.* disinterest, unconcern, apathy, coldness ★**interest**

indifferent *adj.* uninterested, cold, casual, apathetic, listless ★**interested**

indignant *adj.* annoyed, resentful, wrathful ▷*angry* ★**pleased**

indirect *adj.* devious, roundabout, incidental ★**direct**

indiscreet *adj.* incautious, thoughtless, ill-advised ▷*hasty* ★**discreet**

indiscriminate *adj.* confused, bewildered, careless ▷*random* ★**deliberate**

indispensable *adj.* necessary, crucial, vital ▷*essential* ★**unnecessary**

indistinct *adj.* faint, dim, unclear, obscure, murky ▷*vague* ★**distinct**

individual ① *adj.* single, odd, special, exclusive ② *n.* person, being *Sharon enjoys the company of other human beings,* creature

indulge *v.* gratify, humor, pamper, satisfy, spoil

industrious *adj.* busy, hard-working, diligent, conscientious ★**lazy**

inedible *adj.* deadly, poisonous, harmful, uneatable ★**edible**

inefficient *adj.* negligent, incapable ▷*incompetent* ★**efficient**

inelegant *adj.* awkward, ungainly, crude, coarse ▷*clumsy* ★**elegant**

inept *adj.* awkward, absurd, unskilled ▷*clumsy* ★**skillful**

inert *adj.* inactive, passive, static, sluggish, listless, dead ★**alive**

inevitable *adj.* unavoidable, certain, sure, necessary ★**uncertain**

inexact *adj.* imprecise, inaccurate ▷*erroneous* ★**exact**

inexpensive *adj.* low-priced, reasonable, economical ▷*cheap* ★**expensive**

inexperienced *adj.* inexpert, unskilled, untrained ▷*inept* ★**experienced**

infallible *adj.* perfect, unerring, faultless ▷*reliable* ★**faulty**

infamous *adj.* notorious, shady, scandalous, shameful, disgraceful ★**glorious**

infant *n.* baby, child, little one, toddler

infatuated *adj.* in love, beguiled, charmed, fascinated, smitten

infect *v.* contaminate, blight, defile, pollute

infectious *adj.* catching, contagious

infer *v.* reason, conclude, judge, understand

inferior *adj.* second-rate, lesser, lower, poor, mediocre, imperfect ★**superior**

infinite *adj.* eternal, unending, endless, immense, unbounded

infirm *adj.* weak, feeble, frail, senile, decrepit ★**healthy**

inflame *v.* inspire, provoke, excite, stimulate, arouse ★**cool**

inflate *v.* expand, dilate, swell, pump up, blow up ★**deflate**

inflict *v.* apply, burden, deal, deliver, force

influence ① *n.* authority, control, guidance, force ② *v.* affect, impress, inspire *After Annie visited her old neighborhood, she was inspired to write a poem,* prejudice

inform *v.* tell, let know, acquaint, warn, enlighten

informal *adj.* casual, easy, familiar, relaxed, simple ★**formal**

information *n.* knowledge, news, intelligence, advice

infrequent *adj.* unusual, uncommon, occasional ▷*rare* ★**frequent**

infringe *v.* disobey, violate, encroach, trespass, flout

infuriate *v.* anger, enrage, madden, incense, vex ▷*annoy* ★**calm**

ingenious *adj.* clever, resourceful, shrewd, adroit, inventive ★**clumsy**

ingenuous *adj.* honest, open, simple, trusting, sincere ★**artful**

ingratiate *v.* curry favor, flatter, grovel, toady *We distrusted Tim, he was always trying to ingratiate himself with the teacher*

Ingratiate

We distrusted Tim, he was always trying to ingratiate himself with the teacher.

ingredient *n.* component, element, part, factor

inhabit *v.* live in, dwell in, reside in, dwell, occupy

inhale *v.* breathe in, inspire, sniff, suck in ★**exhale**

inherit *v.* succeed to, acquire, take over, receive

inhospitable *adj.* unfriendly, desolate, unkind, unsociable ★**hospitable**

inhuman *adj.* barbaric, brutal, beastly, heartless, savage

inhumane *adj.* callous, cruel, pitiless, ruthless ▷*inhuman* ★**humane**

initiate *v.* start, launch, teach, instruct, train ▷*begin*

initiative *n.* ambition, drive, enterprise, resourcefulness

inject *v.* inoculate, infuse, vaccinate

injure *v.* hurt, mar, spoil, wound, blemish, deform, disfigure

inkling *n.* suspicion, impression, notion, clue

inlet *n.* bay, gulf, basin, bight, estuary, harbor

inn *n.* hotel, motel, lodge, tavern IN

innocent *adj.* guiltless, faultless, stainless, virtuous, blameless ★**guilty**

inoffensive *adj.* harmless, safe, gentle, quiet ▷*innocent* ★**malicious**

inquire *v.* ask, examine, inspect, check, question

inquisitive *adj.* nosy, snooping, eager, inquiring, ▷*curious*

insane *adj.* demented, mad, frenzied, crazy, wild, lunatic ★**sane**

inscribe *v.* write, stamp, cut, carve, etch

inscription *n.* heading, caption, legend, epitaph, label

insecure *adj.* perilous, unsafe, hazardous, dangerous, unconfident, uncertain ★**secure**

insensible *adj.* ① unconscious, stunned, knocked out *The reigning champion was knocked out in the third round* ② insensitive, numb, stupefied

insensitive *adj.* impassive, indifferent, thick-skinned, unruffled, insensible ★**sensitive**

inseparable *adj.* indivisible, devoted, intimate, close

insert *v.* put in, inset, introduce, place, interleave ★**remove**

inside *adv.* indoors, inner, inward, within ★**outside**

insight *n.* awareness, intelligence, judgment, knowledge ▷*wisdom*

insignificant *adj.* unimportant, non-essential, meager, irrelevant ▷*humble* ★**important**

insincere *adj.* pretended, deceptive, dishonest, two-faced, false ★**sincere**

insinuate *v.* suggest, imply, signify, get at, intimate

insipid *adj.* tasteless, flat, flavorless, bland, banal ★**tasty**

insist *v.* assert, maintain, request, require, demand, persist ★**waive**

insolent *adj.* impudent, impertinent, discourteous, insulting, fresh, rude ★**respectful**

inspect *v.* examine, check, oversee, supervise, superintend

inspiration *n.* motive, stimulus, brain wave, ▷*encouragement*

inspire *v.* hearten, prompt, provoke, excite ▷*encourage* ★**deter**

install *v.* establish, plant, set, position, fix, introduce

instance *n.* example, case, occasion, occurrence INSTANTS

instant ① *adj.* immediate, instantaneous *I pressed the button, and there was an instantaneous explosion,* rapid ② *n.* moment, minute, flash, jiffy

instantly *adv.* at once, right away, immediately, now ▷*forthwith* ★**later**

instead *adv.* alternatively, preferably, rather

instead of *adv.* in place of, in one's place, on behalf of

instinct *n.* ability, knack, intuition, feeling, sixth sense

institute ① *n.* association, college, establishment, organization ② *v.* begin, start *The people raised enough money to start a new program to help the poor,* found, open

Musical Instruments

Accordion
Bagpipes
Balalaika
Banjo
Bassoon
Bells
Bugle
Castanets
Cello
Clarinet
Cornet
Cymbals
Didgeridoo
Double bass
Drum
Dulcimer
Electric
  guitar

Fiddle
Fife
Flute
French horn
Glockenspiel
Guitar
Harmonica
Harp
Harpsichord
Hurdy-gurdy
Kazoo
Kettledrum
Lute
Lyre
Mandolin
Maraca
Oboe

Organ
Piano
Piccolo
Recorder
Saxophone
Synthesizer
Tambourine
Triangle
Trombone
Trumpet
Tuba
Ukulele
Viola
Violin
Whistle
Xylophone
Zither

instruct *v.* teach, direct, order, educate, coach, drill, train

instrument *n.* device, gadget, implement, contraption, tool

insufferable *adj.* unbearable, intolerable, impossible ★**tolerable**

insufficient *adj.* inadequate, lacking, scanty, wanting ▷*sparse* ★**sufficient**

insulate *v.* protect, shield, isolate, set apart

insult *n. & v.* slander, slight, snub, abuse, outrage ★**compliment**

insure *v.* guarantee, protect, warrant, assure

intact *adj.* whole, unharmed, uncut, complete, in one piece, sound ★**damaged**

integrity *n.* honor, uprightness, honesty, goodness, purity ★**dishonesty**

intellectual *adj.* scholarly, studious, thoughtful ▷*intelligent* ★**foolish**

intelligent *adj.* acute, astute, brainy, brilliant, intellectual ▷*clever* ★**stupid**

intend *v.* mean, aim, determine, ordain, plan, project

intense *adj.* extreme, ardent, earnest, forcible, passionate ▷*keen* ★**mild** INTENTS

intention *n.* aim, intent, project, design, notion, end, goal

intercept *v.* stop, arrest, confiscate, delay, obstruct ▷*thwart*

interest *n.* appeal, fascination, zest, activity, concern ★**boredom**

interesting *adj.* appealing, fascinating, absorbing, entertaining ★**boring**

interfere *v.* meddle, intrude, interrupt, butt in, tamper ★**assist**

interior *adj.* internal, inner, inside, inward ★**exterior**

interlude *n.* pause, interval, intermission, spell, recess

internal *adj.* inner, inward ▷*interior* ★**external**

interpret *adj.* explain, define, construe

interrogate *v.* question, examine, ask, inquire, quiz ▷*investigate*

interrupt *adj.* break in, butt in, interject, disturb, hold up, suspend

interval *n.* space, period, term, intermission ▷*interlude*

intervene *v.* break in, interrupt, intrude, mediate, arbitrate ▷*interfere*

interview *n.* conference, inquiry, meeting, consultation, talk

intimate ① *adj.* near, close, familiar, private, secret ★**distant** ② *v.* hint at, suggest *The evidence suggests that the defendant has not been telling the truth* ▷*insinuate*

intimidate *v.* daunt, overawe, cow, bully, frighten, browbeat ★**persuade**

intolerant *adj.* bigoted, unfair, small-minded, dogmatic ★**tolerant**

intoxicated *adj.* drunk, inebriated, tipsy

intrepid *adj.* daring, heroic, unafraid, bold, gallant ▷*fearless*

intricate *adj.* complex, complicated, elaborate, tricky ★**simple**

intrigue ① *n.* plot, scheme, affair, liaison ② *v.* attract, enchant *The old man enchanted us with his stories,* captivate, scheme

introduce *v.* ① put in, insert, inject ② acquaint, present

intrude *v.* interrupt, interfere, invade, trespass ★**withdraw**

inundate *v.* flood, deluge, engulf, immerse, submerge, swamp *We advertised for a new assistant and were swamped with replies*

invade *v.* break in, penetrate, assault, assail ▷*enter* ★**withdraw** INVEIGHED

invalid ① *adj.* (*in-val*-id) null, void *These tickets are void, for they are more than a year old,* useless ② *n.* (*in*-val-id) patient, sufferer, sick person, disabled person

invaluable *adj.* precious, costly, priceless, valuable ★**worthless**

invent *v.* fabricate, conceive, devise, make up, originate, concoct

invention *n.* creation, gadget, contrivance, discovery

investigate *v.* explore, examine, research, inquire, search, study

invisible *adj.* hidden, concealed, out of sight, unseen, masked ★**visible**

invite *v.* ask, beckon, attract, summon, urge, encourage ★**force**

involve *v.* comprise, complicate, entangle, include, take in

inward *adj.* hidden, inner, internal, secret, inside ★**outward**

irate *adj.* incensed, cross, annoyed, furious, infuriated ▷*angry* ★**calm**

irksome *adj.* annoying, irritating, disagreeable ★**pleasing**

ironic *adj.* satirical, derisive, mocking, scornful

irregular *adj.* uncertain, unsettled, disordered, singular ▷*odd* ★**regular**

irrelevant *adj.* immaterial, unnecessary, unrelated ★**relevant**

irresistible *adj.* charming, compelling, overpowering, fascinating ★**resistible**

irresponsible *adj.* undependable, unreliable, feckless, flighty ★**responsible**

irritable *adj.* bad-tempered, edgy, fretful, peevish ▷*cross* ★**cheerful**

irritate *v.* annoy, vex, irk, offend, provoke ▷*bother* ★**please**

island *n.* isle, islet, key, atoll, cay

issue ① *v.* flow, ooze, bring out, circulate, publish ② *n.* edition, printing, publication *My book of poems was ready for publication,* impression ③ problem, question, concern

itch ① *v.* prickle, tingle, irritate ② *n.* impulse, motive, desire *I have always had a strong desire to work in a hospital*

item *n.* point, particular, thing, object, article

J j

jab *v.* poke, prod, push, stab, dig

jabber *v.* chatter, gabble, mumble, babble

jacket *n.* coat, jerkin, cover, case, sheath

jagged *adj.* rough, broken, snagged, notched, uneven ★**smooth**

jail *n.* prison, penitentiary, lockup, brig

jam ① *n.* jelly, preserves, conserve, marmalade ② *v.* crowd, pack *All the buses were full, and we were packed in like sardines,* crush, squeeze JAMB

jar ① *n.* jug, beaker, ewer, vase, pitcher, pot ② *v.* jog, rattle, grate *That singer's voice really grates on me,* grind

jaunt *n.* & *v.* trip, journey, cruise, travel, tour

jaunty *adj.* lighthearted, showy, dapper, spruce, debonair

jealous *adj.* envious, covetous, grudging

jealousy *n.* envy, covetousness, distrust, spite

jeer *v.* laugh at, deride, mock, ridicule, insult ▷*taunt*

jeopardy *n.* peril, risk, hazard, plight ▷*danger* ★**safety**

jerk *n.* & *v.* yank, pull, drag, jog, jolt, tug

jersey *n.* pullover, sweater

Jewels

Agate
Amethyst
Aquamarine
Bloodstone
Carbuncle
Carnelian
Coral
Diamond
Emerald
Garnet
Jasper
Moonstone
Onyx

Opal
Ruby
Sapphire
Topaz
Turquoise
Zircon

jest *n.* joke, jape, spoof, banter, chaff

jester *n.* clown, buffoon, merry-andrew, prankster, comedian

jet *n.* & *v.* spurt, squirt, flow, gush

jetty *n.* wharf, dock, quay, pier

jewel *n.* gem, stone, trinket, charm, locket

jibe *v.* mock, scoff, scorn, sneer, taunt ▷*jeer*

jiffy *n.* instant, flash, minute, moment

jilt *v.* abandon, brush off, desert, drop, forsake

jingle *v.* tinkle, clink, chink, ring, jangle

job *n.* task, work, chore, place, office, post, position

jocular *adj.* gleeful, hilarious, witty, humorous, jolly ▷*funny* ★**serious**

jog *v.* ① prod, nudge, shove, shake ② run, sprint, canter, trot, exercise

join *v.* ① unite, link, combine, connect, attach ★**separate** ② enlist, sign up *Gaby and Bill have signed up for tennis lessons*

joint ① *n.* junction, knot, union, connection ② *adj.* shared, united, mutual *It's in our mutual interest to keep expenses down*

joke *n.* gag, trick, frolic, lark, jape, game, prank ▷*jest*

jolly *adj.* jovial, cheerful, blithe, frisky ▷*merry* ★**sad**

jolt *n.* & *v.* jar, shock, shove, rock, jerk, bump

jostle *v.* push, shove, shoulder, thrust, elbow

jot ① *n.* atom, bit, grain, particle ② *v.* note, scribble, take down

journal *n.* ① ledger, account book ② diary, newspaper, magazine *I've just become editor of the natural history society's magazine*

journey *n.* excursion, trip, tour, jaunt, ramble

jovial *adj.* jolly, festive, cordial, affable, cheerful ▷*merry* ★**sad**

joy *n.* rapture, enchantment, delight, pleasure, charm ▷*bliss* ★**sorrow**

joyful *adj.* joyous, enjoyable, pleasurable, happy, jovial, delighted ★**sorrowful**

jubilant *adj.* exultant, gleeful, happy, overjoyed, excited ★**depressed**

judge ① *n.* justice, magistrate, referee, umpire ② *v.* assess *We can ask the jeweler to assess the value of these pearls,* decide, find, appraise, estimate

judgment *n.* ① decision, opinion, verdict *The*

K k

Key

Keys

jury gave a verdict of "not guilty," decree, finding ② intelligence, understanding, valuation

judicious *adj.* prudent, discreet, expedient, wise ★**indiscreet**

jug *n.* beaker, ewer, urn, vase ▷*jar*

juggle *v.* conjure, manipulate

juice *n.* essence, extract, sap, fluid, nectar

jumble *n.* medley, mixture, muddle, tangle, clutter

jump *v.* spring, bound, hop, skip, vault, ▷*leap*

junction *n.* ① union, combination, joint, connection ② crossroads, intersection, juncture, crossing

jungle *n.* forest, bush, wilderness

junior *adj.* lesser, lower, younger, subordinate ★**senior**

junk *n.* trash, debris, rubbish, waste, clutter, litter, scrap, garbage, refuse

just ① *adj.* sound, regular, orderly, exact, fair, honest, impartial ② *adv.* exactly, precisely ③ *adv.* only, merely, simply

justice *n.* equity, impartiality, fairness, right ★**injustice**

justify *v.* vindicate, acquit, condone, uphold, legalize

jut *v.* bulge, extend, stick out, overhang, project *We took shelter where the cliff projects over the path* ★**recede**

juvenile ① *adj.* adolescent, youthful, young, childish ★**mature** ② *n.* boy, girl, child, youngster, youth

keen ① *adj.* eager, ardent, earnest, diligent ② sharp *Her wit is as sharp as a razor,* acute, fine ★**dull**

keep ① *v.* hold, retain, collect, possess ★**abandon** ② *v.* care for, maintain, shelter *We have arranged to shelter the refugees* ③ *n.* tower, dungeon, castle, fort, stronghold

keeper *n.* jailer, warden, attendant, caretaker, janitor, custodian

keeping *n.* compliance, obedience, accord

keep on *v.* continue, go on, endure, persist ★**give up**

keepsake *n.* souvenir, token, memento, reminder, relic

keg *n.* barrel, cask, tub, drum, container

ken *n.* grasp, grip, understanding, mastery, knowledge

kerchief *n.* scarf, headscarf, shawl, neckcloth

kernel *n.* core, heart, hub, center, gist, nub COLONEL

kettle *n.* boiler, cauldron, cooking pot, teakettle

key ① *n.* opener ② *n.* solution, clue, answer ③ *n.* cay, isle, island, atoll ④ *adj.* essential, fundamental, vital, critical QUAY

kick *v.* ① boot, strike with the foot, punt, hit ② complain, grumble, rebel *The people rebelled against the harsh rule of the new king,* resist

kidnap *v.* abduct, capture, seize, snatch, steal, hijack

kill *v.* slay, assassinate, destroy, massacre, slaughter ▷*murder*

killjoy *n.* spoilsport, wet blanket *I don't want to be a wet blanket, but I'm tired and want to go home,* grouch, complainer ★**optimist**

kin *n.* race, kindred, offspring, kind, family, relative

kind ① *adj.* gentle, kindly, genial, good-natured, amiable ★**unkind** ② *n.* style, character, sort, variety

kindle *v.* ① light, ignite, set fire to ② inflame

A Little Knowledge is a Dangerous Thing—and Other Misquotes

Many of the familiar quotations we use from literature, history, or the world of entertainment are incorrect adapations of the original. Greta Garbo did not say "I want to be alone." Her true words were: "I like to be alone." Shakespeare did not say "Discretion is the better part of valor." The correct quotation is: "The better part of valor is discretion." Here are some more, with the correct original version printed in italic type:

From Shakespeare
Alas, poor Yorick: I knew him well.
Alas, poor Yorick; I knew him,
Horatio: a fellow of infinite jest.
(Hamlet)

O Romeo. Romeo! wherefore art thou, Romeo?
O Romeo. Romeo! wherefore art thou
Romeo? (Romeo and Juliet)
(Note the position of the comma.
"Wherefore" means "why" not "where.")

To gild the lily . . .
to gild refined gold, to paint the lily . . .
(King John)
Screw your courage to the sticking-point
But screw your courage to the sticking-
place (Macbeth)

All that glitters is not gold
All that glisters is not gold
(The Merchant of Venice)
Discretion is the better part of valor.
The better part of valor is discretion.
(King Henry IV, part I)

From the King James Bible
Pride goes before a fall
Pride goeth before destruction and an
haughty spirit before a fall (Proverbs)

Money is the root of all evil
For the love of money is the root of
all evil (Timothy)

To go the way of all flesh
And, behold, this day I am going the
way of all the earth (Joshua)

The mayor's words only inflamed the
people even more, excite, provoke, rouse
kindness *n.* good nature, charity, amiability, affection, tenderness ★**cruelty**
king *n.* monarch, sovereign, majesty, ruler, emperor
kink *n.* ① knot, loop, bend, coil ② freak, eccentricity, whim *This strange tower was built as the result of a whim by the eccentric designer*
kiss *v.* salute, embrace, smooch, buss
kit *n.* set, outfit, baggage, effects, gear, rig
knack *n.* flair, talent, ability, genius, gift ▷ *skill*

knave *n.* cheat, rascal, villain, scamp, scoundrel ▷ *rogue* NAVE
knead *v.* form, squeeze, mold, shape, press NEED
kneel *v.* bend the knee, genuflect *The nun genuflected before the altar, then said her rosary,* bow down, worship
knife *n.* scalpel, blade, dagger, cutter
knight *n.* cavalier, champion, soldier, warrior, baronet NIGHT
knit *v.* weave, crochet, spin, twill, link, loop
knob *n.* boss, bump, handle, opener, button
knock *v.* hit, slap, punch, bang, smite, strike
knock out ① *v.* stun, make insensible, render

L l

Other sources

Water, water, everywhere, and not a drop to drink
Water, water, everywhere, Nor any drop to drink (The Rime of the Ancient Mariner)

A little knowledge is a dangerous thing *A little learning is a dang'rous thing* (Alexander Pope)

Tomorrow to fresh fields and pastures new *Tomorrow to fresh woods, and pastures new* (Paradise Lost)

They shall not grow old as we that are left grow old
They shall grow not old, as we that are left grow old (Laurence Binyon)

Play it again, Sam (Humphrey Bogart, in the film *Casablanca*)

Play it, Sam. Play "As Time Goes By" (Ingrid Bergman, in the film *Casablanca*)

---

unconscious ② *n.* success, hit, triumph

knoll *n.* barrow, hill, mound, hillock

knot *n.* ① tie, bond, join, loop, kink, snarl, tangle ② cluster, group NOT

know *v.* perceive, discern, notice, identify ▷ *understand* NO

know-how *n.* skill, knowledge, talent

knowing *adj.* astute, knowledgeable, intelligent, perceptive ★**ignorant**

knowledge *n.* understanding, acquaintance, learning, wisdom, scholarship, information, sapience ★**ignorance**

kudos *n.* prestige, distinction, fame, glory, recognition

label *n.* badge, tag, ticket, sticker, docket, slip

labor *n. & v.* toil, work, drudge, strain, struggle

laborious *adj.* ① hard-working, diligent ② strenuous, arduous *Digging potatoes is arduous work,* hard ★**easy**

lack ① *n.* need, want, absence, deficiency, scarcity *During the hot weather there was a scarcity of water* ② *v.* need, require, want, miss

laconic *adj.* terse, curt, brief, concise ★**wordy**

lad *n.* boy, fellow, kid, youth, chap

laden *adj.* loaded, burdened, hampered, weighed down ★**empty**

ladle *v.* dip, scoop, dish, shovel

lady *n.* woman, female, dame, damsel, matron, mistress

lag *v.* dawdle, loiter, tarry, saunter ▷ *linger* ★**lead**

lagoon *n.* pool, pond, lake, basin

lair *n.* den, nest, retreat, hideout, hole

lake *n.* lagoon, loch, pond, spring, reservoir

lam *v.* beat, hit, clout, knock ▷ *strike*

lame *adj.* ① crippled, hobbled, disabled ② weak, feeble *That's a feeble excuse for missing school,* inadequate, unconvincing

lament *v.* deplore, mourn, grieve, sorrow ▷ *regret* ★**rejoice**

lamp *n.* lantern, light, flare, torch, flashlight

lance ① *n.* spear, pike, javelin, shaft ② *v.* puncture, pierce, cut

land ① *n.* country, district, tract, area, nation, region ② *v.* alight, arrive, carry, touch down *We had engine trouble, so the aircraft touched down in the desert*

landlord *n.* host, hotelier, innkeeper, owner

landmark *n.* milestone, milepost, beacon, monument, signpost

landscape *n.* scenery, view, prospect, countryside, panorama

lane *n.* alley, drive, passage, way LAIN

language *n.* tongue, speech, utterance, dialect, jargon

languid *adj.* leisurely, unhurried, sluggish, slow, easy ★**lively**

languish *v.* decline, droop, flag, pine, suffer, yearn ★**flourish**

lanky *adj.* tall, rangy, gangling, scrawny ★**squat**

lantern *n.* lamp, flashlight, torch

lap ① *v.* lick, drink, sip, sup ② *n.* circuit, course, distance ③ *n.* thighs, knees

lapse *v.* expire, die, pass, elapse, go by, deteriorate LAPS

larder *n.* pantry, storeroom, cellar

large *adj.* big, ample, substantial, great, broad ▷*huge* ★**small**

lark *n.* adventure, escapade, spree, joke, frolic, gambol

lash ① *v.* beat, cane, whip, flay, flog ② *n.* prod, goad, drive, whip

lass *n.* girl, maiden, maid, young woman

last ① *adj.* final, concluding, latest, utmost, aftermost ★**first** ② *v.* remain, linger *The foggy weather lingered for most of the morning,* endure, stay

latch *n.* bolt, bar, padlock, fastener

late *adj.* tardy, behindhand, departed, slow ★**early**

lately *adv.* recently, latterly, formerly

lather *n.* suds, foam, bubbles, froth

latter *adj.* final, last, latest, recent, closing ★**former**

laud *v.* compliment, praise, applaud, glorify ★**blame**

laugh *v.* chuckle, giggle, guffaw, snicker ★**cry**

launch ① *v.* start, begin, commence, establish, initiate ② *n.* motorboat

lavish ① *adj.* abundant, generous, liberal, extravagant ② *v.* waste, squander *My parents left me a small fortune, but I squandered it all,* give

law *n.* rule, ordinance, regulation, edict, decree

lawful *adj.* legal, legitimate, rightful ★**illegal**

lawyer *n.* attorney, counsel, jurist, barrister, solicitor, advocate

lax *adj.* careless, casual, slack, relaxed, vague ★**strict** LACKS

lay ① *v.* put, set *It's time for dinner; let's set the table,* deposit, place, spread ② *v.* impute, charge ③ *adj.* nonprofessional, amateur

layer *n.* seam, sheet, thickness, tier

lazy *adj.* idle, inactive, slothful, slow, sluggish ★**active**

lead *v.* conduct, guide, escort, direct, command ★**follow**

leader *n.* guide, pilot, conductor, chief, head, master

leaf *n.* frond, blade, sheet LIEF

league *n.* band, association, society, guild, group

leak *v.* trickle, ooze, seep, exude, flow out LEEK

lean ① *adj.* spare, slim, thin, skinny *Lina has no flesh on her; she is very skinny,* ② *v.* bend, curve, tilt, incline LIEN

leap *v.* spring, bound, jump, hop, skip

learn *v.* find out, ascertain, determine, acquire knowledge, understand

learned *adj.* cultured, educated, scholarly, literate ★**ignorant**

learning *n.* scholarship, education, knowledge ▷*wisdom* ★**ignorance**

least *adj.* fewest, smallest, slightest, lowest, tiniest ★**most** LEASED

leave ① *v.* abandon, desert, forsake, quit, go ② bequeath, bestow ③ *n.* vacation, furlough *Jack is on a furlough from the army,* permission

lecture *n.* talk, speech, address, sermon

ledge *n.* shelf, ridge, step

legacy *n.* bequest, inheritance, gift

legal *adj.* legitimate, lawful, valid, sound ★**illegal**

legend *n.* ① fable, myth, tale, fiction ② inscription *The box bore a brass plate with an inscription,* heading, caption

legible *adj.* clear, readable, understandable, distinct ★**illegible**

legitimate *adj.* legal, lawful, proper, rightful ▷*genuine* ★**illegal**

Lights

Arc lamp
Candle
Chandelier
Desk lamp
Electric light
Flashlight
Fluorescent lamp
Footlights
Gaslight
Headlight
Lantern
Nightlight
Reading light
Spotlight
Sunlamp
Table lamp
Torch

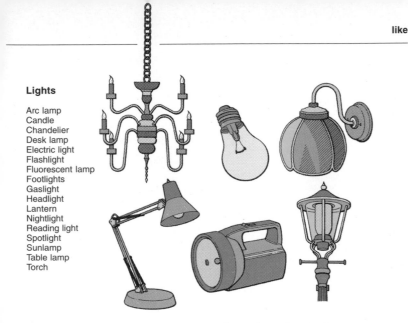

leisurely *adj.* unhurried, slow, easy, carefree, tranquil ★**hectic**

lend *v.* loan, advance, provide, supply, grant, lease ★**borrow**

lengthen *v.* extend, elongate, stretch, draw out, prolong ★**shorten**

lengthy *adj.* long, drawn out, longwinded ▷*tedious* ★**short**

lenient *adj.* tolerant, merciful, sparing, forbearing, indulgent ★**severe**

less *adj.* lesser, smaller, inferior, lower

lessen *v.* reduce, cut, become smaller, diminish, decrease ★**increase** LESSON

lesson *n.* instruction, lecture, information, teaching, exercise LESSEN

let ① *v.* allow, permit, suffer, authorize *The mayor authorized our school to hold the celebrations in the park,* grant ② lease

let down *v.* ① lower, take down ② betray, abandon, disappoint ★**satisfy**

letter *n.* ① dispatch, communication, epistle, message ② character *The book was printed in Hebrew characters,* sign, symbol

level ① *n.* plane, grade ② *adj.* even, flat, smooth ★**uneven** ③ *v.* aim, direct, point ④ *v.* demolish *Many houses were demolished*

during the earthquake, destroy

liable ① *adj.* answerable, accountable, responsible ② apt *My parents are apt to be annoyed if I play loud music,* prone, inclined

liar *n.* deceiver, fibber, teller of tales LYRE

libel *v.* slander, malign, blacken, defame, slur ★**praise**

liberal *adj.* open-handed, generous, open-hearted, free, lavish

liberate *v.* set free, save, release, ★**restrict**

liberty *n.* freedom, independence ★**slavery**

license *v.* allow, permit, entitle ★**ban**

lie ① *n.* untruth, falsehood ② *v.* recline *I shall recline on the sofa for the afternoon,* lounge, repose ▷*loll* ③ *v.* tell a lie, fib, invent LYE

life *n.* being, existence, activity, energy, ★**death**

lift *v.* raise, erect, hoist, elevate, hold up ★**lower**

light ① *n.* radiance, glow, shine, glare, brightness ② *n.* lamp, beacon, flame ② *v.* ignite, illuminate, kindle *The scouts kindled a fire to cook their food* ③ *adj.* fair, light-colored, sunny ★**dark** ④ lightweight, buoyant, airy ★**heavy**

like ①*adj.* similar, resembling, akin ★**unlike**

② v. admire, love, adore, cherish, prize ★**dislike**

likely adj. probable, expected, possible

likeness n. ① resemblance, appearance ② photograph *That's a wonderful photograph of my grandmother,* portrait

likewise adv. also, too, furthermore, further

limb n. leg, arm, extension, branch, shoot, bough

limit ① n. barrier, boundary, border, edge, end, restraint ② v. reduce, restrict *The heavy rain was restricted to the hilly country,* confine ★**free**

limited adj. restricted, reduced, narrow, confined ★**unrestricted**

limp ① adj. flabby, flimsy, flexible ② v. hobble, falter, shuffle

line n. ① stripe, streak, dash, bar ② cord, thread ③ row, queue, file ④ calling *Being an opera singer is a noble calling but a difficult one,* occupation

linger v. loiter, lag, dally, tarry, delay ▷*dawdle* ★**speed**

link ① n. bond, tie, connection, joint ② v. unite, join, couple, bracket ★**separate**

liquefy v. liquidize, melt

liquid n. fluid, liquor, solution, juice

list ① n. schedule, table, catalog, register ② v. tilt, lean, heel *The yacht heeled over as it turned into the wind,* careen, slope

listen v. hear, hearken, hark, heed

listless adj. languid, dull, lethargic, lifeless ▷*sluggish* ★**lively**

literally adv. actually, faithfully, precisely, really ★**loosely**

literate adj. educated, well-educated, learned, lettered ★**illiterate**

lithe adj. agile, nimble, flexible, supple ★**stiff**

litter n. clutter, jumble, rubbish, mess, refuse

little ① adj. small, tiny, short, slight, trivial, petty ▷*small* ★**large** ② adv. hardly, rarely, seldom

live ① adj. alive, living, existing, active, alert ★**dead** ② v. be, subsist, breathe, exist

lively adj. active, brisk, vivacious, animated, agile ★**listless**

livid adj. ① angry, enraged, furious, mad ② ashen *We were really scared, and Bob's face was ashen,* grayish, pale, leaden

living ① adj. alive, existing ② n. job, occupation, work, livelihood

load ① n. freight, cargo, goods, burden ② v. fill, pack, burden, pile up, stack LODE, LOWED

loaf ① v. waste time, idle, dally, dawdle ② n. block, cube, lump, cake

loan ① n. credit, advance, allowance ② v. allow, lend, advance *The bank advanced me the money to pay the mortgage* LONE

loath or **loth** adj. reluctant, disinclined, opposed

loathe v. abhor, detest, despise, dislike ▷*hate* ★**like**

lobby n. hallway, entrance, vestibule, foyer

local adj. regional, district, provincial

locate v. find, discover, detect, unearth

lock ① n. bolt, fastener, latch, clasp ② v. bolt, fasten, secure ③ n. floodgate, weir ④ n. curl, braid, tress *I kept a tress of her hair in a locket*

lodge ① v. stay at, put up, shelter, get stuck *A fishbone got stuck in his throat,* remain ② n. inn, hotel

lofty adj. ① tall, high, noble, great ② proud, exalted, arrogant ★**modest**

logical adj. fair, justifiable, reasonable, sound ★**illogical**

loiter v. lag, trail, linger, dally, dawdle, hang around

loll v. recline, sprawl, lounge, lie, rest, flop

lone adj. single, sole, lonely, separate, unaccompanied LOAN

lonely adj. alone, forsaken, friendless, remote, forlorn, lonesome

long ① adj. lengthy, extended, expanded ★**short** ② v. crave, hanker, yearn, desire

look ① v. appear, seem ② v. peer, glance, watch, behold ③ n. appearance, glance, gaze *Her gaze fell upon me, and I had to answer the next question*

loom v. menace, portend, rise, emerge, appear

loop n. bend, circle, coil, noose, twist

loophole n. escape, way out, excuse, get-out

loose *adj.* ① slack, separate, apart, flimsy, flabby, baggy ② free, relaxed, ③ vague, indefinite

loosely *adv.* freely, separately, vaguely

loosen *v.* slacken, relax, undo, detach, release, unfasten ★**tighten**

Loot   Lute

loot *n.* booty, haul, swag, spoils, plunder LUTE

lord *n.* noble, ruler, duke, marquess, earl, viscount, baron

lose *v.* ① mislay, misplace, miss ★**find** ② be defeated, suffer defeat *The rebels suffered defeat at the hands of the army,* fail ★**win**

loser *n.* failure, dud, flop ★**winner**

loss *n.* damage, harm, forfeit, ruin, misfortune ★**gain**

lost *adj.* mislaid, missing, gone, vanished, strayed, ruined ★**found**

lot *n.* ① group, batch, assortment ② fate, portion, fortune ③ plot, patch, land

lotion *n.* balm, salve, ointment, cream, liniment

loud *adj.* ① noisy, blatant, shrill, blaring, deafening ② gaudy, vulgar, tasteless ★**quiet**

lounge ① *v.* recline, lie, loll, sprawl, laze ② *n.* lobby *Tea was served in the hotel's lobby,* reception room, waiting room

lout *n.* oaf, clod, boor, lummox

lovable *adj.* winsome, charming, attractive, fascinating ★**hateful**

love ① *v.* adore, idolize, worship, dote on, cherish, treasure ② *n.* affection, passion, devotion, ardor ★**hate**

lovely *adj.* charming, delightful, beautiful, adorable ★**hideous**

low *adj.* ① base, vulgar, crude, improper ② not high, flat, level ③ soft, faint, muffled, deep ④ humble, modest, lowly ⑤ cheap, inexpensive ★**high** LO

lower ① *v.* let down, fall, descend ② *v.* debase, disgrace, degrade ③ *adj.* inferior, lesser, smaller, minor

loyal *adj.* constant, staunch *Bill was Kathy's staunch friend for years,* true ▷ *faithful* ★**disloyal**

lucid *adj.* clear, obvious, intelligible, bright ▷ *transparent* ★**murky**

luck *n.* chance, fortune, success, windfall ★**misfortune**

lucky *adj.* fortunate, successful, blessed, charmed, favored ★**unlucky**

ludicrous *adj.* absurd, foolish, silly, outlandish, ▷ *ridiculous*

lug *v.* pull, draw, drag, haul, tow, heave

luggage *n.* baggage, suitcases, trunks, boxes

lull ① *v.* calm, dwindle, cease, slacken, subside ② *n.* calm, hush, respite

lumber ① *n.* timber, wood, boards, logs ② *v.* plod, shuffle, stomp

luminous *adj.* shining, radiant, bright

lump *n.* bit, piece, chunk, block, knob, swelling *I noticed a rather mysterious swelling on my arm*

lunatic *n.* insane person, maniac, psychopath

lunge *v.* push, thrust, plunge, charge, pounce

lurch *v.* lean, list, reel, rock, stagger, stumble

lure *v.* attract, draw, decoy, ensnare, invite ▷ *tempt* ★**repulse**

lurid *adj.* ghastly, disgusting, grim, grisly, melodramatic, sensational

lurk *v.* slink, skulk, crouch, hide, prowl, snoop

luscious *adj.* juicy, succulent, mellow, delicious, scrumptious ★**nauseous**

lush *adj.* wild, luxuriant, green, rich, abundant

lust *n.* desire, passion, craving, greed

luster *n.* brightness, brilliance, gleam, sheen

lusty *adj.* hale, hearty, vigorous, energetic, rugged, tough ★**weak**

luxury *n.* affluence, wealth, richness, comfort, bliss

lyre *n.* harp, zither LIAR

M m

Mail

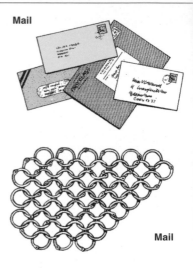

macabre *adj.* ghastly, grisly, hideous, horrible ▷ *ghostly*

machine *n.* engine, contrivance, device

mad *adj.* ① angry, furious ② lunatic, crazy ▷ *insane* ★**sane**

madcap *adj.* flighty, reckless, thoughtless, impulsive

magazine *n.* ① periodical, publication ② storehouse, depot, arsenal

magic ① *n.* wizardry, witchcraft, sorcery, conjuring ② *adj.* bewitching *She greeted me with a bewitching smile,* fascinating, miraculous

magician *n.* conjuror, wizard, witch, sorcerer, juggler

magistrate *n.* judge, justice, bailiff

magnanimous *adj.* forgiving, generous, charitable, liberal ★**paltry**

magnate *n.* industrialist, merchant, tycoon, VIP, leader MAGNET

magnet *n.* lodestone, attraction, bait, draw MAGNATE

magnetic *adj.* attracting, attractive, absorbing, entrancing, alluring, mesmerizing ▷ *charming* ★**repulsive**

magnificent *adj.* majestic, noble, grand, brilliant, superb ▷ *splendid* ★**modest**

magnify *v.* enlarge, increase, exaggerate ▷ *enhance* ★**diminish**

maid *n.* ① maiden, virgin, miss, damsel ② maidservant, domestic help, waitress MADE

mail *n.* ① letters, post, correspondence, epistles ② armor *The knight's armor was made of breastplates and chain mail,* shield MALE

maim *v.* mutilate, injure, mangle, crush ▷ *disable* ★**heal**

main ① *adj.* leading, principal, head, chief, central *Such important matters are dealt with at our central office,* ② *n.* channel, duct, line, pipe

mainly *adv.* chiefly, generally, mostly, on the whole, usually

Mail

maintain *v.* ① sustain, keep, support, provide for ② affirm, advocate *The chairman advocated an increase in charges,* assert

majestic *adj.* dignified, grand, noble, august, elevated ▷ *magnificent* ★**unimportant**

major ① *adj.* senior, chief, leading, more important, greater ★**minor** ② *n.* officer, soldier

majority *n.* greater number, most part, bulk, mass ★**minority**

make *v.* ① build, construct, fabricate, fashion ② compel, drive, coerce ③ designate *Two days after her boss retired Liz was designated as the new head of the department,* appoint

make up *v.* ① invent, fabricate, create ② forgive and forget, bury the hatchet *At last, my brother and sister stopped arguing and decided to bury the hatchet*

makeshift *adj.* improvised, temporary, stopgap *I fixed the car engine, but it was only a stopgap repair* ★**permanent**

malady *n.* illness, sickness, ailment, affliction, disease

malevolent *adj.* malign, baleful, venomous, malicious ▷ *hostile* ★**benevolent**

malice *n.* bitterness, rancor, spite, enmity ▷ *hatred* ★**kindness**

malicious *adj.* malignant, spiteful, resentful, bitter ▷ *hateful* ★**kind**

maltreat *v.* bully, harm, abuse, injure ▷ *hurt* ★**assist**

mammoth *adj.* giant, colossal, enormous, massive ▷ *huge* ★**small**

man ① *n.* male, sir, mankind, gentleman ② *n.* valet, manservant ③ *v.* equip, fit out, arm, crew

manage *v.* ① direct, control, administer ② get along *I get along quite well on my own,* fare, cope with ★**fail**

manager *n.* director, superintendent, overseer, supervisor, boss

mandate *n.* authority, command, instruction, warrant

maneuver *v.* direct, drive, guide, handle ▷ *manipulate*

mangle *v.* crush, deform, destroy, maul ▷ *maim*

mania *n.* madness, delirium, craze, fad, enthusiasm, passion

manifest *v.* signify, suggest, demonstrate, display ▷ *show* ★**hide**

manipulate *v.* work, handle, wield, use, conduct, control ▷ *operate*

manly *adj.* male, masculine, brave, bold, strong ▷ *fearless*

manner *n.* fashion, style, form, mode, demeanor, bearing, way MANOR

manor *n.* estate, country house, château, hall MANNER

mansion *n.* house, castle, residence ▷ *manor*

mantle *n.* canopy, cape, covering, hood, shroud, cloak MANTEL

mantel *n.* fireplace shelf, mantelpiece MANTLE

manual ① *adj.* hand-operated, physical *We found the electric typewriter easier to use than the manual typewriter* ② *n.* guide, guidebook, handbook

manufacture *v.* make, build, fabricate, create, produce ▷ *construct*

manuscript *n.* ① script, article, essay, theme ② handwriting, autograph

many *adj.* numerous, varied, various, frequent, countless ★**few**

map *n.* chart, plan, diagram, outline

mar *v.* deface, disfigure, injure, blemish, damage ▷ *spoil* ★**enhance**

march *v.* stride, walk, pace, step, file, trek

margin *n.* edge, border, rim, side, boundary, brim, brink ★**center**

mariner *n.* seaman, sailor, seafarer, deckhand, tar, seadog

mark ① *n.* feature, emblem, impression *The letter had a hand-stamped impression on it,* blemish ② *v.* scratch, blemish, stain ③ *v.* take notice of, observe

marked *adj.* noticeable, conspicuous, apparent, clear, striking ★**slight**

market *n.* grocery store, supermarket, bazaar

maroon *v.* desert, beach, strand, abandon, cast away ★**rescue**

marry *v.* wed, get married, espouse, mate, unite ★**separate**

marsh *n.* swamp, mire, moor, morass, bog

marshal *v.* gather, group, deploy, assemble MARTIAL

martial *adj.* military, militant, hostile, warlike ★**peaceful** MARSHAL

marvel *n.* miracle, wonder, spectacle, sensation

marvelous *adj.* wonderful, wondrous, fabulous, spectacular ▷ *remarkable* ★**ordinary**

masculine *adj.* manlike, manly, strong, robust, strapping ▷ *male* ★**feminine**

mash *v.* crush, squash, pulverize, grind

mask ① *n.* camouflage, veil, domino ② *v.* conceal, disguise *Aladdin went to the marketplace disguised as a beggar,* shield ★**uncover**

mass *n.* batch, combination, hunk, load, quantity, lump

massacre *v.* exterminate, butcher, murder, slaughter, kill

massive *adj.* big, large, bulky, enormous ▷ *huge* ★**small**

master ① *n.* controller, director, leader, captain, champion ② *v.* tame *Our job on the* *ranch was to tame the wild horses,* control, defeat, subdue

match ① *n.* light, fuse, taper, lucifer ② *v.* copy, pair, equal, tone with

mate ① *n.* spouse, husband, wife, companion, chum, comrade ② *v.* breed, join, wed, yoke

material ① *n.* fabric, textile, cloth, stuff, matter ② *adj.* actual, real, concrete *There was concrete evidence of the prisoner's innocence*

maternal *adj.* motherly, parental, kind, affectionate, protective

matter ① *n.* affair, concern, subject, topic ② *n.* stuff, material, substance *This rock contains some sort of mineral substance* ③ *n.* trouble, distress ④ *v.* signify, count, affect

mature *adj.* ripe, mellowed, seasoned, developed, grown-up, adult ★**immature**

maul *v.* batter, beat, molest, paw ▷ *mangle*

maxim *n.* saying, motto, axiom, proverb

maximum *adj.* supreme, highest, most, greatest, top, largest ★**minimum**

maybe *adv.* possibly, perhaps, perchance

maze *n.* labyrinth, puzzle, tangle, confusion ▷ *muddle* MAIZE

meadow *n.* grassland, field, mead, pasture

meager *adj.* thin, spare, slight, flimsy, sparse ▷ *scanty* ★**substantial**

meal *n.* repast, dinner, lunch, breakfast, supper ▷ *feast*

mean ① *v.* signify, denote, express, suggest ② *adj.* cruel, base, low, paltry, miserly ★**generous** ③ average, medium mien

meaning *n.* significance, explanation, sense

means *n.* ① resources, money, wealth ② technique, ability *She has the ability to become a professional player,* method

measure ① *n.* meter, gauge, rule ② *n.* limit, extent, amount ③ *v.* estimate, value, quantify *It is hard to quantify how much damage has been done*

meat *n.* flesh, viands, victuals, food, muscle,

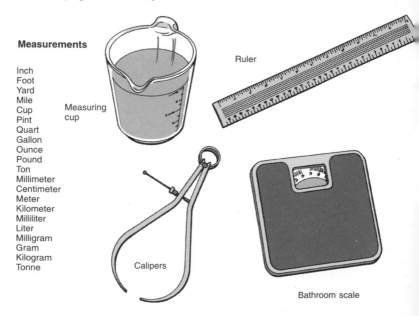

Measurements

Inch
Foot
Yard
Mile
Cup
Pint
Quart
Gallon
Ounce
Pound
Ton
Millimeter
Centimeter
Meter
Kilometer
Milliliter
Liter
Milligram
Gram
Kilogram
Tonne

Measuring cup

Ruler

Calipers

Bathroom scale

brawn MEET, METE

mechanical *adj.* ① automatic, machine-driven ② routine, unthinking

medal *n.* award, decoration, ribbon, prize, trophy MEDDLE

meddle *v.* interfere, intervene, intrude, tamper MEDAL

medicine *n.* remedy, cure, physic, medicament, nostrum, drug

mediocre *adj.* average, common, inferior, middling ▷*ordinary* ★**excellent**

meditate *v.* ponder, puzzle over, think, reflect, contemplate

medium ① *n.* means, agency, center ② *n.* conditions, setting, atmosphere *I like school because it has such a wonderful atmosphere of learning* ③ *adj.* average, fair ▷*mediocre*

medley *n.* assortment, jumble, collection, hodgepodge

meek *adj.* docile, humble, quiet, patient, uncomplaining ▷*mild* ★**arrogant**

meet *v.* come together, converge, join, flock, assemble, encounter MEAT, METE

meeting *n.* gathering, assembly, convention

melancholy *adj.* glum, gloomy, unhappy, sad ▷*miserable* ★**cheerful**

mellow *adj.* ① ripe, rich, full-flavored ★**unripe** ② jovial, cheerful ③ smooth, soothing, delicate *The wine had a smooth, delicate flavor*

melodious *adj.* sweet, mellow, silver-toned, rich, resonant ★**harsh**

melody *n.* tune, air, lay, song, chant, theme

melt *v.* dissolve, liquefy, soften, thaw ★**solidify**

member *n.* ① fellow, associate, representative, comrade ② limb, part, portion, leg, arm

memorable *adj.* unforgettable, fresh, indelible, noticeable, striking ▷*conspicuous*

memorial *n.* monument, memento, relic, mausoleum *The emperor was buried in the state mausoleum*

memorize *v.* learn, commit to memory, remember

memory *n.* recall, recapture, recollection, renown ▷*fame*

menace *v.* threaten, intimidate, frighten, alarm ▷*bully*

mend *v.* restore, correct, promote, improve, rectify, heal ▷*repair* ★**damage**

menial ① *adj.* servile, ignoble, base ② *n.* flunky, underling, lackey

mental *adj.* intellectual, theoretical *Edward's knowledge of music is purely theoretical; he can't play or sing,* abstract ★**physical**

mention *v.* declare, announce, observe, disclose, speak of, say

mercenary ① *adj.* acquisitive, grasping, greedy ▷*selfish* ② *n.* soldier of fortune *The men who were killed were not patriots, but soldiers of fortune,* freelance, hireling

merchandise *n.* wares, goods, commodities, cargo, freight, stock

merchant *n.* dealer, trader, marketeer, vender, retailer, tradesman

merciful *adj.* humane, clement, lenient, compassionate, sparing, forgiving ★**merciless**

merciless *adj.* callous, cruel, pitiless, unrelenting, inhuman ★**merciful**

mercy *n.* compassion, clemency, forgiveness,

Metals

Aluminum
Brass
Bronze
Chromium
Copper
Gold
Iron and Steel
Lead
Manganese
Mercury
Nickel
Platinum
Silver
Tin
Zinc

Trophy

Girder

forbearance, grace ▷*pity* ★**cruelty**

mere *adj.* pure, unmixed, absolute, unaffected, simple, paltry

merge *v.* mix, mingle, combine, fuse, blend, weld ▷*unite*

merit ① *n.* excellence, quality, virtue, worth, caliber ▷*talent* ★**failing** ② *v.* deserve, be worthy of

merry *adj.* jolly, gleeful, cheerful, mirthful, sunny ▷*happy* ★**melancholy**

mesh *n.* net, lattice, snare, netting, tangle, trap, web

mess ① *n.* muddle, confusion, clutter, jumble, chaos ▷*plight* ★**order** ② dining hall, mess hall, dining room

message *n.* communication, letter, missive, notice, note, dispatch *The reporter sent a dispatch to her paper in Lisbon*

messenger *n.* courier, runner, agent, bearer, carrier, herald

mete *v.* measure, apportion, distribute, divide, deal MEAT, MEET

meter *n.* ① measure, gauge, rule ② cadence *He recited some of his poems, which had a peculiar cadence to them,* rhythm, lilt, swing

method *n.* routine, usage, way, means, system, rule, manner ▷*mode*

mettle *n.* spirit, life, fire, animation, ardor, boldness ▷*courage*

middle ① *n.* center, heart, midst ② *adj.* medium, average, normal

midget ① *n.* dwarf, gnome, pygmy ② *adj.* little, miniature, small ▷*tiny* ★**giant**

mien *n.* appearance, air, look, manner, expression MEAN

miffed *adj.* annoyed, nettled, offended, hurt ▷*upset* ★**delighted**

might ① *n.* strength, ability, power, force, energy ② *v.* past tense of **may** *She might not have gone had she known it would snow* MITE

mighty *adj.* strong, powerful, potent, stupendous ▷*hefty* ★**weak**

mild *adj.* moderate, calm, gentle, genial, docile ▷*meek* ★**harsh**

military *adj.* martial, soldierly, warlike

mill ① *n.* grinder, works, factory, plant ② *v.* crush, grind, pulverize *The rock was pulverized and used for making roads,* grate, pound

mimic *v.* impersonate, copy, simulate, imitate

mince *v.* shred, chop, crumble, grind, hash MINTS

mind ① *n.* brain, intellect, soul, spirit ② *v.* listen to, obey, follow orders ③ *v.* take care of, look after ④ *v.* be careful, watch out for

mine ① *n.* quarry, colliery, shaft, deposit, tunnel ② *n.* bomb, explosive ③ *v.* excavate, dig out ④ *pron.* belonging to me *This store is mine*

mingle *v.* mix, blend, combine ▷*merge*

miniature ① *adj.* tiny, small, dwarf, midget, minute ② *n.* small portrait

minimum *adj.* least, smallest, lowest, slightest ★**maximum**

minister *n.* ① clergyman, vicar, priest ② ambassador, diplomat *My aunt was a diplomat working in the Brazilian embassy* ③ secretary, cabinet member

minor *adj.* lesser, smaller, lower, junior, trivial, trifling ★**major** MINER

mint ① *v.* stamp, forge, cast ② *adj.* new, perfect, untarnished ③ *n.* peppermint, plant

minute ① *n.* (*min*-it) flash, instant, moment ② *adj.* (my-*nyute*) slight, tiny, small ▷*miniature* ★**huge**

miracle *n.* marvel, wonder, phenomenon

miraculous *adj.* supernatural, amazing, wondrous, prodigious ★**ordinary**

mire *n.* slime, muck, ooze, mud

mirror ① *n.* looking glass, reflector ② *v.* imitate, simulate, reflect *The essay reflected my feelings about my old home,* copy

mirth *n.* hilarity, laughter, jocularity, fun, frolic, jollity ★**melancholy**

misbehave *v.* do wrong, disobey, offend, be naughty ★**behave**

miscellaneous *adj.* various, varied, divers, sundry, mixed, jumbled

mischief *n.* roguery, pranks, damage, hurt, annoyance, harm

mischievous *adj.* rascally, villainous, naughty, destructive, spiteful ★**good**

misconduct *n.* misbehavior, wrongdoing, naughtiness, rudeness

miser *n.* niggard, skinflint, scrooge, pennypincher, tightwad ★**spendthrift**

miserable *adj.* forlorn, wretched, pitiable, desolate, suffering ★**cheerful**

misery *n.* sorrow, woe, grief, anguish, distress ▷*unhappiness* ★**happiness**

misfit *n.* eccentric *Professor Jones is something of an eccentric and comes to lectures in her slippers,* drop-out, oddball, nonconformist

misfortune *n.* adversity, bad luck, hardship, evil, calamity ▷*disaster* ★**luck**

misgiving *n.* distrust, mistrust, doubt, apprehension, anxiety ▷*qualm* ★**confidence**

mishap *n.* misadventure, blow, accident ▷*misfortune*

misjudge *v.* underestimate, overestimate, overrate, underrate ▷*mistake*

mislay *v.* lose, misplace, miss

mislead *v.* deceive, lead astray, hoodwink, take in, outwit ▷*bluff*

miss ① *v.* fail, fall short of, skip, pass over, mistake ② *v.* grieve over, yearn for, lament ③ *n.* girl, young woman, damsel

missile *n.* projectile, arrow, dart, pellet, shot, rocket

mission *n.* errand, task, assignment, object, objective, end, aim ▷*quest*

mist *n.* moisture, dew, vapor, fog, cloud MISSED

mistake ① *n.* error, fault, lapse, blunder, oversight ② *v.* slip up, misunderstand, confuse

mistaken *adj.* erroneous, untrue, false, fallacious ▷*wrong* ★**correct**

mistrust *v.* disbelieve, distrust, doubt, fear ▷*suspect* ★**trust**

misunderstand *v.* mistake, misinterpret, take wrongly ★**grasp**

misuse *v.* exploit, abuse, corrupt

mite *n.* ① grain, atom, morsel, particle ② bug, parasite *The plants were infested with parasites* MIGHT

mitigate *v.* allay, ease, abate, moderate, justify ★**aggravate**

mix *v.* blend, whip, mingle, combine ▷*stir*

mix up *v.* confuse, confound, muddle, jumble ▷*bewilder*

mixture *n.* miscellany, medley, jumble, blend

moan *v.* wail, groan, grouse, grumble, grieve

mob *n.* crowd, mass, gang, flock, rabble, company, throng

mobile *adj.* active, portable, wandering, movable ★**immobile**

mock ① *v.* mimic, imitate, jeer at, laugh at, ridicule ▷*flatter* ② *adj.* pretended, artificial

mode *n.* fashion, style, vogue, manner, way, form ▷*method* MOWED

model *n.* ① pattern, original, prototype *This car is a prototype, and we will produce many like it* ② mannequin ③ replica, representation

moderate *adj.* reasonable, medium, gentle, mild, quiet, modest ▷*fair*

modern *adj.* new, up-to-date, modish, stylish, recent

modest *adj.* bashful, demure, diffident, unassuming, humble ★**vain**

modesty *n.* humility, diffidence, reserve, shyness, decency ★**vanity**

modify *v.* transform, convert, change, alter, revise, redesign

moist *adj.* damp, humid, watery, clammy, dank ▷*wet* ★**dry**

moisture *n.* damp, dampness, liquid, wetness

mold ① *v.* form, shape, fashion, cast, create ② *n.* pattern, matrix ③ *n.* earth, loam

moldy *adj.* mildewed, putrid, bad

molest *v.* annoy, bother, pursue, attack, torment ▷*harry*

moment *n.* ① second, instant, twinkling ② importance, worth, weight *I think your argument has some weight, and I agree with you*

momentous *adj.* notable, outstanding, decisive, important ★**insignificant**

monarch *n.* king, sovereign, ruler, emperor, prince *The head of state in Monaco is a prince*

money

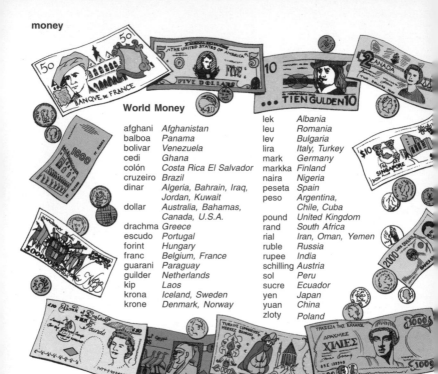

World Money

afghani	Afghanistan	lek	Albania
balboa	Panama	leu	Romania
bolivar	Venezuela	lev	Bulgaria
cedi	Ghana	lira	Italy, Turkey
colón	Costa Rica El Salvador	mark	Germany
cruzeiro	Brazil	markka	Finland
dinar	Algeria, Bahrain, Iraq,	naira	Nigeria
	Jordan, Kuwait	peseta	Spain
dollar	Australia, Bahamas,	peso	Argentina,
	Canada, U.S.A.		Chile, Cuba
drachma	Greece	pound	United Kingdom
escudo	Portugal	rand	South Africa
forint	Hungary	rial	Iran, Oman, Yemen
franc	Belgium, France	ruble	Russia
guarani	Paraguay	rupee	India
guilder	Netherlands	schilling	Austria
kip	Laos	sol	Peru
krona	Iceland, Sweden	sucre	Ecuador
krone	Denmark, Norway	yen	Japan
		yuan	China
		zloty	Poland

money *n.* wealth, cash, coin, legal tender

mongrel *n.* hybrid, mixed, crossbreed, dog

monitor ① *n.* listener, auditor, watchdog, prefect ② *v.* check, supervise, oversee

monologue *n.* lecture, oration, speech, recitation, sermon

monopolize *v.* control, take over, appropriate ▷*dominate* ★**share**

monotonous *adj.* tedious, uninteresting, dull, prosaic *His speech was so prosaic that I almost dropped off to sleep,* repetitive ▷*tiresome*

monster *n.* beast, fiend, villain, brute

monstrous *adj.* hideous, frightful, dreadful, terrible, criminal ▷*wicked*

mood *n.* state of mind, humor, temper, disposition *My grandmother's gentle disposition won her many friends*

moody *adj.* morose, sulky, sullen, peevish, cantankerous *I didn't like Uncle Harry; he was a cantankerous old man* ★**cheerful**

moor ① *v.* tether, picket, tie, chain, anchor, secure ② *n.* heath, moorland MORE

mop *n.* ① sponge, swab, towel ② hair, tresses, locks, mane

mope *v.* be dejected, grieve, moon, pine, sulk

moral *adj.* virtuous, good, honest, honorable ▷*upright* ★**immoral**

morbid *adj.* gruesome, macabre, melancholy

more ① *adj.* in addition, also, beyond, extra, further ② *adv.* better, again, longer MOOR

morning *n.* dawn, daybreak, daylight, cockcrow *I rose at cockcrow, saddled my horse, and was off to Richmond,* sunrise ★**evening** MOURNING

morose *adj.* glum, sullen, sulky, broody, taciturn ▷*moody* ★**cheerful**

morsel *n.* bit, bite, piece, scrap, nibble

mortal *adj.* ① human, feeble, ephemeral ② fatal, final, deadly, severe

most ① *adj.* greatest nearly all ② *adv.* mostly, chiefly, mainly, utmost

mostly *adv.* as a rule, principally, usually, normally

mother ① *n.* female parent, mom, mommy, mama ② *v.* nurse, protect, rear, care for

motherly *adj.* caring, comforting, loving, maternal, gentle

motion *n.* ① movement, locomotion, action, passage ② proposal *I vote that we accept the proposal,* suggestion

motionless *adj.* stationary, still, transfixed, stable, inert ★**moving**

motive *n.* reason, purpose, occasion, impulse, cause ▷*spur*

mottled *adj.* speckled, spotted, pied, piebald

motto *n.* saying, slogan, watchword, maxim *My mother's maxim was "Always look on the bright side,"* proverb

mound *n.* hillock, pile, knoll, rise, mount

mount *v.* ascend, climb, rise, vault

mourn *v.* lament, deplore, sorrow, regret, weep ▷*grieve* ★**rejoice**

mournful *adj.* doleful, somber, cheerless, sorrowful ▷*melancholy* ★**joyful**

mouth *n.* aperture, opening, entrance, orifice, inlet, jaws

mouthful *n.* bite, morsel, sample, taste, tidbit

move *v.* ① march, proceed, walk, go ② propose, suggest, recommend ③ propel, drive, impel

moving *adj.* touching, affecting, stirring *The band played a stirring rendition of "Amazing Grace,"* emotional

much ① *adj.* abundant, considerable, ample ② *adv.* considerably, greatly, often ③ *n.* lots, loads, heaps, plenty

muck *n.* dirt, filth, mire, ooze, mud, scum

muddle ① *n.* confusion, clutter, jumble, mix-up ② *v.* bungle, tangle, confound ▷*bewilder*

muff *v.* botch, mismanage, miss, spoil ▷*muddle*

muffle *v.* ① deaden, mute, muzzle, silence ② wrap, envelop, wind, swaddle

mug ① *n.* face, looks ② *n.* cup, beaker, tankard ③ *v.* attack, beat up, rob

muggy *adj.* clammy, dank, damp, humid, close ★**dry**

mull *v.* meditate *I meditated over the weekend before deciding what to do,* consider, study, think about

multiply *v.* increase, spread, grow, extend, intensify ★**decrease**

multitude *n.* crowd, legion, throng, swarm, horde ★**handful**

mum *adj.* dumb, silent, quiet, mute

munch *v.* crunch, chew, bit, nibble ▷*eat*

murder *v.* slay, assassinate, butcher, destroy, slaughter ▷*kill*

murky *adj.* foggy, cloudy, dark, gloomy, dull, misty ★**bright**

murmur *n. & v.* whisper, mutter, mumble, drone

muscular *adj.* brawny, athletic, burly, beefy, powerful ▷*robust* ★**puny**

muse *v.* meditate, ponder, puzzle over, brood, deliberate

must ① *v.* ought to, should, be obliged to ② *n.* duty, necessity, requirement

muster *v.* marshal, collect, assemble, rally *The troops rallied and prepared to attack again,* enroll

musty *adj.* moldy, rank, mildewy, decayed

mute *adj.* silent, speechless, voiceless, soundless ★**loud**

mutilate *v.* injure, hurt, cut, damage, hack ▷*maim*

mutiny *n. & v.* protest, revolt, strike, riot

mutter *v.* mumble, grouse, grumble ▷*murmur* ★**exclaim**

mutual *adj.* common, reciprocal, interchangeable ▷*joint* ★**one-sided**

mysterious *adj.* obscure, unrevealed, unexplained, secret ▷*hidden* ★**clear**

mystery *n.* puzzle, enigma, secrecy, riddle, problem

mystify *v.* confuse, bamboozle, hoodwink, puzzle, mislead ▷*baffle* ★**enlighten**

myth *n.* fable, legend, supposition, fabrication, tradition, fantasy ★**fact**

mythical *adj.* fabulous, fabled, legendary, traditional, imaginary ★**true**

N n

nab *v.* arrest, apprehend, seize, catch, capture, grab

nag ① *v.* pester, hector, heckle, badger, annoy, henpeck, scold *My parents scolded me for coming home late* ② *n.* horse, pony

nail ① *n.* brad, peg, pin, spike, tack ② *v.* hammer, fix, tack, peg ③ *v.* capture, catch, seize

naive *adj.* innocent, unworldly, unsophisticated, simple, trusting ★**cunning, sophisticated**

naked *adj.* nude, bare, unclothed, undressed ★**clothed**

name ① *n.* title, description, designation ② *n.* character, reputation *A good reputation is very important to me,* distinction ③ *v.* christen, style, term, entitle

nap ① *v.* sleep, doze, drowse, rest ② *n.* down, fiber, fuzz *Velvet is a cloth with a kind of fuzz on the surface*

narrate *v.* describe, tell, recite, yarn

narrow *adj.* slender, fine, small ▷*thin* ★**wide**

nasty *adj.* dirty, mucky, foul, offensive, unpleasant ▷*squalid* ★**nice**

national *adj.* civil, governmental, public, general

native *adj.* natural, inborn, aboriginal, domestic, local

natural *adj.* frank, genuine, innate, instinctive, ordinary, usual

naturally *adj.* absolutely, certainly, frankly, normally

nature *n.* ① temper, personality, disposition ② the world, the outdoors, landscape

naughty *adj.* mischievous, rascally, wicked, disobedient ▷*bad* ★**well-behaved**

nauseous *adj.* disgusting, sickening, repulsive, revolting ★**pleasant**

nautical *adj.* maritime *Ancient Greece was a great maritime nation,* seamanlike, naval, sailing

navigate *v.* voyage, cruise, sail, guide, pilot

navy *n.* ships, fleet, armada, flotilla

near *adj.* close, nearby, adjacent, bordering, beside ▷*nigh* ★**remote**

nearly *adv.* about, almost, all but, thereabouts, roughly

neat *adj.* ① tidy, spruce, smart, stylish ★**untidy** ② skillful, clever, adroit *I admire your adroit handling of that tricky situation,* ingenious

necessary *adj.* needed, essential, basic, required, compulsory ★**optional**

need ① *v.* require, want, crave ▷*demand* ★**have** ② *n.* distress, want, necessity, deprivation *During the long war, the people suffered many deprivations* KNEAD

needed *adj.* wanted, desired, lacking ▷*necessary* ★**unnecessary**

needless *adj.* pointless, unnecessary, superfluous, useless ★**necessary**

needy *adj.* destitute, down-and-out, deprived ▷*poor* ★**well-off**

neglect *v.* overlook, ignore, scorn, slight, disregard ▷*spurn* ★**cherish**

neglected *adj.* unkempt, abandoned, dilapidated, uncared for ★**cherished**

negligent *adj.* neglectful, forgetful, slack, indifferent ▷*careless* ★**careful**

negotiate *v.* bargain, deal, treat, haggle, mediate

neighborhood *n.* vicinity, surroundings, district, area, locality *There are many fine houses in this locality*

neighborly *adj.* hospitable, friendly, kind, obliging ▷*helpful*

nerve *n.* ① mettle, guts, pluck, courage ② audacity, impudence *Mr. Thompson already owes us money and yet he has the impudence to ask for more*

nervous *adj.* tense, taut, jumpy, flustered, anxious, timid ★**confident**

nest *n.* den, burrow, haunt, refuge, resort

nestle *adj.* cuddle, snuggle, huddle, nuzzle

net ① *v.* catch, trap, lasso, capture ② *n.* mesh, lattice, trap, web, lace *I have some new lace curtains* ③ *adj.* clear *I made a clear $15,000 after taxes,* final, lowest

nettle *v.* exasperate, annoy, ruffle,

National and Religious Holidays

Advent, All Saints' Day, Ascension Day, Ash Wednesday, Australia Day, Bastille Day, Canada Day, Candlemas, Carnival, Christmas, Columbus Day, Commonwealth Day, Diwali, Day of the Dead, Easter, Father's Day, Gandhi's Birthday, Good Friday, Guy Fawkes Day, Halloween, Hanukkah, Independence Day, Kwanzaa, Labor Day, Lent, Mardi Gras, Martin Luther King Day, Memorial Day, Mother's Day, Muhammad's Birthday, New Year's Day, Palm Sunday, Passover, Pentecost, Presidents' Day, Purim, Ramadan, Rosh Hashanah, Saint Patrick's Day, Shavuot, Sukkot, Thanksgiving Day, Valentine's Day, Veterans' Day, Yom Kippur

A puppet from the Mexican Day of the Dead Festival

pique ▷ *vex*

neutral *adj.* impartial, unbiased, fair-minded, unprejudiced ★**biased**

never *adv.* at no time, not at all, under no circumstances ★**always**

new *adj.* recent, just out, current, latest, fresh, unused ▷*novel* ★**old** GNU, KNEW

news *n.* information, intelligence, tidings, account, bulletin

next *adj.* ① following, succeeding, after, later ② adjacent, adjoining *I live on Park Street, and my friend lives on the adjoining street,* beside

nibble *v.* bite, peck, gnaw, munch ▷*eat*

nice *adj.* ① pleasant, agreeable, amiable, charming, delightful ★**nasty** ② precise, accurate, fine, subtle

niche *n.* compartment, hole, corner, recess, place

nick *v.* dent, score, mill, cut, scratch

nigh *adj.* next, close, adjacent, adjoining ▷*near* ★**distant**

night *n.* dark, darkness, dusk, evening ★**day** KNIGHT

nimble *adj.* active, agile, spry, lithe, skillfull ▷*deft* ★**clumsy**

nip *v.* cut, snip, pinch, twinge, bite

no ① *adj.* not any, not one, none ② *adv.* nay, not at all KNOW

noble *adj.* dignified, lofty *My aunt is very important and has a lofty position on the council,* generous, grand, stately, elevated ★**base**

nod *v.* ① beckon, signal, indicate, salute ② sleep, doze, nap

noise *n.* din, discord, clamor, clatter, hubbub, tumult, uproar ★**silence**

noisy *adj.* loud, boisterous, turbulent, rowdy, clamorous ★**quiet**

nominate *v.* appoint, assign, elect, choose, propose, suggest

nonchalant *adj.* casual, unperturbed, calm, blasé *We enjoyed the new musical, but Sue has been to so many shows she was very blasé about it,* cool, detached ★**anxious**

nondescript *adj.* commonplace, colorless, dull, ordinary ▷*plain* ★**unusual**

none *pron.* not one, not any, not a part, nil, nobody NUN

nonsense *n.* absurdity, balderdash, drivel, rot, garbage, twaddle ★**sense**

nook *n.* compartment, hole, corner, alcove,

crevice, cubbyhole, cranny ▷ *niche*

noose *n.* loop, bight, snare, rope, lasso

normal *adj.* usual, general, average, sane, lucid, rational, standard ★**abnormal**

nose *n.* ① beak, bill, neb, snout ② prow, stem, bow, front

nosy *adj.* inquisitive, curious, prying, snooping, intrusive

nostalgia *n.* homesickness, longing, pining, regret, remembrance

notable *adj.* eventful, momentous, outstanding, great, celebrated ▷ *famous* ★**commonplace**

notch *n.* dent, nick, score, cut, cleft, indentation

note *n.* ① letter, message, communication ② remark, record, report ③ fame, renown, distinction ④ banknote, bill

noted *adj.* eminent, renowned, celebrated, great ▷ *famous* ★**obscure**

nothing *n.* zero, naught, null, nil, zip ★**something**

notice ① *n.* announcement, advice, sign, poster ② *v.* note, remark, observe *After observing that his bike had a flat tire, Joel knew he would have to walk to school,* perceive, make out, see ★**ignore**

notify *v.* inform, tell, intimate, announce, declare ★**withhold**

Notice

After observing that his bike had a flat tire, Joel knew he would have to walk to school.

notion *n.* idea, conception, opinion, belief, judgment

notorious *adj.* infamous, questionable, scandalous, blatant

notwithstanding *adv.* nevertheless, nonetheless, however, despite

nourish *v.* feed, sustain, nurture, comfort, support ★**starve**

nourishing *adj.* beneficial, healthful, nutritious, wholesome

novel ① *adj.* fresh, unusual, original, unique, rare, uncommon ② *n.* fiction, story, book, romance, tale

novice *n.* beginner, learner, apprentice, tyro, pupil ★**expert**

now *adv.* at this moment, at present, at once, instantly, right away

now and then *adv.* from time to time, sometimes, occasionally

nude *adj.* bare, naked, unclothed, stripped, undressed

nudge *v.* poke, push, prod, jog, shove, dig

nuisance *n.* offense, annoyance, plague, trouble, bore, pest, irritation

nullify *v.* annul, invalidate, cancel, quash ▷ *abolish* ★**establish**

numb *adj.* deadened, insensible, dazed, stunned, unfeeling ★**sensitive**

number ① *n.* figure, amount, volume, quantity, sum ② *n.* crowd, throng, multitude *The new president's visit to the town was watched by a multitude of people* ③ *n.* figure, symbol ▷ *numeral* ④ *v.* count, reckon, tally

numeral *n.* symbol, figure, character, cipher

numerous *adj.* many, divers, several, plentiful ▷ *abundant* ★**few**

nun *n.* sister, religious, abbess, prioress NONE

nurse ① *v.* attend, care for, foster, support, sustain ② *n.* hospital attendant, caretaker

nursery *n.* ① children's room, baby's room ② greenhouse, hothouse, garden

nurture *v.* feed, nourish, cherish, foster, tend ▷ *nurse*

nutritious *adj.* healthful, substantial, health-giving ▷ *nourishing* ★**bad**

O o

oaf *n.* brute, lout, blockhead, dolt, ruffian, lummox

obedient *adj.* respectful, obliging, lawabiding, servile, dutiful ★**rebellious**

obey *v.* comply, conform, submit, heed, mind, behave ★**disobey**

object ① *v.* (ob-*ject*) protest, complain, argue, oppose, refuse ★**agree** ② *n.* (*ob-*ject) thing, article, commodity, item ③ *n.* mission, purpose *The purpose of my visit is to end this conflict,* end,

objectionable *adj.* displeasing, distasteful, disagreeable, repugnant ★**pleasant**

obligation *n.* responsibility, liability, commitment ★**choice**

oblige *v.* ① require, compel, force, make ② gratify, please, help ▷*assist* ★**displease**

obliging *adj.* helpful, polite, agreeable, courteous ▷*willing* ★**unkind**

obliterate *v.* blot out, efface, erase, wipe out, destroy

oblivious *adj.* unmindful, absentminded, heedless, unaware ★**aware**

obnoxious *adj.* repulsive, revolting, offensive ▷*unpleasant* ★**pleasant**

obscene *adj.* dirty, unclean, vile, filthy, nasty, immoral, indecent ★**decent**

obscure ① *adj.* indistinct, dim, vague, hidden, confusing *The language of a legal document can be very confusing* ▷*doubtful* ★**clear** ② *v.* conceal, hide, cloud, darken, cover ▷*hide* ★**clarify**

observant *adj.* attentive, watchful, heedful ▷*alert* ★**inattentive**

observation *n.* ① attention, study, supervision ② utterance, comment, remark, statement *The police issued a statement*

observe *v.* ① abide by *I intend to abide by the laws of this country,* adhere to, carry out, keep up ② note, notice, perceive, watch ▷*see* ③ utter, remark, mention

obsolete *adj.* dated, outmoded, unfashionable, out-of-date ★**current**

obstacle *n.* obstruction, barrier, bar, hindrance ▷*drawback* ★**advantage**

obstinate *adj.* determined, dogged, unyielding, perverse *As a child I upset my parents by my perverse behavior* ▷*stubborn* ★**docile**

obstruct *v.* hinder, impede, block, bar, choke ▷*restrain* ★**help**

obstruction *n.* hindrance, restraint, impediment, snag

obtain *v.* acquire, achieve, gain, procure, attain ▷*get* ★**lose**

obtuse *adj.* dull, stupid, unintelligent, stolid, thick, blunt ★**bright**

obvious *adj.* plain, evident, self-evident, explicit, apparent ▷*clear* ★**obscure**

occasion *n.* ① affair, episode, occurrence, circumstance ② reason, purpose, motive

occasional *adj.* casual, rare, infrequent, periodic ★**frequent**

occult *adj.* hidden, unrevealed, secret, mysterious, supernatural *Edgar Allan Poe wrote tales of the supernatural* ★**open**

occupant *n.* owner, resident, proprietor, tenant

occupation *n.* ① activity, employment, calling, job ② possession, tenancy, residence

occupied *adj.* ① busy, employed, active ② settled, populated, peopled ★**unoccupied**

occupy *v.* inhabit, live in, reside, dwell in, own, possess, hold

occur *v.* take place, befall, turn out, come to pass, result ▷*happen*

occurrence *n.* happening, affair, circumstance, incident, occasion ▷*event*

ocean *n.* sea, main *The pirates of the Spanish Main were the curse of shipping,* deep, tide

odd *adj.* ① single, unmatched ② singular,

Oceans and Waters

Antarctic	Bay	Sound
Arctic	Fjord	Straits
Atlantic	Gulf	
Indian	Lagoon	
Pacific	Loch	

peculiar, quaint, queer ★**ordinary** ③ surplus, left over, remaining

odds and ends *n.* leavings, debris *The police found the debris of the crashed airplane,* leftovers, oddments, remains

odious *adj.* hateful, offensive, detestable ▷*abominable* ★**pleasant**

odor *n.* ① scent, aroma ▷*fragrance* ② stink, stench, reek ▷*smell*

odorous *adj.* fragrant, perfumed, aromatic, sweet-smelling

off ① *adv.* away from, over, done ② *prep.* along, against, opposite, distant ★**on** ③ *adj.* bad, moldy, rotten

offend *v.* ① insult, hurt, wound, outrage, displease ② transgress, sin ★**please**

offense *n.* insult, outrage, attack, crime, hurt

offensive *adj.* insulting, offending, rude, repugnant, hurtful, distasteful

offer ① *v.* propose, proffer, present, tender, attempt ② *n.* bid, endeavor, proposal

offering *n.* sacrifice, donation, gift, present

offhand *adj.* ① brusque, casual, curt, informal, abrupt ② informal, improvised, impromptu *My sister, who is a singer, gave an impromptu performance* ★**planned**

office ① *n.* bureau, department, room ② position, appointment, post

officer *n.* ① official, administrator, functionary, executive ② military rank, policeman, minister *A minister from the French Embassy called*

official ① *adj.* authorized, authentic, proper, formal ★**unofficial** ② *n.* executive, officeholder, bureaucrat *The city bureaucrats take months to get a job done*

officious *adj.* interfering, meddlesome, self-important

offspring *n.* child, children, descendant, heir, family

often *adv.* frequently, regularly, recurrently, time after time, repeatedly ★**seldom**

ointment *n.* lotion, salve, cream, balm, embrocation, liniment

old *adj.* ① ancient, antique, aged, antiquated ② crumbling, decayed *Beneath the ivy were the decayed remains of the castle wall,*

decrepit ★**new** ③ out-of-date, old-fashioned, passé ④ aged, mature, elderly ★**young**

ominous *adj.* menacing, threatening, foreboding, sinister

omit *v.* leave out, neglect, let go, overlook, skip ★**include**

once *adv.* formerly, at one time, previously

one ① *adj.* sole, alone, lone, whole ② *n.* unit, single thing

one-sided *adj.* unequal, unfair, unjust, biased

only ① *adj.* exclusive, single, sole, lone, solitary ② *adv.* solely, barely, exclusively

onset *n.* start, outbreak, assault, attack, onslaught

onslaught *n.* charge, attack, bombardment

ooze ① *n.* mire, muck, slime ② *v.* bleed, discharge, emit, exude, leak

open ① *v.* uncover, unlock, unfasten ② *v.* start, commence, begin ③ *adj.* uncovered, clear, evident, apparent ★**closed** ④ *adj.* frank, honest, candid, fair

opening *n.* ① aperture, mouth, crevice, recess, hole ② commencement, beginning

openly *adv.* candidly, frankly, plainly, sincerely ★**secretly**

operate *v.* function *Despite its age, the old millwheel continued to function,* work, manipulate, drive, ▷*perform*

operation *n.* performance, movement, action, motion, proceeding

opinion *n.* view, concept, judgment, belief, point of view

opponent *n.* antagonist, rival, competitor, contestant, foe ▷*enemy* ★**ally**

opportune *adj.* timely *It had started to rain, thus the timely arrival of the bus was welcome,* convenient, fortunate, suitable ★**untimely**

opportunity *n.* occasion, chance, opening, scope, moment

oppose *v.* withstand, resist, obstruct, confront, hinder ▷*defy* ★**support**

opposite *adj.* ① facing, fronting ② conflicting, opposing, contrary, adverse ★**same**

opposition *n.* antagonism, defiance, hostility, difference ▷*resistance* ★**cooperation**

oppress *v.* crush, depress, harass, overpower, overwhelm

optimist *n.* hopeful person, perfectionist ★**pessimist**

optimistic *adj.* hopeful, cheerful, confident, positive ★**pessimistic**

option *n.* preference, choice, alternative

optional *adj.* possible, voluntary, unforced, open ★**compulsory**

opulent *adj.* rich, affluent, prosperous, well-to-do ▷*wealthy* ★**poor**

oration *n.* sermon, lecture, speech, discourse

orb *n.* globe, ball, sphere

orbit *n.* ① path, passage, trajectory ② province, realm, domain *The river, the forest, and the castle were all within her domain*

ordeal *n.* trial, nightmare, torment, agony

order ① *n.* arrangement, pattern, grouping, organization ② *n.* command, law, rule, decree *A decree was issued forbidding the killing of deer* ③ *n.* shipment, consignment ④ *v.* direct, instruct, command ⑤ *v.* arrange, control, conduct

orderly *adj.* regular, methodical, trim, neat, well-mannered ★**messy**

ordinary *adj.* common, usual, commonplace, general, customary ★**extraordinary**

organization *n.* ① association, group, institute, establishment ② structure, arrangement, system

organize *v.* arrange, form, structure, establish, classify ★**disorganize**

origin *n.* beginning, start, basis, foundation, root, source ★**end**

original *adj.* ① first, aboriginal, ancient, former, primary ② fresh, new, novel *Traveling by camel was a novel experience*

originate ① *v.* create, conceive, compose ② arise, begin ▷*start* ★**end**

ornament ① *n.* decoration, adornment, tracery, pattern ② trinket, curio, knick-knack

ornate *adj.* decorated, adorned, flowery,

Original

Traveling by camel was a novel experience.

embellished, showy, garish ★**plain**

oust *v.* expel, eject, evict, dismiss, propel ▷*overthrow*

out ① *adj.* away, outside, absent ★**in** ② *adj.* open, revealed, uncovered ③ *adv.* loudly, aloud, audibly

out of order *adj.* broken, not working

out of sorts *adj.* sick, ill, poorly, gloomy, fed up

outbreak *n.* epidemic *An epidemic of cholera had hit the village,* rebellion, eruption, explosion, flare-up

outburst *n.* eruption, explosion ▷*outbreak*

outcast *n.* exile, castaway *Robinson Crusoe was a castaway on a desert island,* derelict, refugee

outcome *n.* effect, consequence, conclusion, result

outcry *n.* commotion, row, uproar, tumult, shouting, hue and cry ▷*clamor*

outdated *adj.* old, antique, old-fashioned, unfashionable, obsolete ★**modern**

outdo *v.* surpass, excel, beat, outclass, eclipse

outfit *n.* ensemble, set *My mother bought a new set of dishes in the sale for half price,* rig, equipment, gear

outing *n.* excursion, picnic, expedition, trip, ramble

outlandish *adj.* strange, erratic, odd, queer, quaint, bizarre ★**ordinary**

outlaw *n.* bandit, highwayman, hoodlum, desperado *Billy the Kid was a desperado in the Wild West,* robber

outlet *n.* exit, egress, way out, vent, spout, nozzle, opening ★**inlet**

outline ① *n.* diagram, plan, blueprint, sketch, framework, summary ② *v.* draw, sketch, describe

outlook *n.* view, prospect, forecast, attitude, aspect, prognosis

output *n.* yield, product, produce, achievement, manufacture

outrage ① *n.* disgrace, injury, offense, affront ② *v.* offend, insult, shock, violate

outrageous *adj.* insulting, offensive, exorbitant, monstrous ★**acceptable**

outright ① *adj.* complete, thorough, absolute, wholesale ② *adv.* at once, completely, entirely, altogether

outset *n.* first, opening, beginning ▷*start* ★**finish**

outside ① *n.* exterior, surface, front ② *adj.* exterior, external, outward, surface

outsider *n.* stranger, foreigner, alien, misfit *Gulliver was something of a misfit in the land of the tiny Lilliputians*

outskirts *n.* limits, bounds, boundary, outpost, suburb

outspoken *adj.* frank, open, straightforward, blunt, direct ▷*candid* ★**tactful**

outstanding *adj.* striking, pronounced, conspicuous, notable ▷*exceptional* ★**ordinary**

outward *adj.* exterior, outside, outer, superficial *From a distance, my father and Bill Jones look alike, but it's really just superficial*

outwit *v.* get the better of, swindle, defraud, dupe ▷*cheat*

over ① *adj.* concluded, ended, done with, settled ② *prep.* above, more than, exceeding ③ *adv.* aloft, above, beyond, extra

overall ① *adj.* complete, inclusive, total, broad ② *adv.* by and large, on the whole

overbearing *adj.* domineering, dictatorial, haughty, pompous ▷*arrogant* ★**modest**

overcast *adj.* cloudy, heavy, dark, murky, dull ★**bright**

overcome *adj.* overwhelm, conquer, crush, defeat, vanquish ▷*subdue*

overdo *v.* overwork, exaggerate, go too far *I didn't mind your eating one of my apples, but taking all four was going too far*

overdue *adj.* delayed, belated, late, behindhand ★**early**

overflow *v.* swamp, deluge, inundate, submerge, soak, spill

overhaul *v.* ① repair, mend, fix, inspect, examine ② overtake, pass, gain on

overhead *adv.* above, upward, aloft, on high ★**below**

overhear *v.* listen, eavesdrop, snoop, spy

overjoyed *adj.* elated, jubilant, rapturous ▷*delighted* ★**disappointed**

overlap *v.* overrun, go beyond, coincide, overlay

overlook *v.* ① disregard, pardon, condone, ignore ② neglect, miss, pass over ③ inspect, check, examine

overpower *v.* conquer, crush, master, subdue, vanquish ▷*defeat*

overseas *adj.* abroad, foreign ★**domestic**

overseer *n.* inspector, supervisor, boss, manager, master, mistress

oversight *n.* omission, blunder, error, fault, lapse ▷*mistake*

overtake *v.* catch up, pass, outdo, outstrip, pass ▷*overhaul*

overthrow *v.* defeat, beat, topple ▷*overpower*

overture *n.* ① (in music) prelude, opening, introduction ② offer, proposal, invitation

overwhelm *v.* overcome, stun, shock, overpower, deluge, inundate *The reply to our advertisement was huge; we were inundated with letters*

overwhelming *adj.* all-powerful, formidable, breathtaking, shattering ★**insignificant**

owe *v.* be in debt, incur, be due

own ① *v.* possess, occupy, hold ② *v.* admit, confess, grant ③ *adj.* individual, personal, private

owner *n.* proprietor, possessor, landlord

P p

pace ① *n. & v.* step, tread, stride ② *n.* speed, rate, velocity, tempo

pacify *v.* appease, calm, moderate, tranquilize ▷*soothe* ★**aggravate**

pack ① *n.* bundle, bunch, swarm, crowd, group ② *v.* cram, load, fill, throng

package *n.* parcel, packet, bundle, box, carton

packet *n.* bag, pack, container, parcel ▷*package*

pact *n.* contract, treaty, agreement, arrangement PACKED

pad ① *n.* tablet, notepad, jotter ② *n.* foot, paw ③ *v.* fill, pack, shape, stuff, cushion

paddle ① *n.* oar, sweep, scull ② *v.* row, steer, propel ③ *v.* wade, splash, swim

pagan *n.* heathen, idol-worshiper, infidel

page *n.* ① sheet, leaf, paper ② boy, attendant, bellhop, messenger

pageant *n.* fair, parade, procession, exhibition, masque ▷*show*

pail *n.* bucket, churn, tub, container PALE

pain ① *n.* ache, pang, throb, twinge, spasm, cramp ② *v.* hurt, sting, ache ▷*ail* PANE

painful *adj.* aching, throbbing, sore, agonizing ★**painless**

painstaking *adj.* scrupulous *Carly kept a scrupulous record of all she spent,* careful, diligent, particular ★**negligent**

paint *v.* color, draw, daub, varnish, stain

painting *n.* drawing, illustration, picture, mural, design

pair *n.* couple, brace, two, twins, twosome PARE, PEAR

pal *n.* chum, friend, buddy, crony ▷*comrade* ★**enemy**

palace *n.* castle, château, stately home *In England you can visit stately homes belonging to the aristocracy,* mansion

pale *adj.* pallid, ashen, pasty, colorless, faint, feeble, white ★**ruddy** PAIL

pallid *adj.* ashen, colorless, livid *The man had a livid scar across his forehead,*

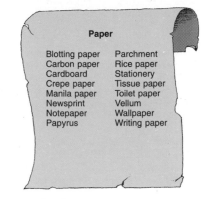

Paper

Blotting paper	Parchment
Carbon paper	Rice paper
Cardboard	Stationery
Crepe paper	Tissue paper
Manila paper	Toilet paper
Newsprint	Vellum
Notepaper	Wallpaper
Papyrus	Writing paper

waxen ▷*pale*

paltry *adj.* petty, mean, shabby, trifling, pitiable, trashy ★**significant**

pamper *v.* humor, indulge, coddle, fondle ▷*spoil* ★**neglect**

pan *n.* container ▷*pot*

pandemonium *n.* uproar, clatter, row, rumpus, din, chaos *The ice storm reduced the airline schedule to total chaos* ▷*noise* ★**calm**

pander *v.* indulge, pamper, please, give in to

pane *n.* panel, glass, window PAIN

panel *n.* ① pane, rectangle, insert ② jury, group, committee, forum *There will be a forum of all the candidates before the election*

pang *n.* ache, throe, twinge, throb ▷*pain*

panic ① *n.* fright, alarm, fear, terror ② *v.* scare, frighten, startle, stampede ★**relax**

pant *v.* puff, snort, blow, gasp, heave

pantry *n.* larder, buttery, storeroom, cupboard

paper *n.* stationery, document, deed, article, dossier *The police have a dossier on all known criminals in this town*

parade ① *n.* procession, march, display ▷*pageant* ② *v.* display, exhibit, flaunt, show off

paralyze *v.* cripple, disable, incapacitate, deaden, stun

paramount *adj.* leading, chief, supreme, outstanding ▷*foremost* ★**minor**

paraphernalia *n.* baggage, equipment, gear

parasite *n.* sponger, hanger-on, leech, scrounger

parcel *n.* batch, bundle, lot ▷*package*

parched *v.* arid, scorched, withered, dry, thirsty

pardon *v.* excuse, forgive, acquit, condone, absolve ★**condemn**

pare *v.* skin, peel, uncover, strip, scrape, shave PAIR, PEAR

parent *n.* father, mother, guardian, originator

park ① *n.* garden, green, grounds, playground, woodland ② *v.* leave *You can leave your car outside our house,* position, station

parlor *n.* drawing room, living room, sitting room

parody *n.* caricature, burlesque, satire, imitation

parry *v.* avoid, avert, fend off, rebuff, repel

parsimonious *adj.* niggardly *The factory workers received a niggardly sum for their work,* sparing, miserly, stingy ▷*frugal* ★**generous**

part ① *n.* piece, fragment, portion, scrap ② *n.* character, role *My sister has a leading role in the play,* duty ③ *v.* separate, divide, detach ④ *v.* depart, quit, leave

partial *adj.* ① imperfect, limited, part, unfinished ② biased, favorable to, inclined

partially *adv.* incompletely, somewhat, in part

participate *v.* take part, share, cooperate

particle *n.* morsel, atom, bit, seed, crumb, grain, scrap

particular *adj.* ① choosy, fastidious, scrupulous ② strange, odd, peculiar ③ special, distinct, notable *Old John Cotton was one of the notable citizens of our city*

partly *adv.* in part, incompletely, to some degree, up to a point ★**totally**

partner *n.* colleague, associate, ally, helper

party *n.* ① function, celebration, festivity, social ② group, faction *A small faction on the committee wanted the park to be closed,* body

pass ① *v.* exceed, overstep, outstrip ② *v.*

experience *He experienced little pain after the operation,* suffer, undergo ③ *v.* neglect, ignore ④ *n.* permit, ticket, passport ⑤ *n.* defile, gap, notch, passage

passage *n.* ① corridor, pathway, alley ② journey, cruise, voyage ③ sentence, paragraph, clause

passenger *n.* traveler, commuter, wayfarer

passing *adj.* casual, fleeting, hasty, temporary, brief ★**permanent**

passion *n.* desire, ardor, warmth, excitement, zeal ▷*emotion* ★**calm**

passionate *adj.* ardent, impetuous, fiery, earnest, enthusiastic ★**indifferent**

past ① *adj.* finished, ended, former, gone ★**present** ② *prep.* after, exceeding, beyond ③ *n.* history, yesterday ★**future** PASSED

paste *n.* glue, cement, gum, adhesive

pastime *n.* recreation, sport, fun, hobby, amusement

pasture *n.* grass, field, meadow, mead

pat ① *v.* tap, caress, fondle, stroke, touch ② *adv.* timely, exactly *Celia arrived at exactly the right moment,* precisely

patch *v.* mend, patch up, sew, darn, cobble

path *n.* way, track, road, route, course, footway

pathetic *adj.* pitiable, sad, wretched, miserable, poor, puny *We picked out the*

Paths and Passageways

Alley	Highway	Path
Avenue	Lane	Road
Boulevard	Mountain	Sidewalk
Freeway	pass	Street
Drive	Passage	Thoroughfare

puniest pup in the litter for a pet

patience *n.* endurance, perseverance, composure, calmness, restraint ★**impatience** PATIENTS

patient *adj.* forbearing, long-suffering, persevering, understanding ★**impatient**

patriotic *adj.* loyal, nationalistic, public-spirited, jingoistic

patrol *v.* police, watch, guard, protect, tour

patronize *v.* ① assist, encourage, foster, buy from ② talk down to, condescend

pattern *n.* ① model, standard, prototype ② arrangement, decoration, ornament

pause ① *v.* halt, cease, suspend, stop, delay ② *n.* lull, intermission, break, interruption, breather, rest PAWS

pay ① *v.* reward, award, support, compensate, discharge ② *n.* payment, salary, wages, compensation

peace *n.* harmony, calm, concord, serenity, quiet, tranquility *We spent the day in total tranquility down by the lake* ★**tumult** PIECE

peaceful *adj.* serene, quiet, restful, harmonious ▷*tranquil* ★**disturbed**

peak *n.* summit, apex, top, crown, pinnacle

peal *v.* ring, strike, clamor, chime, resound, toll, clang PEEL

peasant *n.* farmer, rustic, sharecropper, countryman, yokel

peculiar *adj.* ① singular, odd, curious, unusual, uncommon, strange ② unique, private, special, distinctive

peddle *v.* sell, hawk, canvas, trade, vend, retail

peddler *n.* hawker, street trader, trader

pedestal *n.* base, stand, plinth, support

peek *n. & v.* glimpse, blink, look ▷*peer*

peel ① *v.* skin, strip, pare, scale ② *n.* skin, covering, rind, coat PEAL

peer ① *v.* peep, stare, look, gaze ② *n.* aristocrat, lord, noble ③ *n.* equal, fellow, counterpart PIER

peerless *adj.* unequaled, unique, beyond compare, unbeatable

peevish *adj.* cross, childish, grumpy, crusty, irritable ▷*testy* ★**good-tempered**

peg *n.* hook, knob, pin, post, hanger, fastener

pelt ① *v.* beat, bombard, thrash, throw ② *v.* rain cats and dogs, teem, pour ③ *n.* skin, hide, fleece, fur

pen ① *n.* quill, ballpoint ② *n.* cage, coop, hutch, stall ③ *v.* write, autograph, scribble

penalty *n.* fine, forfeit, punishment, price ★**reward**

pending *adj.* awaiting, unfinished, doubtful, uncertain, undecided

penetrate *v.* ① pierce, perforate, stab, permeate *The aroma of lilacs and roses permeated the house* ② discern, see through, comprehend

penetrating *adj.* ① sharp, perceptive, understanding ② shrill, stinging

pennant *n.* flag, streamer, bunting, banner

penniless *adj.* destitute, needy, poverty-striken ▷*poor* ★**wealthy**

pensive *adj.* thoughtful, reflective, wistful, preoccupied

people ① *n.* folk, society, the public, populace, inhabitants ② *v.* populate, inhabit, settle

pep *n.* punch, energy, high spirits, vigor ▷*vitality*

peppery *adj.* ① biting, caustic *I'm afraid your essay wasn't very good; the teacher made some very caustic comments,* hot-tempered, angry ② hot, pungent, sharp

perceive *v.* feel, sense, observe, notice, make out, understand ▷*see*

perch ① *v.* alight, light, sit, squat, roost ② *n.* rod, pole, staff, roost ③ *n.* fish

perfect ① *adj.* (*per*-fect) absolute, ideal, sublime, excellent, splendid, faultless ★**imperfect** ② *v.* (per-*fect*) complete, finish, fulfill, refine

perforate *v.* puncture, drill, punch, penetrate

perform *v.* ① carry out, do, fulfill, accomplish ② play, act, stage, present *The local drama group will present a new play next week*

performer *n.* actor, player, singer, entertainer, artist

perfume *n.* scent, essence, aroma, odor

perhaps *adv.* possibly, perchance, maybe, conceivably

peril *n.* hazard, jeopardy, menace, risk, insecurity ▷*danger* ★**safety**

period *n.* spell, time, duration, term, interval, course, span, age

periodical ① *n.* magazine, publication, journal, gazette, review ② *adj.* regular, routine, recurring, repeated

perish *v.* die, pass away, wither, disintegrate, expire, shrivel

perky *adj.* bouncy, bright, cheerful, lively ▷*sprightly* ★**dull**

permanent *adj.* endless, ageless, timeless, constant ▷*durable* ★**fleeting**

permission *n.* authorization, sanction, privilege, warrant *The police have a warrant for your arrest* ★**prohibition**

permit ① *v.* (per-*mit*) allow, grant, agree, empower ② *n.* (*per*-mit) warrant, license, pass

perpendicular *adj.* upright, erect, sheer, steep, vertical ★**horizontal**

perpetrate *v.* commit, do, inflict, perform, practice, execute

perpetual *adj.* everlasting, ceaseless, eternal, never ending ▷*endless* ★**fleeting**

perplex *v.* mystify, baffle, bewilder, confound ▷*puzzle* ★**enlighten**

persecute *v.* harass, molest, plague, badger ▷*bother* ★**pamper**

persevere *v.* persist, hold out, hang on, endure, continue ★**give up**

persist *v.* remain, stand fast, abide, carry on ▷*persevere* ★**stop**

persistent *adj.* tenacious, relentless, stubborn, obstinate ★**weak**

person *n.* individual, human, being, somebody, personage, character

personal *adj.* individual, intimate, private, special, peculiar

personality *n.* individuality, character, disposition, nature

perspective *n.* outlook, aspect, proportion

perspire *v.* sweat, exude, ooze

persuade *v.* convince, wheedle, blandish, entice, cajole *I cajoled my mother into buying me a new swimsuit,* induce ▷*coax* ★**discourage**

pert *adj.* saucy, flippant, jaunty, cheeky, brash ★**shy**

perturb *v.* upset, disturb, trouble, distress, fluster ▷*bother* ★**reassure**

peruse *v.* read, study, pore over, browse, inspect, scrutinize, examine

pervade *v.* penetrate, permeate, spread, saturate, soak

perverse *adj.* contrary, wayward, opposite, disobedient ▷*stubborn* ★**reasonable**

pessimist *n.* defeatist, killjoy, wet blanket, cynic *Uncle Bert is a real cynic; he even thinks the lottery is fixed* ★**optimist**

pessimistic *adj.* cynical, dismal, fatalistic, defeatist, downhearted ★**optimistic**

pest *n.* nuisance, plague, blight, curse, vexation, bug

pester *v.* nag, hector, badger, annoy, disturb, harass ▷*bother*

pet ① *v.* fondle, caress, baby, cosset, cuddle ② *n.* favorite, beloved, dear ③ *adj.* endearing, cherished, dearest

petition *n.* plea, appeal, entreaty, round robin, request

petrified *adj.* spellbound, frightened, scared, terrified

petty *adj.* ① paltry, cheap, inferior, trifling ▷*trivial* ★**important** ② mean, measly, stingy

petulant *adj.* fretful, displeased, querulous, irritable ▷*peevish*

phantom ① *n.* apparition, specter, spook, ghost ② *adj.* spooky, ghostly, imaginary

phase *n.* aspect, appearance, angle, view, period, point FAZE

phenomenal *adj.* remarkable, outstanding, marvelous, miraculous, incredible

phenomenon *n.* marvel, rarity, curiosity, sensation, spectacle

philanthropic *adj.* charitable, kind, generous, humane, benevolent, bountiful, public-spirited ★**selfish**

philosophical *adj.* calm, cool, logical, thoughtful, impassive, unruffled

phobia *n.* dread, fear, awe, neurosis, hang-

Pine

The flowers in the pot are languishing from lack of water.

up *My father has a hang-up about bats; he can't stand them,* horror

phrase *n.* expression, idiom, saying, utterance, sentence FRAYS

physical *adj.* ① material, substantial, solid, concrete ② bodily, personal, sensible

pick ① *v.* select, choose, single out, gather ② *n.* pike, pickax

picket ① *n.* patrol, scout, sentinel, lookout, guard ② *n.* post, rail, panel, fence ③ *v.* strike, demonstrate

pickle ① *n.* preserve ② *n.* difficulty, predicament ③ *v.* cure, salt, preserve, souse

picture ① *n.* painting, tableau, portrait, illustration, drawing ② *n.* movie, film ③ *v.* illustrate, imagine, fancy

picturesque *adj.* attractive, artistic, pictorial, scenic

piece *n.* portion, fragment, lump, morsel, bit ▷*scrap* PEACE

pier *n.* wharf, dock, quay, jetty PEER

pierce *v.* perforate, drill, bore ▷*penetrate*

piercing *adj.* ① loud, deafening, shrill, penetrating ② keen, sharp, cutting

pigment *n.* color, dye, hue, paint, stain

pile *n. & v.* heap, mass, stack, load, store

pilfer *v.* purloin, rifle, rob, filch ▷*steal*

pilgrim *n.* traveler, wanderer, wayfarer

pilgrimage *n.* excursion, journey, mission, tour, trip, crusade

pillage *v.* plunder, ravage, loot, ransack *Thieves broke into the museum and ransacked all the cases,* rifle

pillar *n.* column, shaft, tower, obelisk, monument

pillow *n.* cushion, bolster, support

pilot *n.* ① guide, steersman, coxswain,

helmsman ② aviator, flyer

pimple *n.* zit, blemish, swelling, boil

pin ① *n.* fastener, clip, spike, peg ② *v.* fix, fasten, attach, join, tack

pinch ① *v.* nip, squeeze, crush, tweak ② *v.* pilfer, steal ③ *n.* dash, drop, splash ④ *n.* crisis, difficulty, jam

pine *v.* hanker, yearn, long for, languish *The flowers in the pot are languishing from lack of water,* sicken

pinnacle *n.* summit, top, crest, peak, apex

pioneer *n.* founder, leader, trailblazer, explorer, innovator

pious *adj.* devout, godly, holy, moral, religious, virtuous

pipe ① *n.* tube, duct, passage, hose, conduit ② whistle, flute

piquant *adj.* appetizing, spicy, tangy, savory, pungent

pique *v.* annoy, displease, irritate, affront, vex PEAK

pirate ① *n.* corsair *In days of old the ships in the Mediterranean were often raided by corsairs,* buccaneer, privateer, sea-rover ② *v.* copy, plagiarize, steal

pistol *n.* gun, revolver, automatic PISTIL

pit *n.* ① hole, hollow, crater, trench, mine ② dent, dimple, depression

pitch ① *v.* fling, throw, cast, sling, toss ② *v.* fall, drop, descend ③ *v.* raise, set up, erect ④ *n.* angle, slope, degree ⑤ *v.* sales message

pitcher *n.* jar, beaker, crock, jug, ewer, vessel

piteous *adj.* pitiful, heartbreaking, mournful ▷*pathetic*

pitiless *adj.* merciless, unmerciful, cruel, unrelenting ★**merciful**

pity ① *n.* mercy, compassion, charity, tenderness ② *v.* spare, forgive, grieve for, sympathize with

pivot ① *n.* axle, axis, hinge, turning point, spindle, swivel ② *v.* revolve, rotate, turn, spin

placate *v.* appease, pacify, soothe, satisfy ▷*humor* ★**infuriate**

place ① *n.* spot, locality, site, situation, position ② *n.* house, apartment, residence ③

Planets

The nine planets of our solar system travel around a star we call the Sun.

Earth
Jupiter
Mars
Mercury
Neptune
Pluto
Saturn
Uranus
Venus

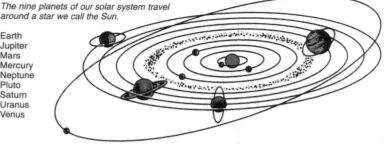

position ② *n.* house, apartment, residence ③ *v.* put, deposit, establish, allocate, arrange

placid *adj.* peaceful, quiet, serene, mild ▷*restful* ★**ruffled**

plague ① *n.* epidemic, disease, contagion, pest, blight ② *v.* persecute, pester *We were pestered by flies,* infest, annoy ▷*badger*

plain ① *adj.* unadorned, simple ② *adj.* obvious, clear, apparent ③ *adj.* blunt, direct, candid ④ *adj.* smooth, level, flat ⑤ *n.* prairie, plateau, tableland PLANE

plan ① *n.* design, chart, diagram, drawing ② *n.* project, proposal, arrangement, scheme ③ *v.* design, prepare, arrange, invent

plane ① *adj.* level, even, flat, smooth ② *n.* aircraft ③ *n.* smoothing tool PLAIN

planned *adj.* prepared, ready, arranged

plant ① *v.* sow, scatter, implant ② *v.* place, set, establish ③ *n.* herb, shrub, vegetable ④ *n.* equipment, machinery, factory

plaster ① *n.* cement, mortar, paste ② *n.* bandage, dressing ③ *v.* spread, smear, daub

plastic ① *adj.* moldable, pliable, malleable, soft, supple ② *n.* thermoplastic

plate ① *n.* dish, platter, palette ② *n.* sheet, panel ③ *v.* laminate, cover, gild, anodize

platform *n.* rostrum *I was called up to the rostrum to receive my prize,* stage, stand, dais

plausible *adj.* believable, credible, convincing, glib, persuasive ★**unlikely**

play ① *v.* sport, gambol, frisk, romp, frolic

② *v.* perform, act, represent ③ *n.* drama, performance ④ *n.* sport, amusement, recreation

player *n.* actor, sportsman, artist, musician, performer, contestant

playful *adj.* frisky, frolicsome, larky, lively, sportive ★**serious**

plead *v.* appeal, argue, ask, implore, request, beseech

pleasant *adj.* affable, agreeable, cheerful, nice ▷*charming* ★**unpleasant**

please *v.* ① gratify, enchant, amuse, entertain ▷*delight* ② like, choose, wish, prefer

pleased *adj.* delighted, gratified, satisfied ▷*contented* ★**annoyed**

pleasing *adj.* agreeable, enchanting, entertaining ▷*satisfying* ★**unpleasant**

pleasure *n.* delight, joy, amusement, entertainment, enjoyment ▷*fun* ★**trouble**

pledge ① *n.* promise, vow, undertaking, warrant, oath ② *v.* bind, contract, promise, undertake

plentiful *adj.* lavish, ample, profuse, bountiful ▷*abundant* ★**scanty**

plenty *n.* enough, profusion, affluence ▷*abundance* ★**scarcity**

pliable *adj.* supple, flexible, pliant, malleable, moldable, bendy ★**rigid**

plight *n.* predicament, difficulty, condition, dilemma *We made it to the train station on time, but when we realized we had forgotten our tickets we were in a real*

plot ① n. scheme, plan, intrigue ② n. story, narrative ③ v. hatch, intrigue, scheme

pluck ① v. gather, pick, pull, yank, catch ② n. courage, determination, bravery

plucky adj. courageous, daring, heroic, hardy ▷*brave* ★**feeble**

plug ① n. stopper, cork, bung ② v. stop, block, choke, cork ③ v. publicize, boost, promote, push

plum ① n. prize, bonus, treasure ② adj. best, choice, first-class

plump adj. buxom, stout, chubby, rotund, pudgy ★**skinny**

plunder ① n. booty, loot, swag, spoils ② v. fleece, rob, ransack, pillage, loot

plunge v. dive, pitch, submerge, duck, immerse, swoop, hurtle

poach v. ① pilfer, steal, filch, purloin ② steam, cook

pocket ① n. compartment, pouch, sack, bag ② v. filch, pinch, steal

poem n. ode, verse, rhyme, ballad, lyric

poetic adj. artistic, elegant, graceful, flowing, lyrical

poignant adj. moving, touching, pathetic, biting, penetrating

point ① n. spike, barb, pike, prong, end, tip ② n. locality, place, spot ③ n. aspect, object, aim, purpose ④ n. headland, cape ⑤ v. aim, direct, level, train

pointless adj. meaningless, senseless, silly, vague, feeble ▷*absurd* ★**significant**

poise ① n. confidence, assurance, dignity, self-possession, balance ② v. stand, hover, brood over

poison ① n. venom, virus, toxin ② v. taint, fester, corrupt, infect

poisonous adj. deadly, evil, lethal *Don't touch those red berries; they're lethal,* noxious, toxic, venomous

poke v. jab, push, nudge, jostle, ram, thrust, stab, prod ▷*shove*

pole n. stick, stave, stake, rod, post, bar, mast, shaft, spar

policy n. course, action, practice, rule, procedure, guidelines

polish ① v. burnish, buff, smooth, brighten, clean ② n. gloss, glaze, shine ③ n. refinement, grace, culture

polished adj. ① glossy, burnished, shiny ② refined, cultivated, cultured

polite adj. courteous, attentive, civil, well-bred, elegant, discreet ★**impolite**

poll ① n. election, vote, count, census, ballot ② v. survey, canvas, vote

pollute v. adulterate, debase, befoul, taint, poison, corrupt ★**purify**

pomp n. ceremony, show, splendor, pageantry, magnificence ★**simplicity**

pompous adj. showy, self-important, bombastic ▷*pretentious* ★**modest**

ponder v. meditate, consider, reflect, deliberate, think about

pool ① n. lagoon, pond, lake ② n. accumulation, funds, reserve, kitty ③ v. combine, contribute, share

poor adj. ① destitute, penniless, miserable ★**rich** ② low quality, faulty, feeble, shoddy *That shirt may be cheap, but it's shoddy and won't last* ★**superior** PORE, POUR

poorly ① adj. ailing, ill, sick, seedy ② adv. badly, inexpertly, crudely ★**well**

pop v. ① bang, burst, crack, explode ② slide, slip, insert

popular adj. ① well-liked, favorite, in favor, fashionable ② current, common, vulgar, prevailing

Poisonous Plants

Aconite
Baneberry
Belladonna
Black nightshade
Deadly nightshade
Foxglove
Hellebore
Hemlock
Henbane
Larkspur
Nux vomica
Poison ivy

fashionable ② current, common, vulgar, prevailing

pore *v.* scan, examine, peruse, scrutinize POOR, POUR

portable *adj.* lightweight, convenient, transportable ▷*handy* ★**awkward**

portion *n.* piece, fragment, share, fraction ▷*part*

portly *adj.* plump, stout, fat, burly, bulky

portrait *n.* likeness, painting, picture, profile

portray *v.* describe, depict, represent, picture, illustrate, impersonate

pose ① *v.* stand, poise, posture, position ② *n.* position, stand, guise, stance *If you want to learn to play golf well, you need a good stance*

position *n.* ① spot, situation, location, place, site ② job, post ③ posture, attitude ④ rank, standing, status

positive *adj.* ① certain, sure, confident ★**doubtful** ② real, true, absolute ★**negative** ③ precise, definite, unmistakable

possess *v.* have, own, hold, occupy ★**lose**

possessions *n.* wealth, assets, property, goods

possible *adj.* conceivable, imaginable, likely, feasible, attainable ★**impossible**

possibly *adv.* perhaps, maybe, perchance conceivably

post *n.* ① rail, pole, beam, banister, stake ② position, employment, job ③ mail

poster *n.* placard, bill, advertisement, sign

posterior *adj.* hind, behind, after, rear ★**front**

postpone *v.* put off, defer, shelve, adjourn ▷*delay* ★**advance**

posture *n.* bearing, stance, attitude, carriage

pot *n.* basin, bowl, pan, vessel, container, jar

potential ① *adj.* possible, probable, latent *The professor discovered that I had a latent talent for languages,* dormant, budding ② *n.* ability, talent, capacity ▷*flair*

potion *n.* beverage, medicine, mixture, tonic, brew

pouch *n.* bag, poke, sack, purse, pocket, wallet

pounce *v.* strike, lunge, spring, swoop, fall upon ▷*attack*

pound ① *v.* beat, batter, crush, hammer ② *n.* enclosure, compound, pen ③ *n.* weight

pour *v.* spout, jet, gush, spill, cascade, rain PORE, POUR

pout *v.* grimace, glower, sulk, scowl, mope ★**smile**

poverty *n.* ① distress, need, bankruptcy, privation ▷*want* ② scarcity, shortage ★**plenty**

powder ① *n.* dust, sand, ash, grit, bran ② *v.* pulverize, crunch, grind

power *n.* ① authority, command, control, ability ② energy, force, strength

powerful *adj.* mighty, vigorous, forceful ▷*strong* ★**weak**

practical *adj.* ① useful, effective, workable ② experienced, qualified, trained ▷*skilled* ★**impractical**

practice *n.* ① custom, habit, usage ② work, conduct, performance, action ★**theory** ② *v.* carry out, apply, do, execute ▷*perform*

praise ① *v.* acclaim, applaud, glorify, exalt ★**criticize** ② *n.* applause, flattery, compliment, approval ★**criticism** PRAYS, PREYS

prance *v.* gambol *I love to watch the lambs gambol in the spring,* frolic, romp, caper, swagger

prank *n.* trick, joke, antic, lark, jape, stunt

prattle *n.* & *v.* chatter, jabber, gossip, drivel, babble

pray *v.* beg, beseech, entreat, implore, request PREY

prayer *n.* petition, entreaty, worship, devotion, supplication

preach *v.* lecture, moralize, advocate *The president advocated a program to feed the poor,* urge, proclaim

precarious *adj.* perilous, hazardous, insecure, dangerous ▷*risky* ★**safe**

precaution *n.* forethought, provision, anticipation, care, providence ▷*prudence*

Prey

Pray

precede v. lead, head, usher, go before, preface ★**follow**

precious adj. valuable, cherished, treasured, dear, beloved ▷*costly* ★**worthless**

precise adj. ① definite, exact, pointed, accurate ② formal, particular, strict ★**vague**

precisely adv. absolutely, just so, exactly, correctly

precision n. exactitude, accuracy, care, detail

precocious adj. fast, smart, clever ★**backward**

predicament n. situation, state, condition, embarrassment, fix ▷*plight*

predict v. foresee, foretell, prophesy, presage, divine

predominant adj. leading, main, powerful, superior, ruling, controlling ★**minor**

preen v. prance, swagger, strut, spruce up, doll up, groom

preface n. introduction, prelude, prologue, preamble, foreword

prefer v. choose, select, desire, like better, fancy ▷*favor* ★**reject**

prejudice ① n. bigotry, intolerance, bias, discrimination ② v. influence, warp, twist, distort, undermine ★**benefit**

prejudiced adj. biased *My opinion of Jessica is biased; she was very cruel to me once*, bigoted, one-sided, unfair, intolerant ★**fair**

preliminary adj. introductory, preparatory, opening, initial ★**final**

premature adj. untimely, previous, early, immature ★**late**

premeditated adj. calculated, planned, prearranged, intentional ★**spontaneous**

premier ① n. prime minister, first minister, head of government ② adj. chief, first, head, leading, principal

premises n. grounds, house, building, lands

prepare v. arrange, adapt, provide, get ready, concoct, plan ★**demolish**

preposterous adj. absurd, ridiculous, laughable ▷*unreasonable* ★**reasonable**

prescribe v. indicate, order, propose, recommend, specify

presence n. ① existence, appearance, aspect ② nearness, neighborhood, proximity

PRESENTS

present ① n. (*pres*-ent) gift, donation, bounty, favor ② (*pres*-ent) adj. here, on the spot, ready, current ③ v. (pre-*sent*) offer, tender, bestow, award, exhibit

presently adv. soon, shortly, before long, immediately

preserve ① v. protect safeguard, conserve, shield ▷*keep* ② n. jam, jelly, relish

press ① v. bear down, depress, clamp, jam, compress, flatten ② n. printing machine ③ n. newspapers, reporters, journalism

pressure n. ① strain, tension, stress, urgency ② weight, compression, force

prestige n. repute, authority, weight, power

presume v. infer *I infer from your smile that you have passed your exam,* suppose, grant, take for granted, assume

presumptuous adj. arrogant, bold, audacious, insolent ▷*forward* ★**modest**

pretend v. ① make believe, simulate, sham, feign, masquerade ② aspire, claim, strive for

pretext n. excuse, pretense, guise, device

pretty adj. attractive, beautiful, comely,

dainty, bonny ▷*lovely* ★**ugly**

prevail *v.* obtain, overcome, predominate ▷*triumph* ★**lose**

prevalent *adj.* current, common, popular, in use, accepted ★**uncommon**

prevent *v.* avert, forestall, ward off, discourage, stop ▷*hinder* ★**help**

previous *adj.* former, prior, earlier, premature, untimely ★**later**

prey *n.* quarry, chase, booty, victim PRAY

prey on *v.* plunder, fleece, oppress, terrorize

price *n.* cost, amount, expense, payment, value, worth

priceless *adj.* ① invaluable, precious, cherished, costly ② amusing, comic, humorous, hilarious *The clown's antics were hilarious*

prick *v.* jab, jag, puncture, stab, pierce

pride *n.* conceit, arrogance, vanity, egotism, self-importance, honor, exaltation, pleasure PRIED

prim *adj.* puritanical, demure, starchy, priggish ★**informal**

primary *adj.* first, original, chief, essential, fundamental

prime *adj.* ① principal, chief, basic, original ② best, finest, choice

primitive *adj.* ① simple, austere, crude ② uncivilized, savage, barbarous

principal ① *adj.* main, chief, head, leading, foremost ② *n.* head, leader, boss, director PRINCIPLE

principle *n.* ① law, regulation, rule, doctrine ② virtue, worth, integrity, rectitude *The president of the club was honored by the mayor as a "person of high moral rectitude"* ★**wickedness** PRINCIPAL

print ① *v.* impress, stamp, brand, publish ② *n.* impression, printing, imprint

prior ① *adj.* previous, former, earlier, preceding ② *n.* abbot, monk

prison *n.* jail, penitentiary, dungeon, lock up

private *adj.* ① particular, personal, special, own ② solitary, remote *He spent his vacations in a remote cabin,* quiet ★**public**

privilege *n.* ① advantage, benefit, exemption

Printing

Collotype
Computer-setting
Cylinder press
Flatbed press
Intaglio
Letterpress
Linotype
Lithography
Monotype
Photogravure
Rotary press
Silk screen
Type
Web offset

② right, authority, entitlement, prerogative *It was the emperor's prerogative to pardon offenders*

prize ① *n.* reward, premium, trophy, honor ② *n.* booty, spoils, plunder ③ *adj.* best, champion, winning ④ *v.* value, appreciate, cherish ⑤ *v.* force, lever, pry, lift, raise PRIES

probable *adj.* likely, presumable, reasonable, possible ★**improbable**

probe *v.* ① poke, prod ② examine, investigate, scrutinize

problem *n.* ① puzzle, question, riddle, poser, quandary ② difficulty, dilemma, snag, predicament, complication

proceed *v.* ① advance, continue, go on, progress ★**recede** ② arise, flow, spring, emanate *A strong sulfurous odor emanated from the crater of the volcano*

process ① *n.* procedure, operation, movement, system, method ② *v.* convert, alter, handle, refine

procession *n.* parade, pageant, march, cavalcade

proclaim *v.* declare, announce, advertise, publish, expound

procure *v.* secure, acquire, win, gain, attain, get ★**lose**

prod *v.* goad, poke, nudge, incite, urge, shove

prodigal *adj.* extravagant, reckless, lavish ▷*spendthrift* ★**thrifty**

prodigious *adj.* ① miraculous, abnormal, amazing, remarkable ▷*extraordinary*

★**ordinary** ② huge, mighty ▷*enormous*
★**tiny**

produce ① *n.* (*pro*-duce) product, output, yield, crop, harvest ② *v.* (pro-*duce*) provide, yield, create, deliver, put forward

product *n.* output, crop, harvest, return, merchandise, commodity

profane *adj.* impious, blasphemous, unholy, worldly, sinful ★**sacred**

profess *v.* declare, avow, acknowledge, own

profession *n.* ① occupation, career, job, calling, employment ② avowal, admission

professional *adj.* skilled, efficient, experienced ▷*expert* ★**amateur**

proffer *v.* present, offer, tender, submit

proficient *adj.* competent, able, skilled, trained ▷*expert* ★**clumsy**

profit ① *n.* benefit, gain, advantage, acquisition ★**loss** ② *v.* improve, gain, reap, acquire ★**lose** PROPHET

profound ① *adj.* deep, penetrating, fathomless ② wise, shrewd, learned, sagacious *The leader of the tribe was old, wise, and sagacious* ★**shallow**

profuse *adj.* bountiful, extravagant, exuberant, prolific, sumptuous ▷*lavish* ★**sparse**

progress ① *n.* (*prog*-ress) advancement, growth, development ★**decline** ② *v.* (pro-*gress*) advance, proceed, go, forge ahead, travel, grow

prohibit *v.* forbid, bar, deny, ban, obstruct, hinder ▷*prevent* ★**permit**

project ① *n.* (*pro*-ject) work, affair, plan, scheme, undertaking ② *v.* (pro-*ject*) propel, hurl, jut, protrude ③ *v.* contrive, scheme, plan ④ *v.* protrude, bulge, stick out

prolific *adj.* fruitful, creative, productive, fertile ★**scarce**

prolong *v.* lengthen, stretch, draw out, spin out ▷*extend* ★**shorten**

prominent *adj.* ① famous, notable, distinguished ★**minor** ② projecting, standing out, bulging, jutting

promise ① *n.* commitment, undertaking, warrant, pledge ② *v.* agree, guarantee, vow

promote *adj.* ① cultivate, advance, assist

▷*encourage* ② dignify, elevate, upgrade, honor ★**degrade**

prompt ① *adj.* punctual, timely, quick, smart, ready ★**tardy** ② *v.* hint, remind, urge ▷*encourage* ★**deter**

prone *adj.* ① inclined, apt, liable, disposed ★**unlikely** ② prostrate *The poor fellow lay prostrate on the ship's deck,* face down, recumbent ★**upright**

pronounce *v.* ① speak, utter, say, articulate ② declare, decree, proclaim

pronounced *adj.* outstanding, striking, noticeable ▷*distinct* ★**vague**

proof *n.* evidence, testimony, confirmation, criterion, scrutiny ★**failure**

prop *n.* & *v.* stay, brace, truss, support

propel *v.* start, push, force, impel, send ▷*drive* ★**stop**

proper *adj.* ① correct, without error, right, accurate, exact ② respectable, decent, becoming, seemly ★**improper** ③ personal, own, special ★**common**

property ① *n.* possessions, wealth, chattels, buildings, belongings ② quality, virtue, characteristic, peculiarity

prophecy *n.* forecast, divination, prediction, prognostication

prophesy *v.* predict, foretell, foresee, declare

proportion ① *n.* ratio, percentage, part, fraction ② adjustment, arrangement

proposal *n.* proposition, offer, outline

propose *v.* ① put forward, offer, suggest ② ask for the hand of, ask to marry, pop the question

proprietor *n.* owner, possessor, landlady, landlord

prosaic *adj.* factual, tedious, uninteresting, boring, unimaginative, everyday, dull, mundane, ordinary ★**interesting**

prosecute *v.* ① indict, put on trial, summon, sue ② continue, pursue, carry on, conduct ★**abandon**

prospect *n.* ① outlook, forecast, promise, expectation ② view, landscape, vista, aspect

prosper *v.* succeed, flourish, grow ★**fail**

prosperous *adj.* affluent, wealthy, rich, successful, thriving ★**unsuccessful**

protect *v.* defend, preserve, guard, secure, shelter, support ★**endanger**

protest ① *v.* (pro-*test*) complain, object, dispute, challenge ★**accept** ② *n.* (*pro*-test) objection, complaint, dissent, outcry

protracted *adj.* extended, drawn out, lengthy, prolonged ★**shortened**

protrude *v.* project, bulge, jut ★**recede**

proud ① *adj.* arrogant, haughty, supercilious, boastful ★**humble** ② lofty, majestic, noble, splendid ★**mean**

prove *v.* show, demonstrate, authenticate, confirm, verify ★**disprove**

provide *v.* supply, furnish, equip, contribute, afford ★**withhold**

province *n.* ① realm, sphere, orbit, place, department ② region, state, county

provoke *v.* prompt, incite, excite, enrage, inflame ▷*aggravate* ★**appease**

prowess *n.* ability, strength, might, bravery ▷*valor* ★**clumsiness**

prowl *v.* stalk *Somewhere in the darkness a large gray cat stalked its prey,* roam, slink

prudent *adj.* careful, cautious, discreet, shrewd ▷*thrifty* ★**rash**

prudish *adj.* straitlaced, narrow-minded, demure, priggish ▷*prim*

prune ① *v.* cut, shorten, trim, crop ② *n.* dried plum

pry *v.* snoop, peep, meddle, intrude

public ① *adj.* communal, civil, popular, social, national ② *n.* the people, the populace, society

publish *v.* broadcast, distribute, circulate, communicate, bring out

pucker *v.* fold, crease, cockle, furrow, wrinkle ★**straighten**

puerile *adj.* callow, immature, juvenile

puff *v.* inflate, swell, blow, pant, distend

pull *v.* ① haul, drag, tow, heave ★**push** ② gather, pluck, detach, pick

pump *v.* ① inflate, expand, swell, inject, siphon ② interrogate, question, grill

punch *v.* ① strike, beat, hit, cuff ② puncture, pierce, perforate, bore

punctual *adj.* prompt, on time, precise, exact, timely ★**tardy**

puncture *n.* perforation, hole, leak, wound

pungent *adj.* sharp, bitter, poignant, biting ▷*acrid* ★**mild**

punish *v.* chastise, correct, discipline, chasten, reprove, scold

puny *adj.* feeble, weak, frail, small, petty, stunted, insignificant ★**large**

pupil *n.* student, scholar, schoolchild, learner

puppet *n.* ① doll, marionette ② cat's-paw *The prisoner was not the true culprit, but only the ringleader's cat's-paw,* figurehead, pawn

purchase ① *v.* buy, procure, secure, obtain, get ▷*buy* ★**sell** ② *n.* bargain, investment

pure *adj.* ① immaculate, spotless, stainless, clear ▷*clean* ★**impure** ② virtuous, chaste, honest, blameless

purely *adv.* simply, barely, merely, only

purge *v.* ① purify, clean, cleanse, scour ② liquidate, exterminate, kill

purify *v.* clean, clarify, wash, purge

purloin *v.* rob, thieve, take, filch, pilfer ▷*steal*

purpose *n.* intent, design, will, goal, target

purse ① *n.* handbag, wallet, pouch, reticule, ② *v.* pucker, crease, compress, wrinkle

pursue *v.* ① follow, track, trace ▷*chase* ② practice, maintain, work for

pursuit *n.* ① hunt, chase, follow, hue and cry ② occupation, hobby, interest *Stamp collecting has always been one of my main interests*

push ① *v.* shove, thrust, press, drive, propel ② *n.* advance, assault, drive

put *v.* ① set, place, deposit, repose, lay ② express, propose, state

put down *v.* ① write, jot down, record, note ② crush, humiliate, subdue, insult

put off *v.* ① postpone, defer, delay, adjourn ② dishearten, unsettle, perturb

putrid *adj.* decomposed, rotten, rancid, rank, stinking ★**wholesome**

putter *v.* dabble, fiddle, tinker, mess around

puzzle ① *v.* baffle, confuse, mystify, perplex ▷*bewilder* ② *n.* conundrum, brainteaser, problem, dilemma

puzzling *adj.* baffling, curious, strange, bewildering ▷*peculiar*

Q q

quack *n.* impostor, charlatan *She pretended to tell fortunes by cards, but she was nothing but a charlatan,* humbug, fake

quaff *v.* imbibe, swallow ▷*drink*

quagmire *n.* bog, mire, marsh ▷*swamp*

quail *v.* tremble, flinch, shrink, cower, succumb ★**withstand**

quaint *adj.* curious, whimsical, fanciful, singular, old-fashioned, droll

quake ① *v.* tremble, quaver, shiver, quiver, shudder ② *n.* shock, convulsion, tremor *The tremors from the earthquake were felt hundreds of miles away*

qualification *n.* ① fitness, capacity, ability, accomplishment ② restriction, limitation, modification *The engineer's design was accepted with certain modifications*

qualify *v.* ① empower, enable, fit, suit ② moderate, limit, restrict

quality *n.* ① characteristic, condition, power ② excellence, worth, goodness

qualm *n.* doubt, misgiving, hesitation

quandary *n.* difficulty, doubt ▷*dilemma*

quantity *n.* amount, number, volume, sum

quarrel ① *n.* dispute, squabble, wrangle, disagreement ★**harmony** ② *v.* argue, bicker, brawl, squabble ★**agree**

quarry *n.* ① game, prey, object, victim, target ② mine, excavation, pit

quarter *n.* ① area, territory, place, district ② one-fourth ③ mercy *The commander of the invading army showed no mercy to the local defenders,* grace, lenience

quarters *n.* lodgings, dwelling, billet, rooms

quash *v.* abolish, nullify, suppress, overthrow, subdue

quaver *v.* shake, tremble, shiver, shudder, vibrate, oscillate, quake

quay *n.* pier, dock, wharf, landing, jetty KEY

queasy *adj.* bilious, squeamish, sick, faint

queer *adj.* strange, odd, whimsical, peculiar

quell *v.* crush, stifle, extinguish, defeat

quench *v.* ① douse *We carefully doused our campfire before leaving the site,* put out, cool, check ② slake *The cattle rushed to the river and slaked their thirst,* cool, allay

query ① *n.* question, doubt, objection ② *v.* ask, inquire, question, doubt ★**accept**

quest *n.* chase, hunt, search, pursuit, venture

question ① *n.* query, inquiry, interrogation, ② *n.* topic, problem, issue ③ *v.* ask, inquire, interrogate ★**answer**

questionable *adj.* doubtful, uncertain, undecided, unbelievable ★**certain**

queue *n.* ① row, line, procession, lineup ② pigtail, coil, braid, ponytail CUE

quibble *v.* argue, trifle, split hairs, carp *If you like our plan, don't carp about the details*

quick *adj.* ① speedy, rapid, express, swift ▷*fast* ② alert, active, agile, lively ★**slow** ③ clever, intelligent, acute ★**dull** ④ hasty, sharp, touchy ★**mild**

quicken *v.* accelerate ▷*hasten* ★**delay**

quiet ① *adj.* silent, soundless, noiseless, hushed ★**noisy** ② *adj.* placid, smooth, undisturbed ★**busy** ③ *n.* peace, rest, tranquility, silence ★**tumult**

quilt *n.* blanket, cover, comforter, eiderdown

quip *n.* joke, gag, gipe, jest, wisecrack, retort

quirk *n.* pecularity, curiosity, foible *Despite his age and one or two foibles, old Uncle Fred was very agile,* mannerism ▷*habit*

quit *v.* ① cease, desist, stop ② leave, depart, relinquish ③ give up, surrender

quite *adv.* absolutely, altogether, wholly

quits *adj.* even *If I pay what I owe, it makes us even,* all square, level, equal

quiver ① *v.* tremble, quake, shiver, shudder ② *n.* holster, scabbard, sheath

quiz ① *v.* question, ask, examine, grill ② *n.* test, examination, contest *Barbara was the winner in the spelling contest*

quizzical *adj.* ① incredulous, skeptical, suspicious ② whimsical, teasing, amused

quota *n.* allowance, allocation, ration

quotation *n.* ① extract, selection, passage ② cost, estimate, price

quote *v.* recite, cite, recount, recollect, tell, mention

R r

rabble *n.* crowd, mob, scum, riffraff

race ① *n.* competition, contest, chase, dash ② *n.* people, nation, folk, stock, breed, tribe ③ *v.* run, speed, hurry, scamper, gallop, sprint

rack ① *n.* shelf, stand, frame, framework ② *v.* distress, strain, torment, pain WRACK

racket *n.* ① uproar, noise, hubbub, tumult ▷ *din* ② fraud, deception, swindle

racy *adj.* ① pungent, piquant, zestful ② spirited, smart, lively

radiant *adj.* ① brilliant, bright, luminous, shining ② splendid, glorious, happy ★**dull**

radiate *v.* ① gleam, sparkle, beam, shine ② emit, spread, diffuse

radical *adj.* ① extreme, fanatical, deep-seated ② original, fundamental *The new teacher made some fundamental changes in our lessons,* natural ★**superficial**

raffle *n.* draw, sweepstakes, lottery

rafter *n.* joist, girder, beam, support

ragamuffin *n.* scarecrow, urchin ▷ *waif*

rage ① *n.* wrath, fury, ferocity, passion, madness ▷ *anger* ② *v.* rave, fret, fume *The mad bull was fuming with rage as we leaped over the fence,* storm, flare up

ragged *adj.* shabby, seedy, shaggy, rough, torn ★**smart**

raid ① *n.* invasion, attack, strike, sortie ② *v.* attack, invade, ransack, plunder, maraud *The ship was attacked and plundered by pirates* RAYED

rail ① *n.* post, picket, fence, railing ② *v.* scold, rant, blast, reproach

rain *n. & v.* deluge, drizzle, flood, shower, torrent REIGN, REIN

raise *v.* ① elevate, lift, erect, hoist *The flag was hoisted as the ship came into port* ★**lower** ② excite, awaken, rouse ③ promote, increase, advance ④ cultivate, grow, breed RAZE

rake *v.* grope, scrape, collect, gather, assemble

rally *v.* ① meet, assemble, convene *The*

members of the club will convene next mont⚫ ★**disperse** ② encourage, restore, reunite

ram *v.* ① cram, crowd, push, pack, stuff, poke, wedge ② charge, beat, crash, drive

ramble *v.* ① stroll, meander, saunter, roam, rove ② chatter, digress *Joe's speech was very long, as he kept digressing from the point,* dodder

ramp *n.* gradient, slope, incline, grade

rampage ① *n.* storm, rage, riot, uproar, tumult ② *v.* rave, rush, run wild *Someone left the gate open, and the pigs ran wild in the cabbage patch*

ramshackle *adj.* unstable, shaky, unsteady, flimsy, rickety ▷ *decrepit* ★**stable**

rancid *adj.* sour, curdled, rank, putrid, musty

rancor *n.* spite, grudge, animosity, hatred ▷ *malice* RANKER

random *adj.* haphazard, vague, casual, accidental ▷ *chance* ★**deliberate**

range ① *n.* extent, length, span, magnitude, area ② *n.* kind, sort, class, order ③ *v.* wander, rove, roam, stray

rank ① *n.* grade, class, position, level ② *adj.* foul, musty, offensive, coarse ③ *adj.* luxuriant, fertile, dense *The whole county was covered with dense forest*

rankle *v.* burn, smolder, fester, be embittered

ransack *v.* plunder, pillage, search, scour

ransom ① *n.* release, deliverance, payoff, price ② *v.* rescue, redeem *Jill was lazy at school to begin with, but later redeemed herself with hard work,* liberate

rant *v.* rave, declaim, bluster, roar, shout

rap *v.* tap, pat, strike, knock

rape *v.* violate, abuse, assault, attack

rapid *adj.* speedy, quick, swift ▷ *fast* ★**slow**

rapt *adj.* engrossed, intent, captivated, fascinated, delighted RAPPED, WRAPPED

rapture *n.* bliss, ecstasy, delight ▷ *joy* ★**sorrow**

rare *adj.* ① unusual, uncommon, scarce, occasional ② valuable, fine, precious ★**common** ③ underdone, lightly cooked

rascal *n.* rogue, knave, villain, scamp, scoundrel, blackguard ★**gentleman**

rash ① *adj.* headstrong, audacious, hasty,

foolhardy ▷ *reckless* ★**cautious** ② *n.*
eruption, outbreak, epidemic *There has
been an epidemic of chicken pox in our
neighborhood*

rashness *n.* audacity, carelessness,
hastiness, recklessness ★**carefulness**

rasp ① *v.* file, grate, grind ② *v.* irk, irritate,
vex ③ *n.* file, tool

rate ① *n.* pace, tempo *It took us a while to
get used to the tempo of life in the city,*
velocity, speed ② *n.* tax, charge, cost ③ *v.*
appraise, assess, estimate, merit, value

rather *adv.* ① somewhat, to some extent, sort
of ② first, preferably, sooner

ration ① *n.* portion, share, allotment, helping
② *v.* allocate, allot, restrict, control

rational *adj.* ① sensible, sound, wise,
intelligent, sane ★**irrational** ② reasonable,
fair, proper ★**absurd**

rattle *v.* ① jangle, jingle, vibrate ② muddle,
confuse, daze ▷ *bewilder*

raucous *adj.* harsh, hoarse, rough, strident,
gutteral

ravage *v.* devastate, destroy, pillage,
ransack, desolate, wreck

rave *v.* ① rant, ramble *The old man rambled
on for hours about his youth,* roar, rage,
storm ② favor, be ecstatic about

ravenous *adj.* hungry, starving, famished,
voracious ▷ *greedy*

ravishing *adj.* beautiful, bewitching,
delightful, charming ▷ *enchanting*

raw *adj.* ① uncooked ② unripe, green *I was
pretty green during the first six months in
the job,* inexperienced ③ sensitive, painful,
tender ④ cold, exposed, chilly

ray *n.* beam, gleam, glimmer, shaft, stream,
spark

raze *v.* demolish, destroy, flatten, obliterate,
ruin RAISE, RAYS

reach ① *v.* arrive at, gain, get to, attain,
grasp ② *v.* stretch, extend ③ *n.* extent,
length, grasp, distance, scope

react *v.* respond, reverberate *The sound of
the church bell reverberated through the
village,* behave, respond

read *v.* ① peruse, pore over, study, browse,

Read

Reed

understand ② recite, orate REED

readily *adv.* easily, eagerly, freely, gladly,
promptly ★**reluctantly**

ready *adj.* ① prepared, alert, prompt, willing
★**reluctant** ② convenient, handy ★**remote**
③ skillful, facile, expert ★**clumsy**

real *adj.* ① genuine, authentic, factual
★**false** ② substantial, existent, actual
★**imaginary** REEL

realistic *adj.* ① authentic, lifelike
② practical, down-to-earth *Sue is a real
romantic type, but her boyfriend is much
more down-to-earth,* unromantic,
businesslike, pragmatic ★**fanciful**

realize *v.* ① understand, comprehend, feel
② earn, gain, obtain, acquire

really *adv.* truly, indeed, actually, absolutely

realm *n.* domain, province, sphere *My
mother has taken up writing and is very
involved in the sphere of books,* region,
territory, field

reap *v.* harvest, gather, obtain, realize,
derive, gain ★**squander**

rear ① *n.* back, end, tail, behind, posterior
② *adj.* hind, after, following ③ *v.* foster,
breed, educate ④ *v.* lift, raise, elevate

reason ① *n.* purpose, motive, basis, cause,
explanation ② *n.* wisdom, sense, intellect ③
v. consider, think, argue

reasonable *adj.* ① sensible, valid, rational
★**absurd** ② moderate, fair, just, modest ③
inexpensive, low-priced *Everything in the
new supermarket is low-priced* ★**excessive**

reassure *v.* inspire, hearten, convince ▷*encourage* ★**discourage**

rebate *n.* refund, repayment, discount, allowance

rebel ① *v.* (re-*bel*) revolt, mutiny, disobey, resist ② *n.* (*reb*-el) revolutionary, mutineer *Fletcher Christian was the leader of the mutineers on the* Bounty, traitor

rebellious *adj.* defiant, disobedient, mutinous, resistant ★**obedient**

rebuke *v.* reprimand, reproach, scold, tell off ★**praise**

recall *v.* ① recollect, remember ② cancel, overrule, countermand *We were just about to pull down the building when our orders were countermanded,* call back

recede *v.* ebb, retreat, flow back, decline, shrink, withdraw, return ★**proceed**

receipt *n.* acknowledgment, voucher

recent *adj.* late, new, fresh, novel, modern, current ★**out-of-date**

recently *adv.* lately, currently, latterly

receptacle *n.* container, holder, vessel, bowl

reception *n.* ① entertainment, function, party ② acceptance, acknowledgment

recess *n.* ① alcove, corner, socket, niche, slot, nook ② intermission, interlude, pause

recession *n.* slump, stagnation, depression ★**boom**

recipe *n.* formula, method *I'll show you my secret method of making angel food cake; it never fails,* prescription

recite *v.* recount, chant, speak, declaim, relate, describe

reckless *adj.* unwary, incautious, daring, brash, heedless ▷*rash* ★**cautious**

reckon ① *v.* calculate, figure, count, tally *I have checked the accounts and my figures tally with yours,* account ② judge, expect, believe, guess, surmise

reclaim *v.* recover, redeem, reform, retrieve, restore, salvage

recline *v.* lounge, sprawl, lie, rest, loll, repose

recognize *v.* ① recall, recollect, remember, identify, know ② see *I will explain my idea slowly and you will see what I mean,* comprehend, understand

recoil *v.* ① rebound, backfire, boomerang ② falter, flinch, shrink, quail *My little brother quailed at the sound of the thunder*

recollect *v.* recall, recognize, place ▷*remember* ★**forget**

recommend *v.* suggest, advise, propose, commend, approve ★**veto**

recompense ① *n.* payment, compensation, remuneration ② *v.* reimburse, repay ▷*reward*

reconcile *v.* ① accept, harmonize, pacify, placate ★**estrange** ② adjust, settle, square

record ① *v.* (re-*cord*) note, register, enter, inscribe, list ② *n.* (*rec*-ord) album, disk, platter, CD, LP ③ chronicle, archive, almanac *We'll get hold of the almanac and check the time of high tide,* register ④ performance, championship

recount *v.* ① (re-*count*) relate, tell, recite, describe ② (*re*-count) count again

recover *v.* ① reclaim, retrieve, redeem, regain ② get better, recuperate, revive ★**worsen**

recreation *n.* pastime, sports, amusement, fun

recruit ① *n.* trainee, beginner, apprentice ② *v.* enlist, enroll, draft, mobilize

rectify *v.* correct, put right, repair, remedy, restore, adjust, reset

recuperate *v.* get better, rally, improve, mend ▷*recover* ★**worsen**

recur *v.* return, reappear, come back, repeat, revert

redden *v.* crimson, color, flush ▷*blush*

redeem *v.* ① buy back, compensate for, exchange ② save, liberate, free

reduce *v.* ① lessen, diminish, curtail, contract ② overcome, defeat, humiliate

reek *v.* smell, stink, fume, exhale, smoke

reel ① *v.* roll, rock, shake, stagger, falter, totter ② *n.* spool, bobbin, spindle REAL

refer *v.* relate, connect, associate, assign, belong

referee *n.* umpire, arbitrator, judge

reference *n.* ① allusion, insinuation, innuendo *From your innuendo, it seems that you think I'm joking!* ▷*hint* ② testimonial, recommendation, credentials

refine *v.* clarify, purify, filter, process, cultivate

refined *adj.* ① civilized, cultivated, cultured ▷ *polite* ② purified, pure, clarified ★**coarse**

reflect *v.* ① think, contemplate, deliberate, consider ② mirror, copy, imitate, image

reform *v.* ① improve, correct ▷ *rectify* ② remodel, reorganize, revamp

refrain ① *v.* avoid, abstain, forbear, resist, keep from ② *n.* chorus, melody, tune

refresh *v.* rejuvenate, renew, restore, cheer, enliven ★**exhaust**

refrigerate *v.* chill, cool, freeze

refuge *n.* haven, harbor, asylum, sanctuary ▷ *shelter*

refugee *n.* exile, fugitive, emigrant

refund *v.* repay, rebate, reimburse *I must reimburse you for everything you spent on my behalf,* pay back, return

refuse ① *v.* (re-*fuze*) decline, say no, demur, repudiate ② *n.* (*ref*-use) trash, garbage, rubbish, waste

refute *v.* deny, dispute, disprove, discredit ★**prove**

regain *v.* recover, get back, retrieve, redeem

regal *adj.* royal, princely, majestic, noble, stately

regard ① *v.* esteem, revere, honor, respect ★**dislike** ② *v.* notice, observe, see, gaze ③ *n.* affection, esteem, fondness, repute ★**contempt**

regardless ① *adj.* heedless, neglectful, indifferent ★**careful** ② *adv.* anyhow, anyway, in any case

region *n.* area, zone, territory, locality, province, country

register ① *n.* roll, roster, record, archives *We can trace the town's history from the ancient archives* ② *v.* enter, record, inscribe, enroll, sign on

regret ① *v.* repent, rue, deplore, lament, mourn, apologize ★**welcome** ② *n.* remorse, sorrow, apology, grief

regular *adj.* ① normal, customary, periodical, formal ★**unusual** ② orderly, steady, unchanging ★**variable**

regulate *v.* ① control, manage, govern, determine ② adjust, measure, time, correct

regulation *n.* ① rule, law, command, bylaw

Rain

Rein

The club bylaws require us to elect a new secretary ② order, control, government

rehearse *v.* repeat, practice, drill, prepare, run through

reign ① *n.* rule, sway, power, control ② *v.* govern, rule, dominate, command RAIN, REIN

rein *v. & n.* bridle, hold, check, harness RAIN, REIGN

reinforce *v.* support, strengthen, toughen, harden, stiffen ★**weaken**

reject ① *v.* (re-*ject*) discard, get rid of, throw out, refuse, repel, deny ② *n.* (*re*-ject) cast-off, scrap

rejoice *v.* glory, exult, cheer, please, triumph ▷ *delight* ★**lament**

relapse ① *v.* revert, backslide, turn back, recede ② *n.* repetition, recurrence, setback

relate *v.* describe, recount, tell, mention, detail

related *adj.* associated, allied, connected, linked, akin ★**different**

relative ① *n.* kinsman, kinswoman, cousin, relation, sibling *I have four siblings—three sisters and one brother* ② *adj.* comparative, approximate, relevant

relax *v.* diminish, loosen, ease, reduce, relieve, unwind ★**tighten**

relaxed *adj.* composed, cool, easygoing, mellow ▷ *casual* ★**tense**

release *v.* let go, loose, liberate, acquit, discharge ▷*free* ★**detain**

relent *v.* relax, soften, yield, ease, give in, unbend ★**harden**

relentless *adj.* unmerciful, remorseless, grim, pitiless ▷*cruel* ★**humane**

relevant *adj.* applicable, pertinent, appropriate, apt ▷*suitable* ★**irrelevant**

reliable *adj.* dependable, trustworthy, responsible, honest ▷*sound* ★**unreliable**

relic *n.* fragment, vestige, antique, keepsake, memento *This brooch is a memento of my great-grandmother; she wore it often*

relief *n.* aid, assistance, respite, support, succor ▷*help* ★**aggravation**

relieve *v.* release, support, comfort, lighten, relax, console ★**aggravate**

religious *adj.* pious, devout, orthodox, devoted, God-fearing, faithful

relinquish *v.* renounce, let go, waive, disclaim, give up ▷*abandon* ★**retain**

relish ① *v.* enjoy, like, approve ▷*appreciate* ★**loathe** ② *n.* savor, flavor, tang, gusto *The fried chicken was a great success; everyone ate with enormous gusto,* zest, sauce

reluctant *adj.* hesitant, averse, loth, disinclined, squeamish ★**willing**

rely on *v.* depend on, count on, believe in

remain *v.* ① stay, tarry, dwell, wait, rest ★**depart** ② persist, last, endure

remainder *n.* remnant, residue, leavings

remark *v.* ① utter, observe, state, mention ▷*say* ② notice, perceive, note ▷*see*

remarkable *adj.* unusual, surprising, curious, prominent ▷*outstanding* ★**ordinary**

remedy ① *n.* cure, restorative, medicine ② *n.* relief, solution, treatment, corrective ③ *v.* relieve, heal, cure, put right

remember *v.* recollect, recognize, think back ▷*recall* ★**forget**

remind *v.* suggest, hint, cue, prompt

remit *v.* ① relax, desist, slacken, modify, excuse, forgive ② pay, square, settle up

remnant *n.* residue, remains, rest ▷*remainder*

remorse *n.* regrets, contrition, pity

remote *adj.* ① distant, far, isolated ★**near** ② unrelated, alien, foreign ★**significant**

remove *v.* dislocate, take away, transfer, withdraw, carry off

rend *v.* split, fracture, tear apart, sever, break

render *v.* ① give, present, surrender, deliver ② play, execute, perform

renew *v.* ① modernize, mend, prolong, renovate ② reissue *Next week we start to reissue some of the old silent movies,* revive

renounce *v.* disown, disclaim, give up, repudiate, forsake ★**retain**

renowned *adj.* eminent, noted, famed, notable ▷*celebrated* ★**obscure**

rent ① *v.* hire, lease, let, charter ② *n.* tear, rip break, crack, fissure ③ *n.* fee, payment

repair ① *v.* fix, mend, correct, remedy, rectify *We are sorry there was an error in your account; we will rectify it right away* ② *n.* restoration, adjustment

repast *n.* meal, food, snack, spread

repay *v.* ① refund, reimburse, pay ② avenge, retaliate, revenge, punish

repeal *v.* revoke, annul, abolish, quash *The man's innocence was proved and his sentence was quashed* ▷*cancel* ★**establish**

repeat *v.* duplicate, renew, reiterate, do again

repel *v.* ① repulse, deter, reject, push back ② revolt, disgust, nauseate ★**attract**

repellent *adj.* distasteful, hateful, discouraging ▷*repulsive* ★**attractive**

repent *v.* sorrow, deplore, grieve ▷*regret*

replace *v.* ① supersede, succeed, follow, substitute ② put back, reinstate, restore

replenish *v.* fill, refill, restock, furnish, provide, top up ★**empty**

replica *n.* facsimile, copy, likeness, duplicate

reply ① *v.* answer, respond, rejoin, retort, acknowledge ② *n.* answer, response, acknowledgment, riposte

report ① *n.* statement, account, message, communication, tidings ② *n.* noise, explosion bang ③ *v.* tell, disclose, reveal, expose

repose ① *v.* rest, settle, lie down, sleep, recline ② *n.* ease, peace, quiet, tranquility ★**tumult**

represent *v.* ① depict, picture, portray, illustrate ② stand for, mean, denote

representative ① *n.* agent, delegate, envoy, deputy ② *adj.* typical, figurative

repress *v.* restrain, suppress, bottle up, smother, stifle

reprimand ① *v.* admonish, blame, rebuke ▷*chide* ② *n.* reproach, talking-to, scolding ★**praise**

reproach *v.* scold, reprove, reprimand, blame ▷*rebuke* ★**approve**

reproduce *v.* ① copy, duplicate, imitate, simulate ② breed, multiply, generate

reprove *v.* reproach, reprimand ▷*rebuke* ★**approve**

repudiate *v.* renounce, disown, disavow, disclaim ★**acknowledge**

repugnant *adj.* unattractive, disagreeable, offensive ▷*repulsive,* ★**pleasant**

repulse *v.* repel, rebuff, drive back, reject ▷*spurn* ★**attract**

repulsive *adj.* obnoxious, disgusting, loathsome ▷*repugnant* ★**attractive**

reputation *n.* standing, position, esteem, honor, good name

request ① *v.* demand, beg, entreat, beseech ▷*ask* ② *n.* petition, entreaty, invitation

require *v.* ① need, want, demand, crave ② expect, cause, instruct

rescue ① *v.* save, set free, liberate, recover, release ② *n.* liberation, deliverance, salvation *Salvation for the shipwrecked crew came when the coast guard lifted them to safety* ★**capture**

research *v.* examine, explore, investigate, inquire ▷*study*

resemble *v.* look like, mirror, take after, be like ★**differ**

resent *v.* resist, begrudge, dislike, take exception to ★**like**

resentful *adj.* offended, bitter, piqued, huffy ▷*indignant* ★**contented**

reserve ① *v.* hoard, retain, withhold ▷*keep* ② *n.* modesty, shyness, restraint ③ *n.* supply, backlog, stock

reservoir *n.* lake, spring, pool, container

reside *v.* live, occupy, inhabit, lodge ▷*dwell*

residence *n.* house, home, habitation, dwelling, mansion RESIDENTS

resign *v.* retire, abdicate, step down, give notice, abandon ▷*quit* ★**join**

resign oneself to *v.* accept, comply, reconcile *Robinson Crusoe became reconciled to loneliness on his island,* yield, give in ▷*submit* ★**resist**

resist *v.* withstand, oppose, defy, refrain, hinder ▷*thwart* ★**submit**

Rescue

Salvation for the shipwrecked crew came when the coast guard lifted them to safety.

resistance *n.* defiance, obstruction, opposition, hindrance ★**acceptance**

resolute *adj.* determined, resolved, obstinate, stubborn, dogged *Despite the bad weather, the climbers were dogged in their will to reach the peak* ★**weak**

resolve ① *v.* determine, intend, decide ② *v.* decipher, unravel, disentangle ③ *n.* resolution, purpose, will

resort ① *v.* frequent, haunt, visit ② *n.* alternative, chance, course ③ *n.* spa, watering place, hotel, vacation spot

resourceful *adj.* clever, ingenious, bright

respect ① *n.* esteem, honor, regard, repute, dignity ② *v.* esteem, honor, revere, venerate *The names of the pioneers and explorers will always be venerated*

respectable *adj.* decent, admirable, honest, honorable, proper ★**disreputable**

respectful *adj.* deferential, courteous, polite, dutiful ★**disrespectful**

respite *n.* break, halt, interval, lull, recess, letup

respond *v.* answer, reply, retort, tally, accord, agree ★**differ**

responsible *adj.* ① accountable, dependable, sensible ▷*reliable* ★**unreliable** ② liable, guilty

rest ① *n.* repose, relaxation, peace, tranquility ② *n.* break, pause, respite, spell ③ *n.* remainder, residue, balance ④ *v.* repose, settle, sleep, relax wrest

restful *adj.* peaceful, quiet, calm, placid ★**disturbing**

restless *adj.* uneasy, fitful, agitated, nervous, fretful ★**calm**

restore *v.* ① replace, reinstate, return ② refurbish, recondition, renovate *We renovated this old sofa which we found in a junk shop*

restrain *v.* stop, prevent, hold back, subdue ▷*check* ★**encourage**

restrict *v.* confine, limit, cramp, handicap ▷*regulate* ★**free**

result ① *n.* effect, consequence, outcome, end ★**cause** ② *v.* ensue, happen, turn out, follow, emerge, occur

resume *v.* renew, recommence, start again, go back to ▷*continue* ★**interrupt**

retain *v.* hold, restrain, withhold, detain ▷*keep* ★**relinquish**

retaliate *v.* avenge, reciprocate, fight back, repay, retort ★**submit**

retire *v.* ① retreat, go back ▷*withdraw* ★**advance** ② abdicate, resign, relinquish

retort ① *n.* riposte, reply, rejoinder ② *v.* return, answer, reply

retract *v.* recant, deny, disavow, take back, revoke ★**maintain**

retreat ① *v.* retire, depart, shrink ▷*withdraw* ★**advance** ② *n.* sanctuary *This section of the park is being made into a bird santuary,* shelter, den, haven

retrieve *v.* redeem, recover, regain, rescue ▷*salvage* ★**lose**

return ① *v.* rejoin, come back, reappear ② *v.* restore, give back, repay, refund ③ *n.* form, tax form, document, list

reveal *v.* disclose, expose, show, display, uncover, divulge ★**hide**

revel ① *v.* make merry, celebrate, have fun ② *n.* celebration, gala, party, spree

revenge ① *n.* vengeance, reprisal, retaliation ② *v.* avenge, get one's own back

revenue *n.* income, receipts, earnings

revere *v.* honor, esteem, regard, adore, venerate, respect ★**despise**

reverse ① *v.* cancel, change, overrule, repeal, revoke ② *n.* adversity, disaster, bad luck, misfortune ③ *adj.* backward, contrary, opposite *We turned the car around and drove back in the opposite direction*

review ① *v.* reconsider, examine, survey ② *n.* inspection, examination ③ *n.* synopsis, journal, magazine REVUE

revise *v.* edit, amend, improve, rewrite, alter

revive *v.* awaken, rally, recover, refresh, restore, invigorate ▷*rouse*

revoke *v.* repeal, abolish *The principal refuses to abolish the school dress code,* cancel, quash, reverse, withdraw

revolt ① *v.* rebel, mutiny, riot ② *v.* nauseate, sicken, disgust ③ *n.* rebellion, uprising, revolution

revolting *adj.* obnoxious *The chemical factory's chimney was giving off obnoxious fumes,* repulsive, offensive ▷*repugnant* ★**pleasant**

revolve *v.* rotate, spin, gyrate, turn

reward ① *n.* award, payment, benefit, bonus, profit ★**punishment** ② *v.* compensate, repay, remunerate ★**punish**

rhyme *n.* verse, poem, ditty, ode RIME

rhythm *n.* beat, pulse, throb, stroke, timing

ribald *adj.* smutty, vulgar, coarse, gross

rich *adj.* ① wealthy, prosperous, affluent, opulent ★**poor** ② fertile, loamy, fruitful, abundant ★**barren** ③ delicious, sweet, luscious, delicate

rid *v.* get rid of, unburden, expel, free

riddle ① *n.* puzzle, cryptogram, enigma ② *v.* puncture, bore, perforate, pierce

ride ① *v.* sit, travel, drive, journey ② *n.* journey, jaunt, lift, trip

ridge *n.* ① groove, furrow, fold ② highland, chain, range *A range of hills could be seen in the distance*

ridicule ① *n.* scorn, derision, travesty, sarcasm, mockery ② *v.* deride, mock, jeer,

Rivers and Waterways

Arroyo
Brook
Canal
Channel
Creek
Lake
Loch
Pool
Pond
River
Spring
Strait
Stream
Surf
Waterfall

banter *His banter can be amusing, but he doesn't know when to stop and sometimes offends people*

ridiculous *adj.* laughable, absurd, foolish, preposterous ▷*silly* ★**sensible**

rife *adj.* common, current, frequent, prevalent ▷*widespread* ★**scarce**

rifle ① *v.* loot, rob, plunder ▷*ransack* ② *n.* gun, musket, firearm

rift *n.* ① fissure, breach, crack ② disagreement, clash, break

right ① *adj.* correct, proper, true ★**incorrect** ② *adj.* honest, upright, fair ③ *adj.* seemly, fit, suitable, becoming ★**improper** ④ *n.* truth, justice, honesty ★**wrong** RITE, WRITE

righteous *adj.* honorable, upright, moral

rigid *adj.* ① stiff, firm, inflexible ② stern, austere, harsh ★**flexible**

rigorous *adj.* stern, severe, strict, rigid

rim *n.* border, margin, edge, verge *We knew we were on the verge of disaster,* brink

ring ① *n.* circle, band, collar ② *n.* bell, chime, tinkle ③ *v.* chime, strike, jingle, sound WRING

riot ① *n.* uproar, tumult, brawl, broil ★**calm** ② *v.* revolt, rampage, rebel

ripe *adj.* ① mellow, mature, seasoned ② developed, adult, full-grown

rise ① *v.* ascend, mount, soar, arise, grow ★**fall** ② *v.* appear, occur, happen ★**vanish** ③ *n.* ascent, advance, increase ★**fall**

risk ① *v.* chance, dare, hazard, gamble ② *n.* adventure, peril, danger, jeopardy ★**safety**

risky *adj.* perilous, chancy, dangerous, tricky, uncertain ★**safe**

rite *n.* custom, ritual, practice RIGHT

rival ① *adj.* opposing, competing, conflicting ② *n.* opponent, adversary ★**associate**

river *n.* stream, waterway, brook, torrent *Before the rains came, this torrent was only a trickle*

road *n.* street, avenue, drive, lane, highway, freeway, route, way RODE, ROWED

roam *v.* rove, ramble, range, stroll, wander

roar *v.* bellow, bawl, yell, blare, cry

rob *v.* cheat, defraud, loot, plunder ▷*steal*

robber *n.* bandit, brigand, thief, crook

robe *n.* costume, dress, gown, habit

robust *adj.* strong, healthy, lusty, sturdy ▷*vigorous* ★**delicate**

rock ① *n.* stone, boulder, cobble, pebble, crag, reef ② *v.* totter, reel, sway, falter ③ *v.* quiet, still, tranquilize, soothe

rod *n.* baton, stick, stave, pole, perch, cane

rogue *n.* rascal, blackguard, scamp, knave ▷*scoundrel* ★**gentleman**

role *n.* character, post, duty, function *At the end of the party, my function will be to clear up*

roll ① *n.* record, register, list ② *n.* spool, scroll, reel ③ *v.* revolve, rotate, turn ④ *v.* smooth, level, press ⑤ *v.* lurch, reel, pitch, ROLE

romance *n.* ① love story, novel, love affair ② adventure, excitement, fantasy, glamour

romantic *adj.* ① amorous, passionate, loving ② visionary, fanciful *Many people have a fanciful idea of how things were in the old days,* fantastic, extravagant ★**ordinary**

romp *v.* gambol, caper, frolic, prance, play

roof *n.* ceiling, covering, cover, canopy

room *n.* ① apartment, chamber, area,

root *n.* ① seed, source, radicle ② basis, element, stem, origin

rope *n.* cable, cord, hawser, line, lasso

rosy *adj.* ① cheerful, encouraging, hopeful, optimistic ② pink, flesh-colored

rot ① *v.* corrupt, crumble, decay, perish ② *n.* bunkum *The last speaker at the meeting was talking a lot of bunkum,* balderdash, bosh

rotate *v.* revolve, turn, spin, pivot, gyrate

rotten *adj.* ① decayed, putrid, decomposed, fetid ② deplorable, despicable, nasty, vicious ③ sick, ill, poorly

rough *adj.* ① wrinkled, craggy, coarse, shaggy, broken ② rude, crude, imperfect ③ blunt, gruff, brusque, discourteous RUFF

round ① *adj.* circular, rotund, spherical ② *n.* ring, circle, loop

rouse *v.* ① waken, arouse, excite, disturb ② anger, inflame, incite ★**calm**

rout *v.* crush, defeat, conquer, overthrow

route *n.* road, track, way, journey, direction

routine *n.* usage, practice, formula, technique, method, habit *After being alone for so long, I have gotten into the habit of talking to myself*

rove *v.* tramp, roam, wander, stroll, drift

row ① *n.* (*ro*) string, line, queue, rank, column ② *v.* paddle, scull ROE ③ *n.* (rhymes with *now*) fight, squabble, noise, quarrel, argument, dispute ★**calm**

rowdy *adj.* rough, unruly, boisterous, noisy, wild ★**quiet**

royal *adj.* sovereign, princely, stately, majestic ▷*regal*

rub *v.* stroke, brush, scrub, wipe, polish

rubbish *n.* debris, trash, junk, garbage

rude *adj.* ① coarse, primitive, ill-bred, impolite, boorish, bad-mannered ② crude, formless, shapeless ★**polished**
ROOD, RUED

rue *v.* be sorry for, deplore, grieve ▷*regret*

ruffian *n.* hoodlum, hooligan, lout, scoundrel, rogue, ▷*rascal*

ruffle *v.* ① fluster, worry, excite, agitate ② crumple, rumple, crease

ruffled *adj.* upset, worried, flustered,

Rulers, Monarchs, and Leaders

Caesar	Prime
Czar	Minister
Czarina	Prince
Emperor	Princess
Empress	Queen
King	Rajah
Mikado	Sultan
Mogul	
Pharaoh	
President	

harassed, bothered, irritated

rugged *adj.* ① rough, craggy, shaggy, ragged ② rigorous, robust, strong, strenuous

ruin *v.* ① demolish, wreck, damage, smash ② bankrupt, impoverish, overwhelm

rule ① *v.* control, govern, command, manage, direct ② *v.* decide, determine, judge ③ *n.* law, regulation ④ *n.* straightedge

ruler ① *n.* leader, director, king, queen, monarch, governor ② rule, straightedge

rumble *v.* roar, thunder, boom, roll

rumor *n.* hearsay, report, gossip, scandal *The bribery scandal, added to high taxes, brought down the government*

rumpus *n.* uproar, racket, riot, commotion, hurly burly ★**calm**

run ① *v.* hurry, hasten, speed, sprint ★**saunter** ② *v.* leak, flow, ooze ③ *v.* operate, propel, drive ④ *n.* race, course

run away *v.* escape, flee, bolt, abscond ★**stay**

rupture *v. & n.* break, burst, puncture, split

rural *adj.* rustic, countrified, pastoral ★**urban**

ruse *n.* dodge, hoax, scheme, trick, ploy RUES

rush *v. & n.* dash, speed, hurry, scramble, stampede, rampage ★**saunter**

rust *n.* corrosion, mold, blight, mildew, stain, deterioration

rustic *adj.* rural, pastoral, country, homely, simple

rustle *n. & v.* crackle, swish, murmur, whisper

rut *n.* furrow, channel, groove, score, track

ruthless *adj.* cruel, savage, harsh, ferocious, pitiless ★**merciful**

S s

sack ① *n.* bag, pouch, pack ② *v.* rob, plunder, pillage ③ discharge, dismiss, lay off SAC

sacred *adj.* holy, blessed, hallowed, spiritual, consecrated, revered ★**profane**

sacrifice ① *n.* offering ② *v.* forfeit, give up, relinquish ▷*abandon*

sad *adj.* sorrowful, melancholy, unhappy, mournful, woeful ▷*sorry* ★**happy**

sadden *v.* mourn, grieve, distress, lament, dishearten, disappoint ★**please**

safe ① *adj.* secure, protected, sure ★**unsafe** ② *n.* vault, coffer, cashbox, strongbox

safety *n.* shelter, security, sanctuary, protection, refuge ★**danger**

sag *v.* bend, slump, curve, bow, decline, flag ▷*droop* ★**bulge**

sage ① *adj.* wise, sensible, shrewd, sagacious ★**foolish** ② *n.* wise person, savant *We were taught by an old savant of the university, Professor Hankins,* philosopher ★**fool**

said *adj.* expressed, stated

sail *v.* cruise, voyage, navigate, float, skim SALE

sailor *n.* seafarer, mariner, pilot, shipmate, captain, jack tar, seadog SAILER

sake *n.* motive, reason, purpose, object, principle

salary *n.* pay, earnings, reward, wages, income

sale *n.* auction, transaction, selling, trade, disposal SAIL

sally *n.* jest, joke, crack, riposte ▷*quip*

salute ① *v.* greet, accost, welcome, hail, honor ② *n.* greetings, welcome, acknowledgment

salvage *v.* save, conserve, rescue, restore, reclaim ▷*preserve* ★**abandon**

same *adj.* ① identical, duplicate, alike, similar ② aforesaid, aforementioned *I leave all my possessions to my wife, the aforementioned Angela Gomez*

sample ① *n.* specimen, example, model, pattern, illustration ② *v.* inspect, try, taste

sanction *v.* permit, allow, authorize, approve

sanctuary *n.* retreat, shelter, shrine, asylum, haven ▷*refuge*

sane *adj.* normal, rational, reasonable, lucid ▷*sensible* ★**insane**

sap *v.* bleed, drain, exhaust, reduce, weaken ★**strengthen**

sarcastic *adj.* biting, cutting, sardonic, cynical, ironic, caustic *My cousins made some caustic remarks after I played the violin*

satire *n.* invective, sarcasm, burlesque, ridicule, parody

satisfaction *n.* contentment, delight, gratification, compensation ★**grievance**

satisfy *v.* gratify, fulfill, appease, suit, please ▷*delight* ★**disappoint**

saturate *v.* soak, steep, drench, souse, waterlog *I am afraid that old canoe is too waterlogged ever to be used again*

saucy *adj.* forward, pert, impudent, cheeky, disrespectful ★**civil**

saunter *v.* roam, loiter, wander, linger, dawdle, amble ▷*stroll* ★**hasten**

savage ① *adj.* barbaric, wild, uncivilized, ferocious, brutal ★**civilized** ② *n.* brute, oaf, barbarian

save *v.* ① liberate, set free, rescue, protect,

Sacred Books

Apocrypha	Koran
Bhagavad-Gita	Talmud
Bible	Torah
Book of Mormon	Tripitaka
Book of Common Prayer	Upanishad
Granth	Veda

guard ② keep, preserve, salvage, hoard, put aside ★**squander**

savory *adj.* appetizing, flavorful, luscious, agreeable ★**tasteless**

say *v.* speak, utter, state, pronounce, talk, tell, assert

saying *n.* proverb, statement, adage, idiom, maxim, aphorism

scale ① *n.* measure, balance, calibration ② *n.* crust, plate, flake ③ *n.* clef, key *I will play this next piece in the key of C,* mode ④ *v.* climb, ascend, clamber up

Scale

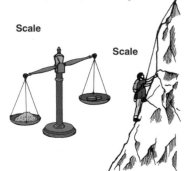

Scale

scamp *n.* knave, rogue, rascal, scoundrel, scalawag *Someone rang our doorbell, but when I opened the door, the scalawag had gone*

scamper *v.* hurry, run, scurry, hasten, sprint, scoot ▷*rush*

scan *v.* examine, glance at, scrutinize, pore over ▷*check*

scandal *n.* disgrace, libel, slander, offense, infamy, rumor, discredit ★**honor**

scanty *adj.* meager, insufficient, sparse, inadequate, poor, scant ★**plenty**

scar ① *n.* blemish, mark, stigma, wound ② *v.* brand, damage, disfigure

scarce *adj.* rare, infrequent, sparse, scanty, uncommon ★**common**

scarcity *n.* lack, deficiency, dearth, rarity, infrequency ★**abundance**

scare *v.* frighten, startle, shock, alarm, dismay ★**reassure**

scatter *v.* spread, disperse, strew, broadcast,

disseminate ▷*sprinkle* ★**collect**

scene *n.* sight, spectacle, vision, view, exhibition, landscape SEEN

scent ① *n.* aroma, tang, fragrance, smell, odor ② *v.* detect, sniff, smell CENT, SENT

schedule *n.* timetable *We checked the timetable before buying our train tickets,* program, catalog, diary

scheme *n.* plot, plan, project, design, proposal, idea

scholar *n.* ① pupil, student, schoolchild, learner ② intellectual *That café is a favorite gathering place for intellectuals,* savant, academic

scholarly *adj.* learned, educated, literate, cultured ★**illiterate**

scoff *v.* sneer, mock, deride, jeer, ridicule ★**respect**

scold *v.* rebuke, admonish, reprove, find fault with ▷*chide* ★**praise**

scoop ① *v.* bail, ladle, spoon, excavate, gouge, hollow ② *n.* exclusive, inside story, coup

scope *n.* extent, margin, compass, range, latitude, field

scorch *v.* sear, burn, singe, blister, shrivel

score *v.* ① cut, mark, scratch ② register, record, win

scorn ① *n.* mockery, disdain, ridicule, disregard ② *v.* despise, mock, spurn, slight ★**respect**

scoundrel *n.* rascal, knave, thief, rogue, villain ▷*vagabond* ★**gentleman**

scour *v.* ① cleanse, rinse, scrub, purge ② search, seek, ransack, rake

scourge ① *v.* beat, whip, thrash, cane ② *n.* curse, evil, misfortune, plague ★**blessing**

scowl *v. & n.* frown, glower, grimace, glare ★**smile**

scramble ① *v.* clamber, climb ② *v.* jostle, struggle, swarm, push ③ *n.* turmoil, bustle, confusion ★**order**

scrap ① *n.* piece, morsel, bit, portion, fragment, grain ② *v.* abandon, discard, junk

scrape ① *v.* scratch, groove, abrade, file, grate, scour ② *n.* predicament, fix, difficulty

scratch *v. & n.* wound, cut, mark, score

scream *v. & n.* screech, cry, shriek, howl, yell

screen ① *n.* awning *Before the ceremony, an awning was erected over the entrance to the hotel,* canopy, shade, protection ② *v.* protect, hide, conceal, veil

screw *v.* twist, turn, wrench, tighten, compress

scribble *v.* write, scrawl, scratch

scribe *n.* writer, penman, clerk, historian

script *n.* handwriting, manuscript, text, words, libretto *Sir Arthur Sullivan wrote the music for* The Mikado, *and W. S. Gilbert wrote the lyrics and libretto*

scrub ① *v.* scour, brush, mop, cleanse ② *n.* brushwood, undergrowth

scruffy *adj.* messy, dirty, frowzy, seedy, shabby, sloppy ▷*slovenly* ★**neat**

scrumptious *adj.* delightful, delicious, appetizing, exquisite

scrupulous *adj.* painstaking, particular, rigorous, strict, conscientious ★**careless**

scrutinize *v.* examine, inspect, peruse, study

scuffle *v. & n.* tussle, skirmish, fight, struggle, squabble

scum *n.* dross, foam, froth, dregs, crust

scuttle *v.* ① scramble, scamper, scoot, hurry ② destroy, smash, wreck

seal ① *n.* signet, stamp ② *n.* cork, bung, closure ③ *n.* sea mammal ④ *v.* fasten, close, shut

seam ① *n.* ridge, scar, lode, furrow ② hem, pleat, tuck SEEM

search ① *v.* seek, quest, hunt, trail, track, scour, explore ② *n.* exploration, investigation, quest, pursuit

season ① *n.* period, time, occasion, term ② *v.* accustom, acclimatize, mature ③ *v.* flavor, spice, salt

seat ① *n.* bench, chair, stool, sofa, couch, throne ② *n.* headquarters, place, site ③ *v.* accommodate, locate, place

secret *adj.* mysterious, hidden, concealed, obscure, private ★**public**

section *n.* division, group, department, segment, portion

secure ① *adj.* safe, protected ② *adj.* confident, certain, sure, stable ★**uncertain** ③ *v.* fasten, protect, close, lock ★**unfasten** ④ *v.* acquire, procure, obtain ★**lost**

sedate *adj.* staid, sober, demure, earnest ▷*steady* ★**flippant**

see *v.* ① behold, witness, sight, observe ② heed, examine, watch, note ③ understand, comprehend, know SEA

seedy *adj.* shabby, squalid, poor, grubby, unkempt ▷*slovenly* ★**spruce**

seek *v.* look for, search, inquire, endeavor, hunt

seem *v.* appear, look like, sound like, look as if SEAM

seemly *adj.* fit, suitable, proper, decent, decorous ★**unseemly**

seethe *v.* simmer, fizz, bubble, boil, foam

seize *v.* grasp, snatch, take, clutch, arrest ▷*grab* ★**abandon** SEAS, SEES

seldom *adv.* rarely, infrequently, hardly, scarcely ★**often**

select ① *adj.* choice, preferred, fine, prime *All the fruit on the trees in the orchard is in its prime,* first-class ★**common** ② *v.* choose, pick out, single out, prefer

selfish *adj.* greedy, self-centered, narrow, illiberal ▷*stingy* ★**generous**

sell *v.* vend, market, retail, trade, peddle ★**buy**

send *v.* transmit, dispatch, forward, mail, direct ★**detain**

send for *v.* command, order, summon, request ★**dismiss**

sensation *n.* ① feeling, perception, impression, awareness ② excitement, commotion, scandal

sensational *adj.* exceptional, scandalous, lurid ▷*exciting* ★**ordinary**

sense *n.* ① sensation, impression, feeling ② understanding, mind, tact, intellect ③ wisdom, significance, meaning CENTS, SCENTS

senseless *adj.* silly, stupid, absurd ▷*foolish* ★**sensible**

sensible *adj.* ① wise, intelligent, astute, shrewd ② reasonable, rational ③ conscious, aware, mindful ★**senseless**

sensitive *adj.* ① susceptible, responsive, acute, impressionable *Because Rachel is at such an impressionable age, her mother does not want her to see the movie* ② thin-skinned, touchy

sentence *n.* ① phrase, clause ② judgment, decision, condemnation, doom

sentimental *adj.* romantic, tender, emotional

separate ① *adj.* disconnected, apart, detached ★united ② *v.* detach, part, divide, break, disconnect ★unite

sequel *n.* continuation, consequence, result, outcome

serene *adj.* tranquil, calm, peaceful, undisturbed, clear ★tempestuous

series *n.* sequence, progression, succession, run, string

serious *adj.* grave, earnest, solemn, thoughtful, severe, grim ★trivial

serve *v.* attend, assist, aid, oblige, help, officiate, act

service *n.* ① aid, help, assistance, attendance, employment ② ceremony, rite *Stuart is at college studying the marriage rites of the Incas*

set ① *n.* group, pack, outfit, series ② *v.* settle, put, place, seat, locate ③ *v.* stiffen, congeal, harden ④ *adj.* decided, resolved, determined, fixed

setback *n.* defeat, delay, problem, snag, holdup ★advantage

settle *v.* ① establish, regulate, fix ② pay, liquidate, finish ③ populate, colonize ④ live, dwell, reside

several *adj.* various, numerous, sundry, separate

severe *adj.* strict, rigid, unkind, hard, austere ▷*stern* ★lenient

sew *v.* stitch, tack, baste, fasten, seam so, sow

shabby *adj.* torn, ragged, mean, shoddy, tacky ▷*squalid* ★neat

shack *n.* hut, cabin, shanty, shed, hovel

shackle *v.* & *n.* manacle, handcuff, chain, rope, fetter

shade *n.* ① shadow, gloom, darkness, dusk ② blind, awning, screen ③ color, tint, hue, tone ④ ghost, spirit, wraith *Out of the darkness, a wraithlike figure loomed up before us*

shadow ① *n.* shade ② *v.* follow, stalk, tail

shady *adj.* ① shadowy, shaded ★sunny ②

crooked, infamous, disreputable ★honest

shaft *n.* ① pillar, column, support ② hilt, handle, rod ③ mine, pit, well, tunnel

shaggy *adj.* hairy, tousled, unkempt, rough ★smooth

shake *v.* flutter, tremble, throb, shudder ▷*quiver*

shallow *adj.* ① not deep ② trivial, empty, silly, empty-headed ★profound

sham *adj.* false, imitation, counterfeit, forged ▷*bogus* ★genuine

shame *n.* & *v.* dishonor, discredit ▷*disgrace*

Ships and Boats

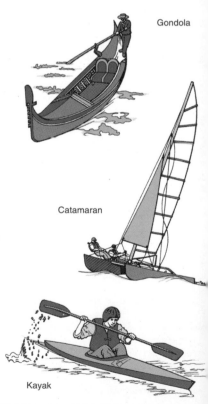

Gondola

Catamaran

Kayak

shameful *adj.* disgraceful, scandalous, outrageous ▷*disreputable* ★**honorable**

shape ① *n.* form, structure, outline, pattern ② *v.* form, fashion, make, create

share ① *v.* allot, divide, participate, co-operate ② *n.* portion, allotment, allowance

sharp *adj.* ① acute, keen, pointed ② clear, distinct, clean-cut ③ painful, severe, intense ④ pungent, acrid, acid ⑤ alert, shrewd, acute ▷*clever* ★**dull**

shatter *v.* smash, wreck, break, fracture, ruin ▷*destroy*

shave *v.* shear, crop, slice, shred, graze, trim

shear *v.* fleece, strip, cut ▷*shave* SHEER

sheath *n.* scabbard, quiver, holster, holder, case, casing

shed ① *n.* hut, barn, lean-to, shanty ② *v.* cast off, molt *Our parrot is molting and is leaving feathers all over the carpet,* spill ③ *v.* beam, radiate

sheepish *adj.* timid, diffident, foolish, embarrassed, shamefaced ★**unabashed**

sheer *adj.* ① absolute, simple, pure, unmixed ② transparent, filmy, thin ③ steep,

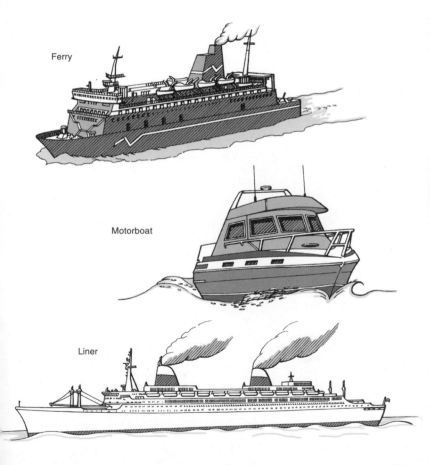

Ferry

Motorboat

Liner

abrupt, perpendicular *The trail ended at the foot of a huge, perpendicular cliff* SHEAR

shell *n.* pod, case, husk, hull, shuck, crust

shelter ① *n.* roof, sanctuary, safety, home, retreat, cover ② *v.* shield, cover, protect, screen ★**expose**

shield *n. & v.* guard, screen, safeguard ▷*shelter*

shift ① *v.* alter, move, change, displace, remove ② *n.* turn, spell, stint

shifty *adj.* untrustworthy, devious, treacherous ▷*wily* ★**honest**

shine *v. & n.* glow, gleam, glitter, sparkle, flash

ship ① *n.* boat, barge, craft, vessel ② *v.* export, send, transport *(see page 114)*

shirk *v.* dodge, avoid, shun, evade, slack

shiver *v.* quaver, quiver, shake, shudder ▷*tremble*

shock ① *n.* blow, jolt, clash, collision ② *n.* scare, start, turn ③ *v.* stupefy, daze, stun

shocking *adj.* scandalous, awful, frightful ▷*horrible* ★**agreeable**

shoot *v.* ① fire, discharge, bombard, propel ② *v.* germinate *We grew some beans in a glass jar and watched them germinate,* grow, bud, sprout ③ *n.* bud, twig, sprout CHUTE

shop ① *n.* store, market, emporium ② *v.* buy, market, purchase

shore ① *n.* beach, coast, strand, seashore, seaside ② *v.* prop, support, bolster up, brace

short *adj.* ① brief, concise, condensed ★**long** ② deficient, incomplete, scanty ★**full** ③ sharp, severe, bad-tempered ④ small, puny, squat, diminutive, tiny ★**tall**

shortcoming *n.* defect, fault, flaw, inadequacy, ▷*weakness*

shorten *v.* cut, crop, abbreviate, lessen ▷*diminish* ★**lengthen**

shortened *adj.* abbreviated, abridged, condensed ★**enlarged**

shortly *adj.* presently, soon, before long, directly

shout *n. & v.* cry, scream, roar, shriek, cheer, whoop, bellow

shove *v.* push, jostle, prod, nudge, move, propel ★**pull**

show ① *v.* display, parade, exhibit, flaunt, reveal ★**hide** ② *v.* prove, testify to, demonstrate ③ *v.* explain, teach, instruct ④ *n.* exhibition, display, ceremony, play

shower ① *v.* scatter, spray, sprinkle, rain ② *n.* downpour, cloudburst ③ *n.* barrage, volley, discharge

shred ① *n.* particle, piece, scrap, tatter, fragment ② *v.* tear, rip, strip

shrewd *adj.* profound, deep, discerning ▷*wise* ★**obtuse**

shriek *n. & v.* screech ▷*shout*

shrill *adj.* treble, high-pitched, screeching, ear-piercing

shrink *v.* ① contract, dwindle, shrivel, become smaller ② flinch, cringe, recoil, withdraw

shrivel *v.* wither, contract, wrinkle, decrease, pucker, parch ▷*wilt*

shudder *v.* shake, quake, tremble ▷*quiver*

shuffle *v.* ① mix, jumble, rearrange ② hobble, limp

shun *v.* avoid, elude, ignore, spurn, steer clear of ★**accept**

shut *v.* fasten, close, secure, slam, bar, latch, lock ★**open**

shut up *v.* ① imprison, cage, intern ② be silent, hold one's tongue, be quiet

shy ① *adj.* bashful, diffident, timid, wary, shrinking ★**bold** ② *v.* flinch, quail, recoil

sick *adj.* ① ill, poorly, ailing, unwell, feeble ② weary, fed up, displeased ③ nauseated

side *n.* ① border, edge, flank, margin, half ② party, sect, group, team SIGHED

sift *v.* strain, drain, separate, screen, sieve, riddle

sigh *v.* ① grieve, lament, moan, complain ② wheeze, breathe

sight ① *n.* appearance, spectacle, scene, mirage ② *n.* seeing, perception, visibiity ③ *v.* behold, glimpse, observe CITE, SITE

sign ① *n.* symbol, emblem, mark ② *n.* omen, token ③ *n.* signboard, signpost, placard ④ *v.* endorse, autograph, inscribe

signal ① *n.* beacon *As soon as the ships*

were sighted, beacons were lit all along the coast, sign, flag, indicator ② *adj.* distinguished, impressive, outstanding

significant *adj.* symbolical, meaningful, weighty ▷*important* ★**unimportant**

signify *v.* denote, indicate, suggest, imply ▷*mean*

silence *n.* quiet, hush, peace, tranquility ★**noise**

silent *adj.* hushed, noiseless, soundless, still, mute ▷*quiet* ★**noisy**

silly *adj.* absurd, senseless, stupid, fatuous ▷*foolish* ★**wise**

similar *adj.* resembling, alike, harmonious, common ▷*like* ★**different**

simple *adj.* ① elementary, plain, uncomplicated ▷*easy* ② trusting, open, naive ★**intricate**

simply *adv.* merely, purely, barely, solely, only

sin ① *n.* misdeed, wrong, vice, evil, wickedness ② *v.* err, offend, trespass, stray, do wrong

since ① *conj.* because, as, for, considering ② *prep.* subsequently, after

sincere *adj.* true, unaffected, frank, open, truthful ▷*genuine* ★**insincere**

sing *v.* vocalize, warble, yodel, trill, croon, chant, carol, hum, chirp

singe *v.* scorch, burn, scald, sear, char

singer *n.* vocalist, minstrel, songster, chorister, crooner

single *adj.* ① one, only, sole ② solitary, alone, separate ③ unmarried, celibate *The priests of the Roman Catholic Church are celibate*

singular *adj.* odd, peculiar, curious, surprising ▷*unusual* ★**ordinary**

sinister *adj.* menacing, threatening, unlucky, disastrous ▷*evil* ★**harmless**

sink ① *v.* drop, dip, descend, decline ▷*fall* ★**rise** ② *n.* basin, drain

sit *v.* perch, seat, squat, roost, rest, settle

site *n.* spot, plot, locality, place, station, post ▷*situation* CITE, SIGHT

situation *n.* ① position, location, place, site, whereabouts, standpoint ② predicament,

Singers

Alto
Baritone
Bass
Basso profundo
Cantor
Chorister
Contrabass
Contralto
Countertenor
Mezzo-soprano
Prima donna
Soprano
Tenor
Treble
Vocalist

plight, state

size *n.* ① dimensions, proportions, measurement ② magnitude, bulk, volume, weight SIGHS

skeptical *adj.* doubtful, unbelieving, incredulous ▷*dubious* ★**convinced**

sketch ① *n.* drawing, picture, cartoon ② *n.* draft, blueprint, outline ③ *v.* draw, portray, depict, outline

skillful *adj.* adroit, able, adept, dexterous, expert, competent ▷*clever* ★**clumsy**

skill *n.* ability, expertness, knack, facility ▷*talent*

skim *v.* brush, touch, graze, float, glide

skimp *v.* stint, scrimp, economize, scrape

skin *n.* peel, rind, hide, husk, pelt

skinny *adj.* thin, lean, scraggy, weedy ★**fat**

skip *v.* ① jump, hop, dance, caper ② pass over, miss, disregard, omit

skirmish *n. & v.* scuffle, fight, affray, scrap, combat, clash

skirt ① *n.* petticoat, kilt ② *n.* border, hem, edge, margin ③ *v.* border, flank, evade, avoid

skulk *v.* lurk, hide, cower, slink, sneak

slab *n.* board, stone, boulder, piece, chunk

slack *adj.* ① limp, flabby, loose, relaxed ★**tight** ② lazy, sluggish ▷*idle* ★**busy**

slander *v.* libel, malign, accuse, abuse ▷*defame* ★**praise**

slant ① *v. & n.* incline, angle, cant ▷*slope*

slap *v.* smack, whack, strike, hit, spank

slash *v. & n.* cut, slit, gash, hack, rip

slaughter *v.* slay, butcher, massacre ▷*kill*

slave ① *n.* bondsman, bondswoman, serf, vassal, drudge, captive ② *v.* drudge, toil, labor, grind

slavery *n.* bondage, enslavement, serfdom, servility, drudgery, captivity ★**freedom**

slay *v.* murder, massacre ▷*kill* SLEIGH

sleek *adj.* shiny, smooth, glossy, slick

sleep *v. & n.* snooze, nap, doze, drowse, repose, slumber

slender *adj.* ① narrow, thin, fine, slight ▷*slim* ★**thick** ② trivial, inadequate, meager

slice ① *v.* shred, shave, cut, strip, segment ② *n.* segment, piece, cut, slab

slick *adj.* ① shiny, smooth ▷*sleek* ② glib, suave, plausible

slide *v.* slip, slither, glide, skim, skate

slight ① *adj.* delicate, tender ▷*slender* ② *adj.* small, little, meager, trifling, trivial ★**significant** ③ *n. & v.* snub, insult, disdain

slim *adj.* fine, slight ▷*slender* ★**fat**

slime *n.* mire, ooze, mud, filth

sling ① *v.* hurl, toss, throw ② *n.* loop, bandage, strap, support

slink *v.* prowl, creep, sidle, sneak ▷*skulk*

slip ① *v.* slide, slither, glide ② *v.* fall, lurch, drop, slip over ③ *v. & n.* blunder, slip up

slippery *adj.* ① smooth, glassy ② tricky, untrustworthy, cunning ▷*shifty* ★**trustworthy**

slit *v.* gash, cut, rip ▷*slash*

slogan *n.* motto, catchword, war cry, saying

slope ① *n.* slant, grade, gradient, incline, ascent, descent, rise ② *v.* lean, incline, descend, ascend

sloppy *adj.* ① careless, slipshod, inattentive ▷*slovenly* ② dowdy, messy, tacky ③ dingy, dirty

slot *n.* recess, opening, hole, groove

slovenly *adj.* slipshod, careless, negligent, disorderly, sloppy, untidy, dowdy

slow ① *adj.* inactive, tardy, late, slack, leisurely ▷*sluggish* ★**fast** ② *v.* slow down, slacken, lose speed, relax ★**accelerate** SLOE

sluggish *adj.* slothful, lazy, inactive,

languid, indolent, lifeless ▷*idle* ★**brisk**

slumber *v.* snooze, doze ▷*sleep* ★**awaken**

sly *adj.* cunning, tricky, furtive, sneaky, artful ▷*wily* ★**frank**

smack *v.* slap, strike, spank ▷*hit*

small *adj.* ① minute, tiny, slight, diminutive ▷*little* ★**large** ② trivial, petty, feeble, paltry, inferior

smart ① *adj.* alert, bright ▷*intelligent* ② *adj.* elegant, neat, spruce, dressy ★**dull** ③ *v.* sting, burn, throb ▷*ache*

smash *v.* break, hit, destroy, wreck, demolish

smear *v.* plaster, daub, coat, varnish, cover, spread, smudge

smell *n.* aroma, fragrance, scent, perfume, stink, stench, odor, tang

smile *v.* grin, simper, smirk, beam ▷*laugh*

smoke ① *n.* vapor, mist, gas ② *v.* fume, reek, whiff, smolder, vent

smooth ① *adj.* level, even, flat, plain, sleek ★**rough** ② *v.* flatten, level, press

smother *v.* choke, throttle, stifle, restrain

smudge *n. & v.* mark, smear, blur, stain, blight

smug *adj.* self-satisfied, content, complacent, conceited

smut *n.* dirt, smudge, blot, spot, smear

snack *n.* lunch, repast, morsel, bite

snag *n.* catch, complication, drawback, hitch

snap *v.* ① break, crack, snip ② snarl, growl

snare ① *v.* trap, catch, seize, net ② *n.* trap, noose, pitfall

snatch *v.* seize, grab, clutch, grip, take, pluck, grasp

sneak ① *v.* slink, prowl, crouch ▷*skulk* ② *n.* wretch, coward, informer

sneer *v.* jeer, scoff, gibe, scorn, ridicule, taunt

sniff *v.* smell, breathe in, inhale, scent

snivel *v.* weep, cry, blub, sniffle

snobbish *adj.* condescending, snooty, lofty, patronizing, stuck-up

snoop *v.* pry, eavesdrop, peep, peek, sneak

snooze *v.* doze, nap, slumber ▷*sleep*

snub *v.* slight, slur, spurn, cut ▷*humiliate*

snug *adj.* cozy, sheltered, secure, safe,

restful ▷*comfortable*

so *adv.* accordingly, thus, therefore, likewise SEW, SOW

soak *v.* moisten, wet, douse, saturate, steep

soar *v.* glide, fly, rise, hover, tower SORE

sob *v.* lament, cry, sigh ▷*weep*

sober *adj.* temperate, abstemious *Uncle Arthur was very abstemious and never drank anything alcoholic,* calm, composed, serious, somber ★**excited**

sociable *adj.* companionable, affable, friendly, genial ★**withdrawn**

social *adj.* neighborly, civic, public ② convivial ▷*sociable*

soft *adj.* ① pliable, plastic, flexible, supple ★**hard** ② kind, gentle, mild ▷*tender* ★**harsh** ③ low, faint, quiet ★**loud**

soften *v.* ① melt, dissolve, mellow ★**solidify** ② moderate, diminish, quell

soil ① *n.* earth, dirt, mold ② *v.* foul, dirty, sully, taint

sole *adj.* only, single, lone, one SOUL

solemn *adj.* ① grim, serious ▷*somber* ② impressive, stately, sedate ★**frivolous**

solid *adj.* ① steady, firm, stable, sturdy ② dense, compact, hard ★**soft**

solidify *v.* congeal, harden, clot, cake, set ★**soften**

solitary *adj.* alone, lonely, remote, separate, only

solution *n.* ① blend, mixture, brew, fluid ② answer, explanation

solve *v.* unravel, untangle, elucidate ▷*explain* ★**complicate**

somber *adj.* dark, serious, solemn, grim, gloomy, funereal ★**bright**

some *adj.* any, more or less, about, several SUM

sometimes *adv.* at times, from time to time, occasionally

somewhat *adv.* in part, a little, not much

song *n.* air, tune, carol, ballad, ode, ditty *The new pop song was based on an old sailors' ditty*

soon *adv.* presently, shortly, before long

soothe *v.* pacify, appease, mollify, ease, lull, comfort ★**irritate**

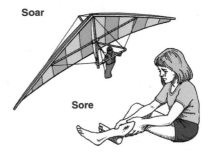

Soar

Sore

sordid *adj.* shabby, miserable, dirty, base ▷*squalid*

sore ① *adj.* tender, aching, painful, inflamed ② *adj.* annoyed, upset, grieved ③ *n.* ulcer, boil, carbuncle SOAR

sorrow ① *n.* grief, woe, remorse, anguish ★**joy** ② *v.* mourn, grieve, lament ★**rejoice**

sorrowful *adj.* sad, disconsolate, mournful, dejected ★**joyful**

sorry *adj.* ① pained, grieved, hurt, dejected, doleful ★**glad** ② wretched, mean, poor, shabby ★**delighted**

sort ① *n.* kind, type, variety, group, class ② *v.* sift, arrange, catalog, classify

soul *n.* spirit, substance, mind, vitality, fire, essence SOLE

sound ① *n.* noise, din, tone ★**silence** ② *v.* blare, blast *We were startled by a blast from the trumpets,* blow ③ *adj.* hearty, virile, whole, perfect ▷*healthy* ★**unfit**

sour *adj.* ① tart, rancid, bitter, acid ★**sweet** ② morose, peevish ▷*harsh* ★**genial**

source *n.* origin, spring, fount, cause, beginning

souvenir *n.* token, memento, keepsake, reminder, relic

sow ① *n.* (rhymes with *how*) female pig ② *v.* (rhymes with *mow*) *v.* plant, scatter, strew SEW, SO

space *n.* ① extent, expanse, capacity, room, accommodation ② the universe, the heavens, firmament

spacious *adj.* roomy, extensive, commodious, broad, wide ★**restricted**

span ① *n.* stretch, reach, extent, length ② *v.*

cross, bridge, link, connect

spare ① *adj.* extra, reserve, surplus ② *adj.* bare, meager, poor, scanty ▷*sparse* ③ *v.* afford, preserve, give, allow

sparkle *v.* glitter, glow, gleam, glint, twinkle

sparse *adj.* scanty, thin ▷*meager* ★**dense**

spate *n.* flood, flow, deluge, rush, torrent

speak *v.* say, utter, talk, pronounce, lecture, express

spear *n.* pike, javelin, lance

special *adj.* distinct, different, unique, individual ▷*particular* ★**common**

species *n.* breed, kind, sort, class, family

specific *adj.* definite, exact, precise ▷*special*

specimen *n.* sample, example, type, model, pattern

speck *n.* dot, speckle, spot, particle

spectacle *n.* sight, scene, exhibition, presentation ▷*display*

spectacles *n.* glasses, eyeglasses

spectacular *adj.* wonderful, fabulous, surprising ▷*marvelous*

spectator *n.* onlooker, witness, observer

speech *n.* ① talk, tongue *The people spoke a strange tongue we had never heard,* language ② address, lecture

speed *n.* velocity, rapidity, dispatch, pace, tempo *The tempo of life in the quiet seaside town was much too slow for us*

speedy *adj.* swift, rapid, fleet, quick, lively ▷*fast* ★**slow**

spell ① *n.* charm, magic, witchcraft ② *n.* period, term, space, time ③ *v.* form words, write out

spend *v.* ① expend, lay out, lavish, pay, disburse ② exhaust, use up

spendthrift *n.* wastrel, squanderer, prodigal ★**miser**

sphere *n.* ① globe, ball, orb, planet ② realm, orbit, domain, field

spice *n.* seasoning, flavoring, zest, relish, savor

spill *v.* pour, stream, run, overflow, spurt, upset

spin *v.* revolve, rotate, turn, whirl, make thread

spine *n.* backbone, needle, quill *The porcupine is covered in sharp quills,* ridge

spirit *n.* ① essence, substance, nature, character ② soul, air, breath ③ vigor, energy, courage ④ phantom, specter, ghost

spiritual *adj.* ① religious, divine, unworldly, holy ② pure, immaterial

spite ① *n.* malice, rancor, hostility, hatred ② *v.* grudge, annoy, offend, injure

spiteful *adj.* vicious, malicious, vindictive ▷*hateful* ★**kind**

splash *v.* wet, spatter, shower, sprinkle

splendid *adj.* grand, brilliant, magnificent, showy, glorious ▷*sumptuous* ★**ordinary**

splendor *n.* glory, pageantry, brilliance ▷*pomp*

split *v.* cleave, sever *Our family quarreled with our cousins and severed relationships for years,* crack, snap, splinter

spoil *v.* ① hurt, injure, harm ② deface, disfigure, destroy ③ rot, decompose, putrefy, decay

spoiled *adj.* decayed, rotten, broken up, corroded

spontaneous *adj.* natural, impulsive, self-generated, voluntary

spoof *n.* ① hoax, joke, bluff, prank, satire ② quip, jest, wisecrack

sport ① *n.* game, amusement, fun, athletics, recreation ② *v.* play, frolic, gambol, romp

Spices

Ginger

Cinnamon

Nutmeg

Pepper

Cloves

Mace

spot ① *n.* dot, speck, mark, stain, blemish ② *v.* espy, notice, recognize, distinguish

spotless *adj.* pure, clean, unstained, faultless, perfect

sprawl *v.* recline, stretch, extend, lie ▷*lounge*

spray *v.* sprinkle, squirt, splash, shower

spread *v.* ① scatter, strew, sow, circulate ② extend, stretch, expand, open

sprightly *adj.* lively, vivacious, cheerful, agile ▷*brisk* ★**sluggish**

spur *v.* arouse, drive, urge, incite

spurious *adj.* fake, counterfeit, false ▷*bogus* ★**genuine**

spurn *v.* reject, scorn, disdain, disregard ▷*snub* ★**respect**

spurt *v.* ① stream, squirt, emerge, gush ② hurry, hasten, rush

spy ① *n.* agent, detective, observer, snooper, scout ② *v.* see, glimpse, pry, peek, spot

squabble ① *n. & v.* quarrel, clash, fight, row ▷*dispute*

squad *n.* group, company, troop, force, band, team

squalid *adj.* foul, dirty, untended, poverty-stricken ▷*sordid* ★**clean**

squall ① *n.* blast, gust, blow, tempest ② *v.* blubber, cry, bawl, howl

squander *v.* misspend, waste, fritter, lavish

squash *v.* ① mash, crush, squelch, pound ② quell, suppress, humiliate

squat ① *adj.* dumpy, stocky, tubby, plump ② *v.* crouch, sit, roost, perch

squeal *v.* squawk, squeak, cheep, grunt, cry

squeamish *adj.* fastidious, delicate, finicky, nauseous

squeeze *v.* compress, press, constrict, force, pinch

squirm *v.* wriggle, fidget, flounder, twist ▷*writhe*

squirt *v.* spray, splash ▷*spurt*

stab *v. & n.* cut, jab, puncture, wound, thrust

stable ① *adj.* firm, steady, solid, constant, durable, lasting ★**unstable** ② *n.* barn, cowshed, shed, stall

stack ① *n.* pile, pack, bundle, sheaf, heap ② *v.* assemble, pile up, amass

staff *n.* ① stick, cane, pole, rod ② team, workers, force, personnel

stage ① *n.* platform, dais, scaffold, podium *The famous conductor stood on the podium and raised his baton,* arena ② *n.* step, degree, position ③ *v.* perform, produce, present, put on

stagger *v.* reel, totter, waver, lurch

stagnant *adj.* motionless, inactive, still, quiet, sluggish

staid *adj.* serious, steady, earnest, sober, demure ▷*sedate* ★**frivolous** STAYED

stain ① *n.* blemish, blur, spot, blot ② *n.* disgrace, shame ③ *v.* tarnish, sully, blemish, defile

stair *n.* step, rung, spoke, footrest STARE

stake ① *n.* stick, stave, paling, spike, pole ▷*staff* ② *n.* bet, claim, wager, involvement ③ *v.* prop, secure, support STEAK

stale *adj.* ① musty, old, tasteless, faded ② common, trite, banal, flat ★**fresh**

stalk *v.* ① hunt, chase, follow, pursue, shadow ② swagger, strut, stride, parade

stall ① *v.* tarry, delay, hedge, obstruct, hamper ★**advance** ② *n.* compartment, booth, stand, bay

stalwart *adj.* rugged, sturdy, stout, lusty ▷*valiant* ★**timid**

stamina *n.* endurance, vitality, strength, power, energy ★**weakness**

stammer *v.* stutter, falter, hesitate, stumble

stamp ① *v.* print, imprint, mark, impress ② *n.* impression, mark, print, brand ③ *n.* kind, make, genus, cast ④ *n.* seal, sticker

stand ① *n.* board, counter, table, platform ▷*stall* ② *v.* rest, put, locate, place ③ *v.* tolerate, put up with, abide, endure ★**oppose** ④ *v.* arise, get up, be erect ★**sit**

standard ① *adj.* normal, regular, uniform ② *n.* pattern, criterion, norm ③ *n.* flag, banner, ensign

staple *adj.* main, principal, important, leading

stare *v.* gaze, gape, look, peer STAIR

stark *adj.* severe, plain, downright, bare, absolute

start ① *v.* commence, begin, found, initiate

② *v.* depart, set out, leave ③ *v.* startle, jump, wince ④ *n.* beginning, commencement ⑤ *n.* shock, scare, fit

startle *v.* frighten, alarm, scare, surprise ▷*start*

starve *v.* be hungry, famish, want

state ① *n.* condition, situation, position ② *n.* country, nation, commonwealth ③ *v.* declare, say, express, utter ▷*speak*

stately *adj.* imposing, grand, dignified ▷*magnificent* ★**commonplace**

statement *n.* ① declaration, utterance, remark, motto ② bill, account, invoice

station ① *n.* post, spot, site, position, terminal ② *v.* park, place, put, establish *We got there early to establish our place in the line*

stationary *adj.* still, unmoving, standing, fixed ★**mobile** STATIONERY

stationery *n.* paper, envelopes, ink, pens, pencils STATIONARY

statue *n.* carving, bust, figure

staunch *adj.* constant, faithful, true, firm

Stationery

Stationary

▷*loyal* ★**unfaithful**

stay ① *v.* endure, last, remain, stand, linger ② *v.* check, curb, prevent ③ *n.* halt, wait ▷*stop*

steady ① *adj.* firm, fixed, established, constant ▷*staunch* ★**uncertain** ② *v.* brace, stabilize, stiffen

steal *v.* ① thieve, pilfer, filch, swipe ▷*rob* ② slink, flit, creep ▷*prowl* STEEL

stealthy *adj.* furtive, sneaky, sly, secret ▷*underhanded* ★**open**

steep ① *adj.* sheer, sharp, hilly, precipitous ② *v.* bathe, soak, souse, submerge

steer *v.* guide, direct, pilot, control

stem ① *n.* stalk, shoot, stock, trunk ② *v.* arise from, flow from ③ *v.* check, resist, restrain

step ① *n.* pace, tread, stride, gait ② *n.* action, method, deed ③ *v.* walk, skip, trip, pace STEPPE

sterile *adj.* ① barren, unfertile, arid ② sanitary, disinfected

stern ① *adj.* strict, severe, harsh, grim ▷*austere* ★**mild** ② *n.* aft end, rear, poop *The name of the ship was displayed in large letters on the poop*

stew *v.* ① cook, simmer, boil ② worry, fuss

stick ① *n.* stave, pole, rod, cane, staff ② *v.* adhere, cling, cleave, glue, paste, seal

sticky *adj.* gluey, gummy, adhesive

stick out *v.* project, bulge, extrude ▷*jut* ★**recede**

stiff *adj.* ① inflexible, firm, stable, unyielding ▷*rigid* ★**flexible** ② formal, stilted, prim, precise ★**yielding**

stifle *v.* suffocate, throttle, gag, muzzle ▷*smother*

stigma *n.* ① blot, blur, scar ▷*blemish* ② disgrace, dishonor ▷*shame* ★**credit**

still ① *adj.* fixed, stable, static ② *adj.* calm, quiet, serene, tranquil, noiseless, hushed ▷*peaceful* ★**agitated** ③ *v.* quiet, hush, muffle ▷*calm* ★**agitate**

stimulate *v.* inspire, provoke, arouse, motivate ▷*excite* ★**discourage**

sting *v.* prick, wound, pain, hurt, injure

stingy *adj.* miserly, tightfisted, selfish,

niggardly ▷ *tight* ★**generous**

stink v. smell, whiff, reek

stint ① n. job, task, chore ② n. turn, spell, share, quota ③ v. limit, stop, scrimp, restrict ★**squander**

stir ① v. move, excite, spur, agitate ▷ *stimulate* ② v. whisk, mix, blend ③ v. waken, arouse ★**calm** ④ n. flurry, fuss, uproar

stock ① adj. standard, regular, established, normal ② n. reserve, hoard, supply ③ v. provide, supply, equip, hoard

stocky adj. thickset, chunky, sturdy, pudgy ▷ *squat* ★**willowy**

stodgy adj. dull, heavy, tedious, boring

stolid adj. stupid, dull, mindless, unintelligent ▷ *stodgy* ★**quick**

stoop v. bend, crouch, kneel, bow

stop ① v. cease, desist, end, terminate, halt ★**start** ② v. prevent, forestall, avoid ③ v. arrest, hold, fix ④ n. pause, end, cessation *A cessation of hostilities came into force after the peace agreement*

store ① v. put by, reserve, hoard, save ★**use** ② n. stock, supply, reserve ③ n. market, shop, emporium

story n. ① yarn, tale, narrative, account, anecdote ② untruth, lie, fib ③ floor, landing, level, flight, deck

storm ① n. tempest, gale, cyclone, hurricane, tornado ★**calm** ② n. turmoil, upheaval, attack ③ v. rage, rant, fume, attack

stout adj. ① sturdy, tough, robust ▷ *strong* ★**weak** ② fat, corpulent ▷ *plump* ★**thin**

stow v. deposit, store ▷ *pack*

straight adj. ① right, undeviating, unswerving ▷ *direct* ② frank, candid, truthful ▷ *honest* ★**crooked** STRAIT

straightforward adj. open, outspoken, reliable, trustworthy ★**devious**

strain ① n. tension, fatigue, exertion ▷ *stress* ★**relaxation** ② n. melody, tune, air ③ v. struggle, labor ▷ *toil* ★**relax** ④ v. wrench, injure ⑤ v. filter, sift, separate

strait n. channel, sound, narrows STRAIGHT

straitlaced adj. prim, prudish, strict, puritanical *My family was rather puritanical and we were not allowed to play any games on Sundays*

strand ① n. coast, beach, shore ② n. hair, fiber, tress, lock ③ v. desert, maroon, abandon

strange adj. ① unusual, incredible, extraordinary, curious ▷ *odd* ★**commonplace** ② foreign, alien, remote

stranger n. outsider, foreigner, visitor, newcomer ▷ *alien* ★**acquaintance**

strangle v. constrict, choke, garrote, throttle

strap n. belt, harness, thong, leash

stray v. ① wander, deviate, depart, rove ② sin, err, do wrong

streak n. stroke, stripe, band, line, bar, strip

stream ① n. current, course, drift, brook, creek, run ② v. flow, gush, spurt, pour

strength n. ① power, force, might ▷ *energy* ② boldness, nerve, intensity ★**weakness**

strenuous adj. laborious, resolute, determined ▷ *earnest* ★**weak**

stress ① n. tension, force, effort ▷ *strain* ② n. accent, emphasis ③ v. emphasize, accentuate

stretch v. expand, reach ▷ *extend* ★**shorten**

strict adj. ① severe, rigorous, rigid, austere ▷ *stern* ★**lenient** ② scrupulous, punctilious, accurate ▷ *precise* ★**inaccurate**

stride n. & v. walk, step, tread, parade, march

strife n. struggle, contest, quarrel, friction ▷ *conflict* ★**peace**

strike ① v. beat, smite, collide, knock ▷ *thump* ② v. discover, unearth ③ n. assault, thrust, attack ④ n. walkout, boycott

striking adj. eye-catching, wonderful ▷ *extraordinary* ★**commonplace**

strip ① v. take off, peel, skin, shave, remove ② n. ribbon, stroke, streak, line

stripe n. streak, band, bar, chevron *Soldiers in the army have chevrons on their sleeves to indicate their rank,* rule ▷ *strip*

strive v. endeavor, attempt, aim, compete

▷*try* ★**yield**

stroke ① *n.* shock, blow, knock, thump ② *n.* seizure, fit, convulsion ③ *v.* pat, rub, caress, smooth, comfort

stroll *v. & n.* walk, promenade, saunter, tramp, ramble

strong *adj.* ① powerful, vigorous, hardy, muscular ▷*robust* ② solid, secure, fortified ★**weak** ③ potent, hot, spicy ▷*pungent*

structure *n.* ① building, edifice, erection ② construction, organization, composition

struggle ① *v.* endeavor, labor, battle, wrestle ★**yield** ② *n.* conflict, battle ▷*fight* ③ *n.* distress, trouble ▷*effort*

strut ① *n.* support, mainstay, prop ② *v.* parade, prance, swagger

stubborn *adj.* ① dogged, persistent, tenacious ② pigheaded, perverse, willful ▷*obstinate* ★**docile**

stuck-up *adj.* vain, conceited ▷*snobbish* ★**modest**

studious *adj.* scholarly, learned, thoughtful ▷*diligent* ★**thoughtless**

study ① *v.* read, peruse, research, scrutinize, examine, train ▷*learn* ② *n.* learning, meditation, thought, contemplation ▷*research*

stuff ① *v.* fill, congest, pack, crowd ② *n.* textile, fabric, material, goods

stumble *v.* ① stagger, lurch, fall ▷*trip* ② stammer, falter ▷*stutter*

stump ① *v.* perplex, mystify, confuse ▷*bewilder* ② *n.* stub, tip, log, root

stun *v.* knock out, overpower, stupefy, dumbfound ▷*confound*

stunt *n.* deed, feat, achievement, performance ▷*exploit*

stupefy *v.* daze, muddle, bewilder, astonish, flabbergast ▷*shock* ★**revive**

stupendous *adj.* astounding, amazing, overwhelming ▷*wonderful* ★**ordinary**

stupid *adj.* simple, stolid, dull, senseless ▷*foolish* ★**clever**

stupidity *n.* inanity, silliness, feebleness, foolishness ★**brilliance**

sturdy *adj.* rugged, stalwart, tough, strapping ▷*hardy* ★**weak**

stutter *v.* stumble, falter ▷*stammer*

style ① *n.* mode, vogue, fashion, way, manner, form ② *n.* name, call, christen STILE

suave *adj.* agreeable, elegant, polite, pleasant, sophisticated *After living in the city for many years, my sister had developed very sophisticated tastes*

subdue *v.* suppress, soften, tame, tone down, moderate, mellow ▷*repress*

subject ① *n.* (*sub*-ject) matter, topic, theme ② *n.* subordinate, dependant ③ *adj.* dependent, subordinate, liable ④ *v.* (sub-*ject*) rule over, subdue, subjugate

submerge *v.* plunge, immerse, sink ★**raise**

submissive *adj.* yielding, servile, meek ▷*obedient* ★**obstinate**

submit *v.* ① yield, give in, accede, surrender, hand over ② offer, tender, present

subordinate *adj.* junior, minor, subject, dependent, secondary ★**superior**

subscribe *v.* sign, enroll, register, agree, assent

subsequent *adj.* later, following, succeeding, after ★**former**

subside *v.* decline, peter out, decrease,

Structures

Molecular

Rope bridge

Spiderweb

diminish, wane *I used to go mountaineering but my interest waned after some years* ▷*abate* ★**rise**

substance *n.* ① matter, object, stuff, material ② essence, kernel, meaning ▷*gist*

substantial *adj.* ① steady, sturdy, firm ▷*stable* ② ample, large, real, solid ★**imaginary**

substitute ① *n.* alternative, makeshift, stopgap ② *v.* swap, change, replace, duplicate

subtle *adj.* ① shrewd, fine, delicate ② clever, crafty, perceptive

subtract *v.* take away, withdraw, deduct, remove ★**add**

succeed *v.* ① flourish, prosper, thrive, triumph ★**fail** ② follow, inherit, replace ★**precede**

success *n.* prosperity, triumph, victory, achievement ★**failure**

successful *adj.* victorious, prosperous, fortunate, thriving ★**unlucky**

suck *v.* inhale, take in, draw in, imbibe

sudden *adj.* unexpected, abrupt, impulsive, swift, prompt ★**gradual**

suffer *v.* ① bear, endure, put up with ② encounter, undergo ▷*sustain*

sufficient *adj.* adequate, ample, plenty ▷*enough* ★**deficient**

suffocate *v.* smother, choke ▷*stifle*

suggest *v.* recommend, advise, submit, hint, intimate

suit ① *v.* fulfill, gratify, please, suffice, accommodate, befit ② *n.* ensemble, outfit, costume

suitable *adj.* fitting, appropriate, correct, proper, becoming ★**unsuitable**

suite *n.* ① set, series, succession ② apartment, rooms

sulk *v.* pout, grouch, brood, mope

sulky *adj.* glum, morose, churlish, moody ▷*sullen* ★**genial**

sullen *adj.* gloomy, heavy, dismal, cheerless ▷*sulky* ★**cheerful**

sum *n.* amount, total, whole, entirety SOME

summary *n.* synopsis, précis, abstract, summing-up, outline, analysis

summit *n.* peak, pinnacle, top, apex, zenith ★**base**

summon *v.* call, beckon, command, invite, muster ★**dismiss**

sumptuous *adj.* profuse, costly, gorgeous, splendid ▷*lavish* ★**frugal**

sundry *adj.* different, separate, several ▷*various*

sunny *adj.* bright, cheerful, light, clear ▷*radiant* ★**gloomy**

superb *adj.* magnificent, stately, gorgeous ▷*grand* ★**commonplace**

supercilious *adj.* contemptuous, haughty, arrogant ▷*snobbish* ★**modest**

superficial *adj.* slight, imperfect, shallow, skin-deep ▷*trivial* ★**profound**

superfluous *adj.* in excess, inessential, spare ▷*surplus* ★**essential**

superior *adj.* ① better, greater, higher, loftier ▷*excellent* ② eminent, conspicuous, principal ★**inferior**

supersede *v.* succeed, replace, displace, suspend, usurp *The president's authority was usurped by the military* ★**continue**

supervise *v.* superintend, control, manage ▷*direct*

supple *adj.* lithe, pliable, flexible, bending

supplement ① *n.* addition, complement, sequel, postscript ② *v.* supply, add, fill

supply ① *v.* provide, furnish, yield, contribute, purvey ★**retain** ② *n.* hoard, reserve ▷*stock*

support ① *v.* uphold, bear, sustain, maintain, help ▷*favor* ★**oppose** ② *v.* hold up, prop, strut, brace ③ *v.* endure, tolerate, suffer ④ *n.* maintenance, upkeep

suppose *v.* assume, presume, believe, imagine, imply ▷*consider*

suppress *v.* restrain, extinguish, destroy, stop ▷*quell* ★**incite**

supreme *adj.* dominant, highest, greatest, maximum ★**lowly**

sure *adj.* ① certain, positive, definite ② secure, steady, safe ③ permanent, abiding, enduring ★**uncertain**

surface *n.* ① area, expanse, stretch ② outside, exterior, covering ★**interior**

surge ① *v.* swell, rise, heave, rush ② *n.* ripple, billow, wave SERGE

surly *adj.* morose, cross, testy, touchy, crusty ▷*sullen* ★**affable**

surmise *v.* guess, speculate, conjecture, suspect ▷*presume* ★**know**

surpass *v.* eclipse, outdo, outstrip, excel, exceed ▷*beat*

surplus *n.* excess, remainder, balance, residue ★**shortcoming**

surprise ① *v.* startle, astonish, amaze ▷*astound* ② *n.* amazement, astonishment ▷*wonder*

surrender *v.* quit, give up, yield, submit ▷*relinquish*

surround *v.* enclose, encircle, encompass

survey ① *v.* (sur-*vey*) look at, examine, scrutinize ▷*study* ② *v.* estimate, measure ③ *n.* (*sur*-vey) assessment, appraisal

survive *v.* live, exist, continue, outlast, abide ★**surrender**

susceptible *adj.* sensitive, impressionable, inclined, capable ★**insensitive**

suspect ① *v.* (sus-*pect*) disbelieve, doubt, distrust ② *adj.* (*sus*-pect) unbelievable, questionable, dubious

suspend *v.* ① interrupt, delay, arrest, adjourn, postpone ▷*stop* ★**continue** ② expel, throw out ③ swing, dangle ▷*hang* ★**drop**

suspense *n.* anticipation, waiting, abeyance *The club couldn't decide on a new leader, so the matter was left in abeyance,* stoppage, uncertainty ▷*tension* ★**decision**

suspicious *adj.* incredulous, skeptical, doubtful, suspecting ★**trustful**

sustain *v.* ① uphold, keep, maintain, provide for ② suffer, undergo, experience ③ nourish, nurture, feed

swagger *v.* ① parade, prance ▷*strut* ② brag, bluster ▷*boast*

swallow ① *v.* absorb, consume, eat, digest, devour, drink ▷*gulp* ② *n.* mouthful, gulp ③ *n.* bird

swamp ① *n.* fen, bog, marsh, morass, quagmire ② *v.* submerge, submerse, overflow, deluge ▷*drench*

swap *v.* exchange, switch, trade, barter

swarm ① *n.* throng, horde, shoal, flock, crowd ② *v.* teem, abound, jam, mass, crowd, cluster

swarthy *adj.* dusky, dark, brown, tawny

sway ① *v.* swing, rock, totter, lean, incline ▷*waver* ② *n.* rule, authority, control ▷*influence*

swear *v.* ① promise, warrant, affirm, attest ② curse, damn, blaspheme

sweat *v.* perspire, ooze, leak, exude, swelter *During that time of the year it was very hot and we sweltered all day*

sweep *v.* brush, scrub, clean, scour

sweet *adj.* ① sugary, syrupy, luscious ★**sour** ② melodic, tuneful, musical, mellow ★**discordant** ③ gentle, tender, mild, lovable ★**unpleasant** ④ fragrant, pure, clean, fresh, wholesome, aromatic ★**putrid**

swell *v.* expand, distend, inflate, bulge ▷*enlarge* ★**contract**

swerve *v.* veer, deviate, skid, skew, lurch ▷*waver*

swift *adj.* speedy, rapid, quick ▷*fast* ★**slow**

swill ① *v.* swig, consume, imbibe, tipple ▷*gulp* ② *n.* refuse, garbage, waste

swim *v.* bathe, wade, paddle, float, glide

swindle ① *n.* trick, fraud, blackmail, racket ② *v.* hoodwink, deceive, hoax, dupe, rip off ▷*cheat*

swine *n.* pig, boar, sow, porker, hog

swing ① *v.* hang, suspend, dangle, lurch, reel ② *n.* tempo, time

switch ① *v.* change, exchange, alter, trade, substitute, swap ② *n.* lever, pedal, control, button

swivel *v.* pivot, spin, rotate, revolve, turn

swoop *v.* pounce, descend, stoop, plummet, plunge

sword *n.* rapier, blade, foil, épée, cutlass, saber, steel SOARED

symbol *n.* character, figure, numeral, letter, sign, token, emblem CYMBAL

sympathetic *adj.* thoughtful, understanding, kind, affectionate ★**indifferent**

system *n.* ① method, plan, order, scheme, arrangement, routine ② network, organization: *a hierarchical system*

T t

table *n.* ① board, stand, slab, tablet, counter, stall ② list, catalog, schedule, index, statement

tablet *n.* ① pill, capsule, lozenge ② board, table, pad

tack ① *n.* thumbtack, nail, pin, brad ② *n.* aim, direction, set ③ *v.* affix, fasten, join, stitch

tackle ① *n.* outfit, gear, rig, harness ② *v.* grasp, halt, intercept, seize ③ *v.* deal with *I dealt with the problem of the school fund shortage,* undertake, set about

tact *n.* diplomacy, judgment, skill, discretion *If you want your secret to be kept, you had better not rely on his discretion* TACKED

tactful *adj.* diplomatic, wise, subtle, prudent ▷*discreet* ★**tactless**

tactics *n.* strategy, campaign, method, procedure

tactless *adj.* inconsiderate, gauche, clumsy, boorish ▷*inept* ★**tactful**

tag *n.* label, ticket, docket, slip, sticker

taint *v.* sully, tarnish, infect, stain, soil, contaminate ▷*defile* ★**purify**

take *v.* ① grasp, grab, seize, procure ② receive, accept, obtain ③ carry, convey, lead, conduct ④ interpret, understand

take place *v.* occur, happen, befall *Our parents were concerned about what might befall us when we left school*

tale *n.* story, fable, anecdote, yarn, narrative TAIL

talent *n.* knack, genius, gift, ability, aptitude ★**stupidity**

talk ① *v.* speak, say, utter, gossip ② *v.* describe, comment on, talk about ③ *n.* speech, chatter, conversation ④ *n.* lecture, speech, discourse

tall *adj.* lanky, lofty, big, high, towering, giant ★**short**

tally *v.* ① count, enumerate, compute ② agree, conform, coincide ★**disagree**

tame ① *adj.* domesticated, gentle, mild, docile *Although we found it in the woods, the kitten was docile* ★**savage** ② *adj.* flat, dull, boring, tedious ③ *v.* train, discipline, domesticate

Tame

Although we found it in the woods, the kitten was docile

tamper with *v.* meddle, interfere, damage, tinker

tang *n.* smell, scent, aroma, flavor, savor, taste

tangible *adj.* concrete, solid, substantial, real, material ★**spiritual**

tangle *n. & v.* twist, muddle, jumble, knot

tantalize *v.* tease, taunt, thwart, disappoint ▷*frustrate* ★**satisfy**

tantrum *n.* rage, fit, hysterics, storm

tap ① *v.* pat, hit, knock, rap, strike ② *n.* faucet, spout, cock, nozzle, bung

tape *n.* ribbon, filament, braid, strip, riband

taper *v.* dwindle, narrow, contract, decline, wane, narrow ★**widen** TAPIR

tardy *adj.* slow, sluggish, reluctant, slack ▷*late* ★**prompt**

target *n.* goal, aim, ambition, purpose, butt, end, victim

tariff *n.* tax, rate, toll, duty, payment, schedule of fees

tarnish *v.* stain, sully *Mark's reputation at school was sullied after he was accused of stealing,* spot, darken, blemish, rust ★**brighten**

tarry *v.* delay, stall, wait, loiter ▷*linger* ★**hurry**

tart ① *adj.* acid, sour, sharp, pungent ② *n.* pie, quiche, pastry, flan

task *n.* job, stint, chore, assignment, undertaking

taste ① *n.* bite, mouthful, flavor, savor, tang ② *v.* try, sip, sample, relish

tasteful *adj.* artistic, graceful, elegant, smart ▷ *refined* ★**tasteless**

tasteless *adj.* ① flavorless, insipid ② gaudy, inelegant ▷ *vulgar* ★**tasteful**

tasty *adj.* appetizing, piquant, savory ▷ *delicious* ★**disgusting**

tattle *v.* gossip, tittle-tattle, blab, prattle

taunt *v.* jibe, reproach, rebuke, ridicule, scoff at ▷ *sneer* ★**compliment**

taut *adj.* tense, tight, stretched ▷ *rigid* ★**relaxed** TAUGHT

tawdry *adj.* flashy, loud, gaudy, showy ▷ *vulgar* ★**superior**

tax ① *n.* levy, duty, impost, tithe, toll ② *v.* load, oppress, overburden TACKS

teach *v.* instruct, educate, tutor, coach, guide, train, drill

teacher *n.* educator, professor, lecturer, schoolmaster, schoolmistress, coach, tutor

team *n.* party, group, gang, crew, company TEEM

tear *v.* ① rip, rend, tatter, shred ② dash, bolt, rush, sprint TARE

tearful *adj.* weepy, moist, wet, sobbing, sad

tease *v.* annoy, harass, vex, irritate, torment ▷ *tantalize* ★**soothe** TEAS, TEES

tedious *adj.* wearisome, tiresome, irksome, exhausting ▷ *boring* ★**fascinating**

teem *v.* abound, swarm, overflow, increase, be full ★**lack** TEAM

tell *v.* ① disclose, speak, state, talk, utter ② discern, discover, distinguish

temper ① *n.* temperament, disposition, nature, humor ② *n.* anger, annoyance, passion ③ *v.* moderate, soften, weaken, restrain

temporary *adj.* short, limited, impermanent, brief ★**permanent**

tempt *v.* entice, invite, attract, persuade ▷ *lure* ★**deter**

tenacious *adj.* ① stubborn, firm, obstinate, unwavering ★**weak** ② adhesive, glutinous

tenant *n.* occupant, householder, occupier

tend *v.* ① take care of, manage, serve, guard ★**neglect** ② affect, lean, incline, verge

★**diverge**

tendency *n.* disposition, leaning, inclination, bent ★**aversion**

tender ① *adj.* delicate, soft ▷ *fragile* ② *adj.* mild, kind, sympathetic ▷ *gentle* ③ *adj.* raw, painful, sore ④ *v.* proffer *Charlotte proffered her services as a babysitter,* present, volunteer, bid

tense *adj.* tight, strained, taut, nervous, edgy ★**relaxed** TENTS

tension *n.* strain, stress, rigidity, suspense, worry ★**relaxation**

term ① *n.* expression, denomination, title, phrase ② *n.* time, season, spell *We stayed in Hong Kong for a spell during our trip to the Far East,* duration ③ *v.* entitle, call, dub

terminate *v.* cease, stop, end, conclude ▷ *finish* ★**begin**

terrible *adj.* frightful, terrifying, fearful, dreadful ▷ *horrible* ★**superb**

terrify *v.* petrify, shock, appall, alarm ▷ *frighten* ★**reassure**

territory *n.* region, area, expanse, dominion, land ▷ *country*

terror *n.* alarm, panic, horror, dismay ▷ *fright* ★**confidence**

terse *adj.* brief, concise, short, pithy, abrupt ▷ *curt* ★**long-winded**

test ① *n.* examination, trial, check, proof, experiment ② *v.* examine, try out, check, quiz, analyze

testy *adj.* irritable, bad-tempered, touchy, peevish ▷ *cross* ★**genial**

tether *n.* rope, cord, lead, leash, chain

text *n.* contents, reading, passage, clause

thanks *n.* gratitude, credit, appreciation

thaw *v.* ① melt, fuse, liquefy, soften ★**freeze** ② unbend, relax

theft *n.* robbery, fraud, larceny, plundering

theme *n.* subject, text matter, topic

theory *n.* idea, supposition, concept, hypothesis

therefore *adv.* consequently, hence, accordingly, thus

thick *adj.* ① dense, solid, bulky, compact ② stiff, set, congealed ③ viscous, gummy, stodgy ★**thin**

thief *n.* crook, robber, burglar, bandit, pirate

thin *adj.* ① slender, slim, slight, lean, skinny ★**fat** ② waferlike, delicate, flimsy ③ watery, dilute, unsubstantial ★**thick**

thing *n.* article, object, something, being, substance

think *v.* ① ponder, consider ▷*reflect* ② conceive, imagine ▷*fancy* ③ surmise, conclude ▷*reckon*

thirsty *adj.* parched, dry, craving, burning

thorn *n.* barb, prickle, bramble, thistle

thorough *adj.* outright, absolute, complete, utter ★**haphazard**

though *conj.* although, even though, notwithstanding, however, yet

thought *n.* reflection, consideration, study, concept, deduction

thoughtful *adj.* ① pensive, studious, contemplative ② considerate, kind, heedful, careful ★**thoughtless**

thoughtless *adj.* heedless, careless, rash, neglectful ▷*indiscreet* ★**thoughtful**

thrash *v.* ① whip, flog, hit ② stir, pitch *The sea was rough—each wave pitched the small boat closer to the rocks,* toss

thread *n.* filament, twist, yarn, fiber

threadbare *adj.* ① shabby, ragged, worn ② commonplace, hackneyed, stale ★**fresh**

threaten *v.* intimidate, bully, blackmail ▷*menace* ★**reassure**

Thrash

The sea was rough—each wave pitched the small boat closer to the rocks.

thrifty *adj.* frugal, careful, economical, saving, sparing ★**wasteful**

thrilling *adj.* exciting, gripping, stimulating

thrive *v.* prosper, flourish, succeed, grow, increase ★**decline**

throb ① *n.* tick, beat, palpitation ② *v.* beat, palpitate, vibrate

throng ① *n.* crowd, horde, mob ② *v.* pack, crowd, swarm, fill

throttle *v.* choke, smother ▷*strangle*

through *prep.* by way of, by means of, as a result of

throw *v.* fling, cast, hurl, project, propel, thrust ★**keep** THROE

thrust *v. & n.* push, project, drive, force, prod

thug *n.* hoodlum, bandit, assassin, mugger, ruffian

thump *v. & n.* beat, hit, knock, bang, wallop

thunderstruck *adj.* open-mouthed, amazed, astounded, staggered

thus *adv.* accordingly, so, therefore, consequently

thwart *v.* frustrate, balk, baffle, hinder, obstruct ★**assist**

ticket *n.* pass, label, card, coupon, token

tickle *v.* ① caress, stroke, pat, brush ② titillate, convulse, amuse ③ delight, gratify

tidbit *n.* delicacy, morsel, dainty, snack, treat

tide *n.* stream, current, drift, ebb, flow TIED

tidings *n.* information, intelligence, report, advice ▷*news*

tidy *adj.* ① neat, well-kept, spruce, orderly ② ample, large, substantial

tie ① *v.* join, attach, secure *Be sure to secure the gate so the dogs can't get out,* unite ▷*fasten* ② *n.* cravat, necktie, bow tie ③ *n.* bond, connection

tight *adj.* ① fast, close, compact, tense ▷*taut* ★**loose** ② miserly, tightfisted ▷*stingy* ★**generous**

tighten *v.* strain, tauten, constrict, cramp, crush ▷*squeeze* ★**loosen**

till ① *prep.* until, up to, as far as ② *v.* plow, cultivate, tend ③ *n.* cash drawer, cash register

tilt *v. & n.* slant, slope, incline, lean, list, tip

time *n.* ① period, duration, season, age, era, term, span ② meter, measure, tempo, rhythm THYME

timid *adj.* fearful, afraid, timorous, diffident, modest ▷*shy* ★**bold**

tinge *v. & n.* color, tincture, tint, stain, shade

tingle *v.* thrill, throb, tickle, vibrate

tinker *v.* meddle, fiddle *Bill fiddled with the old clock for ages, trying to make it work,* patch up, putter, trifle

tinkle *v.* jingle, jangle, ring, clink

tint *n.* dye, hue, tinge, shade ▷*color*

tiny *adj.* small, diminutive, puny, wee ▷*little* ★**huge**

tip ① *n.* apex, peak, point, extremity ▷*top* ② *n.* gratuity, gift, donation, reward ③ *n.* information, hint, tip-off ④ *v.* list, lean, tilt ▷*slope*

tipsy *adj.* inebriated, drunk, drunken

tire *v.* exhaust, bore, fatigue, harass, weaken

tiresome *adj.* wearisome, tedious, boring ▷*humdrum* ★**interesting**

title *n.* ① name, denomination, term, style, designation ② claim, interest *When my father died, I was left an interest in his business,* ownership

toady *v.* fawn, crawl, grovel, crouch, cringe

toast ① *n.* pledge, compliment, salutation ② *v.* brown, roast, heat

together *adv.* collectively, jointly, simultaneously, at the same time ★**separately**

toil ① *v. & n.* struggle, labor, travail ▷*work* ★**relaxation**

token *n.* memento, keepsake, symbol, omen ▷*souvenir*

tolerable *adj.* endurable, supportable, bearable, passable ★**unbearable**

tolerant *adj.* forbearing, indulgent *Sally's parents are very indulgent with her and buy her whatever she wants,* liberal, easygoing ▷*lenient* ★**intolerant**

tolerate *v.* accept, bear with, put up with, endure, suffer ▷*allow* ★**resist**

toll ① *v.* ring, strike, chime, clang ② *n.* charge, duty, tax, levy

tone *n.* ① pitch, loudness, noise, note ②

emphasis, accent, inflection ③ temper, manner, attitude ④ color, cast, hue, shade

too *adv.* ① also, as well, besides ② extremely, very, unduly

tool *n.* ① implement, utensil, machine, agent ② pawn, puppet, cat's-paw, stooge TULLE

top *n.* ① summit, pinnacle, peak ② lid, cover, stopper, cap ③ upper surface ★**bottom** ④ *n.* spinning toy ⑤ *adj.* highest, best, uppermost *After climbing for four days, we reached the uppermost part of the range*

topic *n.* subject, motif, question ▷*theme*

topical *adj.* contemporary, popular, up-to-date

topple *v.* collapse, founder, overturn, totter ▷*fall*

topsy-turvy *adj.* upside-down, overturned, confused, chaotic

torment *v. & n.* pain, distress ▷*torture* ★**ease**

torrent *n.* flood, stream, cascade, cataract, waterfall ★**trickle**

torture *v.* agonize, rack, anguish ▷*torment*

toss *v.* fling, hurl, pitch, cast, project, heave ▷*throw*

total ① *n.* aggregate, whole, sum, completion ② *v.* add, tot up, reckon ③ *adj.* complete, entire

totally *adv.* completely, absolutely, entirely, utterly ★**partially**

touch ① *v.* feel, finger, fondle, handle, stroke ② *v.* move, affect, concern ③ *v.* beat, hit, collide with ④ *v.* adjoin *Our house is situated at a spot where three counties adjoin,* meet, border ⑤ *n.* tinge, hint, suspicion

touchy *adj.* peevish, petulant, snappish ▷*moody* ★**genial**

tough ① *adj.* hard, strong, vigorous, rugged, sturdy ② *adj.* arduous, difficult ③ *n.* hoodlum, hooligan, bruiser, bully

tour *n.* trip, journey, jaunt, excursion, voyage, ride, visit

tournament *n.* contest, championship, competition ▷*match*

tow *v.* haul, drag, tug, haul, heave ▷*pull* TOE

Titles

admiral	lord
ambassador	madame
archbishop	maharajah maharani
baron baroness	major
brigadier	marshal
cardinal	mayor
chancellor	mogul
colonel	monsieur
commodore	pope
count countess	priest
czar czarina	prince princess
dame	professor
dean	queen
duchess duke	rabbi
earl	senator
emir	señor señora
emperor empress	sergeant
general	shogun
governor	signor signora
infanta	shah
kaiser	sheik
khan	sheriff
king	sultan sultana
knight lady	
lama	
lieutenant	

Toys

Wheeled toy
ancient Egypt

Top and whip
1700s

Electronic game
1900s

Doll
1800s

tower ① *v.* soar, dominate, surmount ② *n.* turret, spire, belfry

toy ① *n.* plaything, doll, game ② *v.* play, tinker, fiddle, twiddle

trace ① *v.* trail, track, follow, pursue, discover ② *v.* sketch, draw, copy ③ *n.* trail, track, spoor ④ *n.* drop, speck, vestige

track *v.* search out, follow ▷*trace*

tract *n.* ① area, space, extent, plot ② booklet, leaflet, pamphlet TRACKED

trade ① *v.* barter, exchange, buy, sell, patronize ② *n.* occupation, work, livelihood, business

tradition *n.* custom, convention, practice

traffic ① *n.* business, barter ▷*trade* ② transportation, vehicles, movement

tragedy *n.* catastrophe, disaster, adversity ▷*calamity* ★**comedy**

tragic *adj.* disastrous, catastrophic, miserable, wretched ▷*deplorable* ★**comic**

trail *n.* spoor, track ▷*trace*

train ① *v.* teach, educate, instruct, drill, school ② *n.* chain, procession, series

traitor *n.* rebel, mutineer, renegade, quisling, betrayer

tramp ① *n.* vagabond, wanderer, vagrant, bum, hobo ▷*beggar* ② *n.* jaunt, stroll, ramble ③ *v.* roam, rove, range, walk, travel

trample *v.* tread on, walk on, flatten ▷*crush*

tranquil *adj.* peaceful, placid, serene, restful ▷*calm* ★**restless**

transaction *n.* business, performance, dealing, negotiation, proceeding

transfer *v.* move *My sister is being moved to the head office after her promotion,* displace, change ▷*exchange*

transmit *v.* dispatch, forward, relay ▷*send* ★**receive**

transparent *adj.* clear, lucid, crystal, diaphanous

transport ① *v.* carry, convey, conduct, transfer ▷*move* ② *n.* transportation

trap ① *v.* ensnare, catch, net ② *n.* snare, pitfall, noose, decoy ▷*ambush*

trash *n.* garbage, junk, debris, rubble ▷*rubbish* ★**treasure**

travel ① *v.* & *n.* trek, voyage, cruise ▷*journey*

treacherous *adj.* ① traitorous, unfaithful, false, deceptive ▷*disloyal* ★**faithful**

tread *v.* ① dangerous, risky, precarious, tricky ★**reliable** ② step, walk, tramp, march, go ③ stride, gait, walk, step

treason *n.* treachery, betrayal, sedition

treasure ① *n.* hoard, fortune, riches, wealth ② *v.* appreciate, esteem ▷*value*

treat ① *v.* deal with, handle, manage, serve ② *v.* regale, entertain ③ *v.* doctor, attend ④ *n.* banquet, entertainment, fun

treaty *n.* agreement, covenant, alliance

tremble *v.* quake, quaver, shudder, flutter ▷*shake*

tremendous *adj.* ① immense, enormous ▷*huge* ② terrible, dreadful, awful

tremor *n.* quiver, shake, flutter, ripple ▷*vibration*

trench *n.* ditch, moat, trough, gully, gutter

trend *n.* tendency, inclination, direction

trespass ① *v.* infringe, overstep, intrude ② *n.* offense, sin, transgression

trial *n.* ① endeavor, testing, experiment ② ordeal, grief, suffering ③ essay, proof ④ hearing, lawsuit

tribe *n.* clan, family, race, group, set

tribute *n.* ① ovation, compliment, praise ② dues, toll, tithe, tax

trick ① *n.* fraud, artifice, wile, cheat, deception ② *n.* jape, prank, frolic ③ *n.* juggling, stage magic, conjuring ④ *v.* deceive, defraud

trickle *v.* leak, ooze, seep, drip, drop, dribble

trifle ① *n.* bauble, plaything, foolishness, nonsense ② *v.* dabble, idle, play with

trifling *adj.* paltry, petty, worthless, slight ▷*trivial* ★**important**

trim ① *v.* prune, clip, shorten, crop ② *v.* ornament, smarten, decorate ③ *adj.* tidy, neat, orderly ★**scruffy**

trinket *n.* bauble, bead, jewel, ornament, toy

trip *n.* ① journey, excursion, jaunt ▷*tour* ② *v.* stumble, fall, slip

tripe *n.* garbage, trash, nonsense, twaddle *This is a silly story; I've never read such twaddle*

trite *adj.* hackneyed, ordinary, corny ▷*stale* ★**novel**

triumph *n.* victory, success, achievement ▷*conquest* ★**defeat**

trivial *adj.* trifling, common, unimportant, ordinary, useless ▷*trite* ★**important**

troop ① *n.* band, gang, group, pack, team, unit ② *v.* flock, crowd, swarm TROUPE

trophy *n.* prize, award, cup, souvenir

trot *v.* canter, jog, scamper, scurry

trouble ① *n.* disturbance, annoyance, calamity, misfortune ▷*misery* ② *v.* disturb, annoy, harass ▷*distress* ★**delight**

true *adj.* ① accurate, precise, factual, correct ★**inaccurate** ② faithful, loyal, constant ③ pure, real ▷*genuine* ★**false**

trunk *n.* ① body, torso, stem, stalk ② chest, case, box ③ proboscis *The tapir's proboscis is not as large as the elephant's trunk,* nose, snout

truss *v.* fasten, secure, strap, tie ▷*bind* ★**untie**

trust ① *n.* faith, confidence, belief ② *v.*

believe in, credit, depend on ★**doubt** TRUSSED

trustful *adj.* trusting, innocent, naive ▷*gullible* ★**cautious**

trustworthy *adj.* dependable, credible, honorable ▷*reliable* ★**unreliable**

truth *n.* ① reality, fact, precision ▷*accuracy* ★**falsehood** ② integrity, faith, honor ▷*fidelity* ★**deceit**

truthful *adj.* reliable, frank, open ▷*honest* ★**false**

try ① *v.* endeavor, attempt ▷*strive* ② *v.* examine, try out ▷*test* ★**abandon** ③ *n.* trial, attempt, effort

trying *adj.* bothersome, annoying, troublesome ▷*irksome*

tub *n.* basin, bowl, pot, barrel, keg, tun

tube *n.* pipe, spout, duct, hose, shaft

tuck *v.* stow, fold, pack, pleat, hem

tug *v.* drag, tow, haul, heave ▷*pull* ★**push**

tumble *v.* drop, descend, trip, topple, stumble ▷*fall*

tumult *n.* noise, rumpus, racket, uproar, disturbance, disorder ★**peace**

tune *n.* melody, harmony, air, strain ▷*song*

tunnel *n.* subway, shaft, passage, gallery

turn ① *v.* spin, revolve, whirl ▷*rotate* ② *v.* bend, curve ▷*twist* ③ *v.* change, alter ▷*convert* ④ *v.* spoil ▷*sour* ⑤ *n.* stint, spell, chance ⑥ *n.* rotation ▷*revolution* TERN

twaddle *n.* balderdash, nonsense, drivel, rigmarole, piffle ▷*bunkum* ★**sense**

twinge *n.* pain, pang, spasm, gripe ▷*ache*

twinkle *v.* glitter, gleam, glisten, glimmer ▷*sparkle*

twist *v.* ① bend, curve, turn ② warp, contort, writhe ③ wind, intertwine *The octopus intertwined its legs around the large clam,* encircle

twitch *v.* jerk, jump, jiggle, blink, flutter

type ① *n.* kind, sort, character, description ② *n.* prototype, model, pattern ③ *n.* letter, symbol ④ *v.* typewrite, keyboard

typical *adj.* characteristic, symbolic, regular, stock, representative ★**abnormal**

tyrant *n.* despot, autocrat, dictator, martinet

U u

ugly *adj.* unsightly, ungainly, frightful, ghastly, hideous, horrid, nasty ★**beautiful**

ultimate *adj.* furthest, farthest, most distant, extreme, eventual ▷*final*

umpire *n.* referee, judge, mediator

unabashed *adj.* brazen, unconcerned, undaunted ▷*composed* ★**sheepish**

unable *adj.* helpless, incapable, powerless ★**able**

unaccustomed *adj.* inexperienced, unfamiliar ▷*strange* ★**familiar**

unaffected *adj.* natural, sincere, true, artless ▷*naive* ★**impressed**

unafraid *adj.* courageous, dauntless, intrepid ▷*fearless* ★**afraid**

unanimous *adj.* harmonious, consenting, agreeing ▷*united*

unassuming *adj.* diffident, reserved, quiet, simple ▷*modest* ★**forward**

unattached *adj.* single, free, loose ▷*separate* ★**committed**

unattended *adj.* alone, unwatched, ignored ▷*abandoned* ★**escorted**

unavoidable *adj.* inevitable, irresistable, certain ▷*necessary* ★**uncertain**

unaware *adj.* ignorant, unheeding, unknowing, forgetful ▷*oblivious* ★**aware**

unbalanced *adj.* ① top-heavy, lopsided, uneven ② insane, unhinged *He seems to have become unhinged ever since he lost his job,* crazy, eccentric

unbearable *adj.* unacceptable, intolerable ▷*outrageous* ★**acceptable**

unbiased *adj.* impartial, fair, just ▷*neutral* ★**prejudiced**

uncanny *adj.* weird, ghostly, unearthly, creepy ▷*eerie*

uncertain *adj.* doubtful, vague, chancy, indefinite ▷*dubious* ★**certain**

uncivilized *adj.* primitive, barbaric, coarse, gross ▷*vulgar* ★**civilized**

uncomfortable *adj.* awkward, embarrassed, cramped, self-conscious ★**comfortable**

uncommon *adj.* rare, scarce, infrequent, extraordinary ▷*unusual* ★**common**

unconscious *adj.* ① ignorant, unheeding ▷*unaware* ② insensible, senseless, stunned ★**conscious**

unconventional *adj.* unorthodox, peculiar *I have my own peculiar way of looking at things,* individualistic ▷*eccentric* ★**conventional**

uncouth *adj.* crude, coarse, clumsy, vulgar ▷*boorish* ★**polite**

uncover *v.* expose, discover, show, divulge ▷*reveal* ★**conceal**

under ① *adv.* underneath, below, beneath ② *prep.* less than, lower than, subject to

undergo *v.* endure, tolerate, bear, suffer ▷*sustain*

underground *adj.* secret, concealed, private, hidden, subversive

underhand *adj.* stealthy, undercover, deceitful ▷*sneaky* ★**honest**

underneath *adj.* beneath, under ▷*below* ★**above**

underrate *v.* undervalue, understate, disparage, belittle ★**exaggerate**

understand *v.* comprehend, appreciate, grasp, sympathize ▷*realize* ★**misunderstand**

understudy *n.* stand-in, deputy, substitute, reserve, replacement

undertake *v.* attempt, commence, contract, embark on ▷*tackle*

undesirable *adj.* objectionable, distasteful ▷*unpleasant* ★**desirable**

undignified *adj.* improper, inelegant, clumsy ▷*unseemly* ★**graceful**

undo *v.* unfasten, disentangle, unravel, free ▷*release* ★**fasten**

undress *v.* disrobe, strip, remove, take off ▷*divest* ★**dress**

unearthly *adj.* eerie, uncanny, supernatural ▷*ghostly*

uneasy *adj.* uncomfortable, restive, self-conscious, edgy ★**calm**

unemployed *adj.* unoccupied, redundant, out of work

uneven *adj.* irregular, rough, bumpy,

lopsided, unequal ★**even**

unexpected *adj.* abrupt, impulsive, chance, surprising ▷*sudden* ★**normal**

unfair *adj.* prejudiced, one-sided, partial, unjust ★**fair**

unfaithful *adj.* faithless, untrue, dishonest ▷*false* ★**faithful**

unfamiliar *adj.* alien, obscure, fantastic, bizarre ▷*strange* ★**familiar**

unfasten *v.* release, open, unlatch, untie ▷*undo* ★**fasten**

unfinished *adj.* incomplete, imperfect, lacking, crude ★**finished**

unfit *adj.* unqualified, unsuitable, incapable, unsuited ★**suitable**

unfold *adj.* open, expand, develop, reveal, disclose, unwrap ★**withhold**

unforeseen *adj.* surprising, sudden, accidental ▷*unexpected* ★**predictable**

unforgettable *adj.* memorable, impressive, noteworthy, exceptional

unfortunate *adj.* deplorable, lamentable, adverse, hapless ▷*unlucky* ★**fortunate**

unfriendly *adj.* antagonistic, surly, cold ▷*hostile* ★**friendly**

ungainly *adj.* gawky, awkward, graceless, unwieldly ▷*clumsy* ★**graceful**

ungrateful *adj.* thankless, selfish, ungracious, ill-mannered ★**grateful**

unhappiness *n.* depression, misery, sadness

unhappy *adj.* miserable, dismal, luckless *Try as he might, the luckless Tom was almost last in the race,* melancholy ▷*sad* ★**happy**

unhealthy *adj.* ① unwholesome, harmful ② sick, ill, diseased ★**healthy**

uniform ① *n.* regalia, livery *It was a very grand affair, with the footmen in full livery,* costume, dress ② *adj.* stable, steady, unchanging, level ★**varied**

unimportant *adj.* puny, trivial, insignificant ▷*petty* ★**important**

unintentional *adj.* inadvertent, involuntary, unwitting ▷*accidental* ★**deliberate**

union *n.* ① alliance, association, league ② agreement, accord, harmony ③ fusion, blend, compound

unique *adj.* original, exceptional, exclusive, single, sole ★**commonplace**

unit *n.* entity, single, one, individual

unite *v.* join, combine, connect, merge, blend, fuse ★**separate**

united *adj.* joined, combined, undivided ▷*unanimous* ★**separated**

unity *n.* union, harmony, uniformity, agreement ★**disagreement**

universal *adj.* general, all-embracing, entire, worldwide *Our company has products that are sold worldwide*

unjust *adj.* partial, prejudiced, unfair, wrong ▷*biased* ★**just**

unkempt *adj.* disheveled, shabby, sloppy, slovenly, ungroomed ▷*scruffy* ★**neat**

unkind *adj.* inhuman, heartless, brutal, callous ▷*cruel* ★**kind**

unknown *adj.* hidden, mysterious, undiscovered, dark ★**familiar**

unless *conj.* if not, except when

unlike *adj.* unrelated, dissimilar, distinct ▷*different* ★**similar**

unlikely *adj.* rare, improbable, doubtful, incredible, unheard of ▷*dubious* ★**likely**

unlucky *adj.* unfortunate, luckless, ill-fated, unhappy ★**lucky**

unnatural *adj.* ① artificial, stilted, strained

Uniform

It was a very grand affair, with the footmen in full livery.

② inhuman, cruel ▷ *heartless* ★**natural**

unnecessary *adj.* nonessential, excess, superfluous ▷ *needless* ★**necessary**

unoccupied *adj.* ① uninhabited, empty, deserted ▷ *vacant* ② idle, spare ▷ *unemployed* ★**occupied**

unpleasant *adj.* disagreeable, displeasing, objectionable ▷ *offensive* ★**pleasant**

unpopular *adj.* obnoxious *I was glad to leave the party, for I had been forced to talk to some obnoxious people,* detested, shunned, rejected ▷ *disliked* ★**popular**

unqualified *adj.* ① unable, incompetent, inadequate ▷ *unfit* ② complete, thorough, absolute

unreal *adj.* imaginary, fictional, artificial, false, fanciful ★**real** UNREEL

unreasonable *adj.* ① extravagant, excessive, extreme ★**moderate** ② far-fetched, absurd, foolish ★**rational**

unreliable *adj.* untrustworthy, undependable, irresponsible ▷ *fickle* ★**reliable**

unrest *n.* ① defiance, disquiet, protest, rebellion ② anxiety, distress, worry ★**calm**

unrestricted *adj.* unrestrained, unlimited, open, free, unhindered ★**limited**

unripe *adj.* green, immature, callow *I was just a callow youth in those days, but I hope I have learned something since then,* unseasoned, unready ★**ripe**

unrivaled *adj.* inimitable, unequaled, matchless, peerless ★**inferior**

unruly *adj.* disorderly, troublesome, restive ▷ *rowdy* ★**orderly**

unseemly *adj.* incorrect, indecent, improper, unbecoming, shocking ★**seemly**

unselfish *adj.* generous, liberal, charitable, hospitable ▷ *kind* ★**selfish**

unstable *adj.* unsteady, shaky, inconstant, fickle, volatile ★**stable**

unsuitable *adj.* improper, unacceptable, unfitting, inconsistent ★**suitable**

untidy *adj.* bedraggled, disorderly, muddled, messy ▷ *slovenly* ★**tidy**

untie *v.* unfasten, unravel, free, release ▷ *undo* ★**tie**

until *prep.* till, as far as, up to

untimely *adj.* inopportune, ill-timed, premature ★**opportune**

unusual *adj.* strange, queer, exceptional, quaint, curious ▷ *odd* ★**normal**

unwilling *adj.* averse, disinclined, grudging, opposed ▷ *reluctant* ★**willing**

upheaval *n.* disturbance, disruption, overthrow, turmoil

uphold *v.* sustain, keep up, endorse ▷ *suppor*

upkeep *n.* maintenance, care, conservation, support, expenses ★**neglect**

upper *adj.* higher, superior, elevated, uppermost ★**lower**

upright *adj.* ① sheer, steep, perpendicular ★**horizontal** ② honorable *Josephine was one of the most honorable people I ever met,* ethical, virtuous ★**dishonest**

uproar *n.* hubbub, noise, disorder, tumult, turmoil ▷ *clamor*

upset ① *v.* bother, perturb, unsettle, annoy ② *v.* overthrow, overturn, topple ③ *adj.* disturbed, confused, worried

upside-down *adj.* ① overturned, upturned ② chaotic, muddled, jumbled

urge ① *v.* goad, plead, spur, beseech ★**deter** ② *n.* encouragement, compulsion ▷ *impulse*

urgent *adj.* important, earnest, intense, vital ★**trivial**

use ① *v.* employ, practice, apply ② *v.* consum exhaust, deplete, expend ③ *n.* usage, wear

useful *adj.* valuable, favorable, practical, beneficial ★**useless**

useless *adj.* trashy, paltry, futile *Trying to train a cat to fetch is a futile activity,* inefficient ▷ *worthless* ★**useful**

usual *adj.* common, general, habitual, familiar ▷ *normal* ★**exceptional**

utensil *n.* tool, implement, instrument, apparatus, device

utilize *v.* employ, apply, exploit ▷ *use*

utmost *adj.* extreme, supreme, greatest, ultimate, last, distant

utter ① *adj.* thorough, absolute, complete ② *v.* declare, pronounce, speak ▷ *say*

utterly *adv.* extremely, completely, entirely, fully, wholly

V v

vacant *adj.* ① empty, unoccupied, exhausted ★**occupied** ② stupid, blank, expressionless, mindless

vacation *n.* holiday, rest, recess

vagabond *n.* vagrant, tramp, loafer, beggar, rover, bum, hobo

vague *adj.* indefinite, imprecise, inexact, uncertain ▷*obscure* ★**certain**

vain *adj.* ① conceited, arrogant ▷*proud* ★**modest** ② fruitless, useless, worthless ▷*futile* VANE, VEIN

valiant *adj.* stout, valorous, worthy, gallant ▷*brave* ★**cowardly**

valid *adj.* genuine, authentic, official *No one is allowed into the meeting without an official pass,* proper

valley *n.* gorge, dale, dell, glen, vale

valor *n.* courage, fortitude, heroism, gallantry ▷*bravery* ★**cowardice**

valuable *adj.* ① costly, precious, priceless, expensive ★**worthless** ② meritorious *She was awarded the medal for meritorious service during the war,* righteous, worthy

value ① *n.* worth, benefit, merit, price ② *v.* appreciate, esteem, prize, treasure ③ *v.* appraise, assess, rate, estimate

van *n.* truck, vehicle, wagon, cart

vandalize *v.* damage, sabotage, harm, ruin

vanish *v.* ① disappear, fade, dissolve ★**appear** ② exit, depart, go

vanity *n.* pride, conceit, pretension ★**modesty**

vanquish *v.* conquer, defeat, overpower, subdue ▷*beat*

vapor *n.* steam, fog, mist, moisture, smoke

variable *adj.* changeable, fickle, unsteady, fitful, wavering ★**invariable**

varied *adj.* various, diverse *She was a woman of diverse interests,* miscellaneous, mixed, assorted ★**uniform**

variety *n.* ① assortment, array, mixture, medley *The singers entertained us with a medley of popular songs* ② sort, type,

Vehicles

Ambulance	Stagecoach	Skateboard
Automobile	Surrey	Streetcar
Bicycle	Tank	Wagon
Bulldozer	Taxi	Wheelchair
Bus	Tractor	
Cab	Tram	
Car	Trap	
Cart	Trolley	
Chariot	Truck	
Fire engine		
Go-cart		
Hearse		
Jeep		
Limousine		
Motorcycle		
Rickshaw		
Roller skates		
Scooter		
Sedan		

kind, class, category, breed, brand

various *adj.* mixed, different, many ▷*varied*

vary *v.* differ, alter, change, diversify, diverge

vase *n.* jug, jar, beaker ▷*pitcher*

vast *adj.* great, enormous, extensive, huge, wide ▷*immense* ★**narrow**

vault ① *n.* grave, mausoleum, cellar, crypt, dungeon ② *v.* jump, clear, bound, leap, hurdle

veer *v.* swerve, skid, turn, tack, deviate, change

vehement *adj.* impassioned, fiery, passionate, ardent, eager, zealous ▷*strong* ★**indifferent**

vehicle *n.* ① automobile, car, conveyance, carriage, cart ② agency, means, expedient

veil ① *n.* cloak, cover, wimple, curtain ② *v.* hide, conceal, shade, screen ★**expose** vale

vein *n.* ① seam, strain, streak, stripe, thread, course ② disposition, mood, style, phrasing VAIN

velocity *n.* rate, pace, tempo, rapidity, impetus *After I won the school prize, I had greater impetus to follow my studies* ▷*speed*

venerable *adj.* respectable, revered, august,

dignified, honored ▷*sage*

vengeance *n.* reprisal, retaliation ▷*revenge* ★**pardon**

venomous *adj.* ① poisonous, toxic, vitriolic ② spiteful, malicious, hostile ▷*vindictive*

vent ① *v.* discharge, emit, express, let fly, release ② *n.* aperture, duct, opening, outlet

ventilate *v.* ① aerate, cool, fan, blow ② express, debate, discuss, examine

venture ① *n.* enterprise, undertaking, endeavor ② *v.* risk, bet, hazard ▷*chance*

verbal *adj.* stated, said, expressed, spoken, unwritten ★**written**

verdict *n.* decision, judgment, finding, conclusion, opinion

verge ① *n.* border, brink, edge, boundary ② *v.* incline, tend, border, come close to

verify *v.* confirm, declare, authenticate, corroborate *The witness corroborated the story told by the defendant* ★**discredit**

versatile *adj.* adaptable, variable, adjustable, handy ★**inflexible**

verse *n.* poem, rhyme, stave, canto, jingle, doggerel *Call this stuff poetry? It's just doggerel!*

version *n.* account, form, interpretation, adaptation, type

vertical *adj.* upright, erect, sheer, perpendicular, steep ★**horizontal**

very ① *adv.* extremely, exceedingly, greatly, intensely, absolutely ② *adj.* exact, real, true, actual, genuine

vessel *n.* ① bowl, pot, canister, container, basin, jar ② craft, ship, boat

vestige *n.* remains, remnant, hint, glimmer, residue, trace

veteran ① *n.* old timer, master, old hand, expert ★**novice** ② *adj.* experienced, practiced, adept ★**inexperienced**

veto ① *v.* ban, reject, prohibit, stop, forbid ★**approve** ② *n.* embargo *The United Nations placed an embargo on the selling of arms to the two countries,* prohibition, disapproval ★**assent**

vex *v.* annoy, provoke, trouble, irritate, harass ▷*displease* ★**soothe**

vibrate *v.* shake, quiver, oscillate, fluctuate

▷*tremble*

vice *n.* evil, failing, fault ▷*sin* ★**virtue**

vicinity *n.* area, environs, neighborhood ▷*surroundings*

vicious *adj.* evil, sinful, malignant, immoral, vile ▷*wicked* ★**virtuous**

victim *n.* sufferer, scapegoat, martyr, prey, pawn, dupe

victor *n.* winner, conqueror, champion, prizewinner ★**loser**

victory *n.* success, triumph, achievement ▷*conquest* ★**defeat**

view ① *n.* landscape, sight, panorama, spectacle ② *n.* estimation, belief, theory, opinion ③ *v.* watch, see, behold, witness

vigilant *adj.* attentive, wary, alert, guarded ▷*watchful* ★**lax**

vigor *n.* energy, vim, stamina, might, power ▷*strength* ★**weakness**

vigorous *adj.* forceful, energetic, powerful, dynamic ▷*active* ★**weak**

vile *adj.* low, wretched, contemptible, miserable, nasty, evil ▷*despicable* ★**noble**

villain *n.* blackguard, knave *You are nothing but a knave who is out to steal my money,* sinner, rascal ▷*rogue* ★**hero**

vim *n.* stamina, zip, strength ▷*vigor*

vindicate *v.* warrant, sustain, support, defend, establish ▷*justify* ★**accuse**

vindictive *adj.* vengeful, unforgiving, grudging, spiteful ▷*malicious* ★**merciful**

violate *v.* ① disobey, oppose, defy, resist, infringe ★**obey** ② abuse, defile, outrage, desecrate

violent *adj.* furious, rabid, rampant, forcible, tempestuous ★**calm**

virile *adj.* manly, masculine, vigorous, vibrant ▷*strong* ★**weak**

virtually *adv.* almost, nearly, practically, substantially

virtue *n.* goodness, honesty, chastity, purity ▷*quality* ★**vice**

virtuous *adj.* chaste, innocent, honorable, moral ▷*righteous* ★**wicked**

visible *adj.* perceptible, discernible, apparent, exposed, obvious ★**invisible**

vision *n.* ① apparition, specter, ghost, mirage ② concept, revelation, foresight

visit ① *n.* call, sojourn, stay, excursion ② *v.* call on, drop in, tarry, stay

visitor *n.* guest, company, tourist, caller

visual *adj.* seeable, observable, visible

vital *adj.* ① essential, indispensible, critical, crucial ▷*necessary* ② alive, vibrant, virile, dynamic *Our team won a number of games after we had been trained by the new dynamic coach,* energetic

vitality *n.* stamina, virility, vigor ▷*strength*

vivacious *adj.* lively, spirited, vital, animated, merry ▷*sprightly* ★**languid**

vivid *adj.* ① clear, bright ▷*brilliant* ② vigorous, strong, lucid ★**dull**

vocal *adj.* articulate, eloquent, spoken, strident, vociferous ★**quiet**

vocation *n.* occupation, calling, job, mission, career, pursuit

vogue *n.* style, fashion, mode, popularity

voice ① *n.* speech, articulation, utterance ② *n.* choice, preference, opinion ③ *v.* utter, express, proclaim, pronounce

void ① *adj.* bare, barren, empty ② *adj.* invalid, canceled, useless ③ *n.* cavity, chasm, space, opening, nothingness

volatile *adj.* ① lively, changeable, fickle, giddy ② elusive, fleeting, evaporable

volley *n.* discharge, fusillade, barrage, shower

volume *n.* ① bulk, capacity, mass, quantity ▷*amount* ② loudness, amplitude ③ book, edition, tome

voluntary *adj.* free-willed, optional, intended, gratuitous ★**compulsory**

vomit *v.* spew, disgorge, puke, throw up

vote ① *n.* ballot, election, poll, referendum ② *v.* ballot, poll, choose, elect

vow ① *v.* promise, swear, assure, vouch, testify ② *n.* oath, pledge, promise

voyage *n.* journey, cruise, passage, trip

vulgar *adj.* ① common, coarse, crude, indelicate, rude ★**elegant** ② native, ordinary, common

vulnerable *adj.* unprotected, unguarded, exposed, defenseless, tender ★**strong**

wad *n.* bundle, chunk, block, plug

waddle *v.* wobble, totter, shuffle, toddle

wag ① *v.* waggle, shake ▷*vibrate* ② *n.* wit, humorist, joker

wage ① *n.* fee, pay, salary, remuneration ② *v.* carry out, fulfill, undertake

wager ① *v.* gamble, bet, speculate, chance, hazard ② *n.* pledge, stake, bet

wagon *n.* cart, truck, van ▷*vehicle*

waif *n.* orphan, stray, foundling *In the old days, children were abandoned in the streets, but some people set up homes for such foundlings*

wail ① *v.* deplore, weep, grieve, lament ▷*cry* ★**rejoice** ② *n.* lamentation, weeping, grief, moan, howl

wait *v.* ① expect, await, bide, stay, stop ▷*linger* ② attend, serve WEIGHT

waive *v.* relinquish, disclaim, disown, forego, defer ▷*renounce* WAVE

wake *v.* awaken, stimulate, excite ▷*arouse*

wakeful *adj.* ① restless, awake ② alert, wary, watchful

walk ① *v.* advance, march, step, progress, move ② *n.* stroll, hike ▷*ramble* ★**run** ③ *n.* lane, alley, way ④ *n.* sphere, field, career *I started my career of journalism, but I later went into politics,* interest

wallow *v.* ① flounder, stagger, tumble ② delight, enjoy, revel

wan *adj.* pale, ashen, feeble, sickly, pallid ▷*weak* ★**robust**

wand *n.* mace, baton, stick, scepter, rod

wander *v.* stray, meander, roam, stroll, deviate

wane *v.* droop, decline, decrease, lessen, ebb *As the little boat neared the rocks, Fred's courage ebbed away,* sink ★**wax** WAIN

wangle *v.* fiddle, contrive, fix, arrange

want ① *v.* desire, covet, crave, need, require ② *n.* need, necessity, demand ③ *n.* dearth, deficiency ▷*scarcity* ★**plenty**

wanton *adj.* ① unscrupulous, irresponsible

② playful, frolicsome, wild ③ dissolute, immoral

war *n.* hostilities, fighting, bloodshed, enmity, strife ★**peace** WORE

ward *n.* ① pupil, minor, charge ② district, quarter WARRED

ward off *v.* prevent, forestall, avoid, stop ▷*avert*

wardrobe *n.* ① locker, cupboard, closet ② outfit, clothes, apparel

warm ① *adj.* tepid, hot, lukewarm ② *adj.* sympathetic ▷*warmhearted* ③ *adj.* eager, hot, zealous ④ *v.* heat, bake, cook, prepare

warn *v.* caution, admonish, advise, alert, apprise WORN

warning *n.* caution, admonition, forewarning, alarm, tip

warp *v.* contort, bend, twist, kink, deform ★**straighten**

warrant ① *v.* guarantee, certify, justify, permit, allow ② *n.* assurance, permit, license, authority *She produced documents that showed her authority on the board of directors*

wary *adj.* cautious, alert, careful, heedful ▷*prudent* ★**rash**

wash ① *v.* bathe, scrub, rinse, cleanse, wet ② *n.* washing, cleaning

waste ① *n.* garbage, debris, trash, rubbish ② *v.* squander, spend, lavish, fritter ③ *v.* wither, decay, shrivel, perish WAIST

wasteful *adj.* lavish, prodigal, spendthrift ▷*extravagant* ★**economical**

watch ① *v.* note, observe, guard ★**ignore** ② *v.* inspect, look at, oversee ③ *n.* timepiece ④ *n.* guard, sentry, watchman

watchful *adj.* attentive, observant, vigilant ▷*wary* ★**inattentive**

water *v.* wet, bathe, wash, douse, drench, sprinkle, spray

wave ① *v.* brandish, flourish, waft, swing ② *n.* breaker, billow, undulation WAIVE

waver *v.* falter, hesitate, vacillate *There's no time to vacillate; make up your mind* ★**decide**

wax *v.* increase, rise, grow, expand, enlarge ★**wane**

way *n.* ① route, road, path, passage, track ② technique *The company introduced a new technique for making glass,* procedure, method, style WEIGH

wayward *adj.* contrary, perverse, obstinate ▷*stubborn* ★**docile**

weak *adj.* ① feeble, frail, puny, helpless, delicate ② foolish, soft, senseless, stupid ③ thin, watery, insipid ④ fragile, flimsy, tumbledown ★**strong** WEEK

weaken *v.* enfeeble, relax, sag, flag ▷*languish* ★**strengthen**

weakness *n.* defect, fault, frailty, flaw ★**strength**

wealth *n.* riches, luxury, prosperity, money, opulence ★**poverty**

wealthy *adj.* rich, affluent, prosperous, opulent ★**poor**

wear *v.* ① dress in, don ② rub, scrape, waste, consume ③ last, endure, remain WARE

weary ① *adj.* exhausted, tired, fatigued ★**fresh** ② *v.* exhaust, tire, bore ★**refresh**

weather *n.* climate, clime, conditions

weave *v.* braid, plait, unite, blend

web *n.* net, tissue, webbing, textile, netting

wed *v.* marry, join, link, splice, tie the knot

wedge ① *n.* block, chock, lump, chunk ② *v.* crowd, force, jam, push, thrust, squeeze

wee *adj.* little, small, minute ▷*tiny* ★**large**

weep *v.* blubber, snivel, sob, whimper *The lost puppy was found at last, whimpering in a corner* ▷*cry* ★**rejoice**

weigh *v.* balance, estimate, ponder, examine, consider WAY

weight *n.* ① load, pressure, burden, heaviness ② importance, onus, significance, gravity WAIT

weighty *adj.* heavy, hefty, ponderous, onerous ★**trivial**

weird *adj.* eerie, supernatural, unearthly, mysterious ▷*uncanny*

welcome ① *adj.* pleasing, desirable ▷*agreeable* ② *v.* greet, accost, hail, salute ③ *n.* greeting, salutation, acceptance

welfare *n.* well-being, comfort, happiness, benefit, advantage ★**harm**

well ① *adj.* robust, healthy, hearty, sound

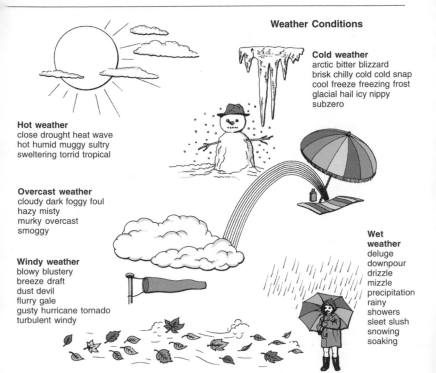

Weather Conditions

Cold weather
arctic bitter blizzard
brisk chilly cold cold snap
cool freeze freezing frost
glacial hail icy nippy
subzero

Hot weather
close drought heat wave
hot humid muggy sultry
sweltering torrid tropical

Overcast weather
cloudy dark foggy foul
hazy misty
murky overcast
smoggy

Wet weather
deluge
downpour
drizzle
mizzle
precipitation
rainy
showers
sleet slush
snowing
soaking

Windy weather
blowy blustery
breeze draft
dust devil
flurry gale
gusty hurricane tornado
turbulent windy

★**ill** ② *adv.* properly, suitable, adequately, accurately ★**badly** ③ *n.* fountain, spring

well-off *adj.* comfortable, prosperous ▷*wealthy* ★**poor**

wet *adj.* ① moist, damp, watery, drenched ② *adj.* drizzling, showery, raining ③ *v.* soak, moisten, dampen

wheedle *v.* coax, cajole, inveigle *We were inveigled into buying some of the local lace,* persuade ★**coerce**

whet *v.* ① sharpen, hone, strop ★**blunt** ② excite, stimulate, rouse ★**dampen**

whim *n.* fancy, humor, desire, urge, notion, impulse

whine *v.* ① howl, wail, whimper, moan ② complain, grouse, grumble

whip *v.* ① flog, lash, thrash, chastise, spank ② whisk, mix, blend

whirl *v.* twirl, spin, rotate, revolve, whir ▷*twist*

whisk *v.* beat, brush, hasten, hurry, sweep ▷*whip*

whisper ① *n.* murmur, hint, suggestion, breath ② *v.* breathe, murmur, divulge, buzz, intimate ★**shout**

whistle *n. & v.* cheep, chirp, warble, call

whole *adj.* ① all, entire, total, intact ② sound, complete, unbroken ★**part** HOLE

wholesome *adj.* healthful, nutritious, beneficial, sound, good ★**noxious**

wicked *adj.* infamous, corrupt, depraved, unrighteous, sinister, sinful ▷*evil* ★**virtuous**

wickedness *n.* corruption, depravity, iniquity, sinfulness, villainy ▷*evil*

wide *adj.* broad, ample, extended, spacious,

roomy, extensive, vast ★**narrow**

widespread *adj.* prevalent, far-flung, extensive, sweeping, universal *The use of a universal language would be of great help in the United Nations* ★**limited**

wield *v.* ① brandish, flourish, manipulate ② control, command, exert, maintain

wild *adj.* ① savage, ferocious, fierce, untamed ★**tame** ② violent, unrestrained, boisterous ★**civilized** ③ careless, insane, reckless ★**sane**

wilderness *n.* desert, jungle, wasteland, wilds, outback

will ① *n.* resolution, decision, zeal, accord ② *n.* order, wish, command, request, demand ③ *n.* legacy, testament ④ *v.* choose, desire, elect

willful *adj.* temperamental, headstrong, deliberate ▷*obstinate* ★**docile**

willing *adj.* disposed, zealous, ready, earnest ▷*agreeable* ★**unwilling**

wilt *v.* wither, waste, sag, dwindle ▷*ebb*

wily *adj.* cunning, sly, tricky, deceitful ▷*crafty* ★**sincere**

win *v.* succeed, gain, get, acquire, procure ▷*triumph* ★**lose**

wince *v.* shrink, quail, flinch *My little sister didn't flinch once when she had her vaccination,* start ▷*cringe*

wind (rhymes with *pinned*) *n.* breeze, blast, gust, gale

wind (rhymes with *mind*) *v.* coil, turn, twist, bend WINED

wink *n. & v.* blink, flutter, flicker, glint

winner *n.* champion, master ▷*victor*

wipe *v.* clean, brush, mop, remove, swab

wire *n.* ① cable, telegraph, telegram ② cable, cord

wisdom *n.* judgment, discretion, tact, thought, reason ★**folly**

wise *adj.* sensible, profound, astute, subtle, discreet ▷*sage* ★**foolish**

wish ① *v.* desire, crave, want, hanker for, long for ② *n.* command, will, desire, liking

wistful *adj.* ① pensive, musing, wishful ② forlorn, melancholy, soulful

wit *n.* ① fun, humor, levity, pleasantry ②

brains, sense, judgment, intelligence ★**stupidity**

witch *n.* enchantress, sorceress, crone, hag

withdraw *v.* ① retire, retreat, depart, leave ▷*flee* ② extract, take out

withdrawn *adj.* unsociable, retiring, reclusive, aloof, solitary ★**sociable**

wither *v.* waste, fade, pine, languish ▷*shrivel*

withhold *v.* retain, reserve, restrain, hold back ▷*keep* ★**grant**

within *adj.* inside, interior, inner

withstand *v.* resist, oppose, confront ▷*defy* ★**support**

witness ① *n.* spectator, onlooker, bystander *One of the bystanders at the accident came forward to give evidence,* signatory ② *v.* behold, observe, see, attest

witty *adj.* funny, jocular, waggish, amusing ▷*comical* ★**dull**

wizard *n.* sorcerer, magician, conjurer

woe *n.* sorrow, sadness, grief, misery, trouble ★**joy**

woman *n.* lady, girl, female, wife

wonder ① *n.* marvel, miracle, rarity, curiosity ② *n.* bewilderment, surprise, amazement ▷*awe* ③ *v.* speculate, question, marvel, muse

wonderful *adj.* marvelous, fabulous, spectacular, superb ▷*splendid* ★**commonplace**

woo *v.* make love, court, pursue

wood *n.* ① lumber, timber, planks ② forest, woods, copse, woodland, grove, thicket WOULD

word *n.* ① expression, term, utterance ② pledge, promise ③ tidings, news, information

work ① *n.* toil, drudgery, labor, grind ② *n.* task, job, stint, chore ③ *v.* operate, function, manipulate, run, drive

world *n.* globe, earth, sphere, planet

worry ① *v.* bother, annoy, disturb ▷*trouble* ★**soothe** ② *n.* vexation, anxiety, concern, fear ★**delight**

worsen *v.* aggravate, decline, deteriorate, degenerate ★**improve**

Borrowed Words

Boomerang

Dutch
boss
brandy
decoy
landscape

Modern French
police
rendezvous
liaison
menu

Scandinavia
fjord
geyser

lemming
ombudsman
ski

Italian
balcony
cameo
fiasco
influenza

German
blitz
delicatessen
dollar
kindergarten

Chinese
kowtow
sampan
typhoon
wok

Japanese
bonsai
judo
karate
origami

Turkish
coffee
kiosk

Spanish
armada
fiesta
macho
patio
siesta
sombrero

Afrikaans
aardvark
apartheid

boer
trek
veldt

Inuit
anorak
igloo
kayak
parka

Gaelic
blarney
bog
brat
brogue
smithereens

Aztec
avocado
cocoa
tomato

Arabic
admiral
alcohol
algebra
alkali
sherbet
sofa
zero

Aboriginal languages
boomerang
dingo
budgerigar
kangaroo

Persian
bazaar
caravan
divan
paradise

tulip
turban

Hindi
bungalow
chintz
cot
pajamas
thug
veranda

Native American
chipmunk
moccasin
moose
papoose
wigwam

worship ① *v.* revere, adore, esteem, honor, praise ★**despise** ② *n.* adoration, devotion, reverence

worth *n.* value, benefit, merit, caliber *This year's students were of a high caliber,* dignity

worthless *adj.* valueless, paltry, trifling, useless ▷*cheap* ★**valuable**

worthwhile *adj.* valuable, helpful, useful, beneficial ★**useless**

worthy *adj.* upright, admirable, excellent, honest, fine ★**vile**

wound ① *v.* hurt, injure, gash, pain, distress ▷*harm* ★**heal** ② *n.* injury, bruise, harm

wrangle *v. & n.* squabble, fight, row, scrap ▷*quarrel* ★**accord**

wrap *v.* fold, envelop, enclose, cover, clothe, conceal ★**unfold** RAP

wrath *n.* fury, ire, rage, passion ▷*anger* ★**pleasure**

wreck ① *v.* demolish, smash, ruin, destroy, spoil, ravage ★**repair** ② *n.* derelict, hulk, shipwreck, ruin

wrench *v.* twist, wring, strain, sprain, pull

wrestle *v.* struggle, battle, combat, grapple, tussle ▷*fight*

wretch *n.* vagabond, blackguard, villain, rogue, ▷*scoundrel*

wretched *adj.* ① dejected, abject, miserable, ▷*despicable* ② saddening, pathetic ▷*pitiful* ★**joyful**

wriggle *v.* twist, writhe, squirm, worm *My hamster wormed his way under the couch and it took some time before we could get him back out,* dodge

wring *v.* choke, squeeze, throttle, strangle, twist RING

wrinkle *n. & v.* crease, pucker, ruffle, rumple, crinkle, furrow

write *v.* inscribe, pen, sign, scrawl, scribble RIGHT, RITE, WRIGHT

writer *n.* ① scribe, penman, clerk ② author, essayist, narrator, playwright, poet, dramatist

writhe *v.* wind, twine, weave, twist ▷*wriggle*

written *adj.* recorded, set down, documentary, transcribed

wrong ① *adj.* unjust, unfair, immoral, wicked ② *adj.* false, mistaken, erroneous ③ *v.* injure, hurt, abuse ④ *n.* offense, atrocity, iniquity, sin, injustice ★**right**

wry *adj.* crooked, askew, awry, aslant, twisted, distorted ★**straight** RYE

Y y

Z z

yank v. draw, pull, snatch ▷*jerk*

yap v. ① bark, yelp ② prattle, blather, gossip, jaw

yard ① n. lawn, garden, courtyard, court, quadrangle ② three feet

yarn n. ① story, account, tale, narrative ② thread, wool, linen, twist

yawn v. gape, open

yearly adj. ① annual, perennial, per annum *We shall pay a salary of $50,000 per annum* ② adv. every year, annually

yearn v. ache, crave, desire, pine, hunger for ★**dislike**

yell v. shriek, squawk, whoop, screech, shout ▷*bellow* ★**whisper**

yield ① v. produce, provide, furnish, supply ② v. surrender, give in, submit ★**withstand** ③ v. abdicate, resign, renounce ④ n. crop, harvest, product, output

yielding ① adj. obedient, submissive, unresisting ★**stubborn** ② plastic, malleable, flexible ★**solid**

yoke ① v. join, couple, link, harness ② n. chain, bondage *The children of Israel moved out of bondage in the land of Egypt,* enslavement YOLK

yokel n. bumpkin, rustic, boor, peasant

young adj. youthful, tender, juvenile, junior, little ★**old**

youngster n. child, youth, boy, girl, kid, lad, adolescent

youth n. ① adolescence, prime, salad days ★**age** ② lad, boy ▷*youngster*

youthful adj. boyish, girlish, young, spry, juvenile, lively ★**aged**

Yule n. Christmas

zany adj. crazy, nutty, droll, goofy, eccentric, wacky, loony, loopy ▷*funny* ★**serious**

zeal n. devotion, eagerness, enthusiasm, keenness, ardor ★**apathy**

zealous adj. devoted, fervent *Dave was a fervent supporter of the school's football team,* fanatical, earnest ▷*eager* ★**apathetic**

zenith n. climax, height, apex, peak

zero n. nothing, nada, zip, naught, nil, nullity, aught

zest n. ① relish, gusto, appetite, keenness ② flavor, piquancy, taste ③ rind, peel

zone n. area, district, region, tract, sector

zoom v. flash, fly, shoot, streak, hurtle, whizz

Words and Synonyms in the English Language

No one can say for sure how many words there are in the English language. A large up-to-date dictionary might include as many as 460,000 entries. Of course, no single person knows or uses all of these words. Native speakers of English might use from 5,000 to 50,000 words and recognize many more. In our daily lives we can often get by with anywhere from a few hundred to a few thousand words. But if we limit ourselves to such a low number, we will soon find that we cannot always say or write precisely what we mean.

Fortunately, many words in English are synonyms—words that mean the same thing or nearly the same thing. And so there are many different words to choose from in order to express yourself clearly and in an interesting manner. Your Thesaurus can help you to find just the word you are looking for to make your writing more interesting to read and to explain yourself more exactly. Sometimes your Thesaurus will simply remind you of a word that you already know but couldn't think of. At other times it might suggest a new word that will help express your meaning more precisely or with more energy and variety. Because the Thesaurus doesn't tell you the meaning of words, it is always a good idea to check a dictionary to make sure that any word that is new to you means what you want it to mean in your sentence. (The opposite is also true—a dictionary will tell you what words mean, but it might not suggest other choices the way your Thesaurus does.)

Where do all these words come from?

The English language is very rich in synonyms. Over the past 1600 years it has changed and grown as new words develop and as others are borrowed from different languages. Many of our most common words are native to English and have been used since the first Anglo-Saxons settled in the island of Britain in the 400s (*man, wife, child, lord, lady, daisy, think, come, home, shirt, word, busy, to, in, ask*). Other common words were borrowed from the Scandinavian settlers who came to Britain during the next few centuries (*sky, scowl, shin, skirt, window*).

In 1066 the French-speaking Normans conquered England. For the next 300 years French was the language of the rulers of England, the aristocracy. During this period speakers of English began to use many French words in their speech and today thousands of these French borrowings have become ordinary English words themselves (*language, conquer, beauty, debt, govern, joy, host, count, plenty, memory*).

Yet when students went to school during these early centuries, they didn't go to study English as we do today, or even French, but to study Latin and then Greek. It is not surprising, therefore, that English now includes many words that came from Latin and Greek. From Latin we get such words as *history, bishop, educate, compose, intelligent, element, solar,* and *pedestrian.* From Greek come *elephant, synonym, system, anthology,* and *geography.* Many of these Greek words came to English through Latin. Modern scientific words are often composed of Greek and Latin elements: *thesaurus, telephone, television, bicycle, radio, dinosaur, pneumonia.*

The age of exploration, travel, and conquest that began in the 1400s greatly increased the number of English words as travelers, soldiers, and settlers came into contact with people speaking different languages all over the world. There are thousands of words that we use today without ever thinking of their widespread origins. Below, for example, are some of our words for different types of storms and the languages they come from:

English: *storm*   Scandinavian: *squall*
Spanish: *tornado*   Arabic: *monsoon*
Latin: *tempest*   Taino (Caribbean): *hurricane*
Greek: *cyclone*   Chinese: *typhoon*

All Sorts of Synonyms

Synonyms don't just come from borrowing words from other languages. People in different places often use different words to mean the same thing. A recent example is found in the words for the bumps that are put on some roads and parking lots to keep cars from going too fast. In the U.S. these are called *speed bumps*, but in Britain they are also known as *sleeping policemen*. Or consider the little insects whose tails light up on summer evenings. Since the 1600s these have been known as *fireflies*, but in the U.S. they are also called *lightning bugs*. In various parts of the U.S., *dragonflies* are known as *mosquito hawks*, *darning needles*, and *snake doctors*. In most of the U.S., a road intersection that goes around a circle is called a *traffic circle*, but in New England it is called a *rotary* and in Britain itself it is called a *roundabout*. Depending on where you live you might sell your old toys at a *tag sale*, a *garage sale*, a *yard sale*, or a *lawn sale*. In Britain you would sell them at a *car boot sale*, because the British sell such things from the *boots* of their cars. What's the *boot* of a car? In the U.S. we call it the *trunk*.

But most synonyms in your Thesaurus are not based on regional or national differences. Synonyms are words that have similar meanings. Their meanings may overlap, but they do not usually express exactly the same thing. Synonyms cluster around a single sense but have different shades of meaning. One of the things your Thesaurus does best is help you to find the right word with just the right shade of meaning so that you can say what you want in the best way. Some words may be formal and some informal. Some may be used in one situation but not in another.

For example, the words *friend*, *companion*, *ally*, and *pal* are all words for someone you like or are friendly with, but each one suggests something slightly different. A *friend* is someone you like, but a *pal* is someone you are particularly close to. The word *ally*, on the other hand, suggests someone who agrees with your position in some matter.

Ally often refers to one country that is on friendly terms with another country and it also suggests the opposite of *enemy*. Thus, a country can be your *friend* and *ally*, but not your *pal* or *companion*. Your *pal*, however, should not only be your *friend* and *companion*, he or she should also be a good *ally*. Each time you choose a synonym you need to think a little about which of the choices in your Thesaurus is the best one for you at the moment. You may know right away when you see it, or you may need to look up some of the choices in a dictionary.

Finding the Differences among Synonyms

On the following pages some entries from your Thesaurus are expanded to show how to choose the word that means the closest to what you wish to say. Definitions are given to show how the synonyms are related and how they are different. Example sentences are included to show one way, at least, in which the word is commonly used. In these expanded entries the main entry is in CAPITALS and its synonyms are listed below it in **bold**. Each synonym is then followed by its meaning and an example sentence. Compare these expanded entries with the entries in the main part of your Thesaurus.

Word	Meaning	Example
FRIEND *n.*	someone you know and like; someone who is not your enemy	*All his **friends** came to the party.* *If you can't trust your **friends**, who can you trust?*
companion	a person or animal who spends a lot of time with you	*Allen has been my constant **companion** for three weeks.*
associate	someone you work with or often mix with socially	*Her **associates** included the mayor and everyone on the town board.*
ally	a country or person who agrees to help and support another	*Canada and Mexico are two of the closest **allies** of the U.S.*

crony	an informal word for someone who has been a close friend for a long time	*One of my old **cronies** showed up at the class reunion.*
pal	an informal word for a close friend	*My **pals** and I go fishing every Saturday.*
chum	an informal word for a close friend	*We've been **chums** for three years.*

HISTORY *n.*	a record, and often an interpretation, of past events and developments	*She wrote a **history** of jazz.* *The doctor wanted to know my medical **history**.*
narration	a detailed telling of what happened	*The **narration** of his escape took over an hour.*
account	a description, report, or explanation	*Paul gave us an **account** of his trip to Peru.*
saga	a long tale of heroic events	*The book is a **saga** of three generations of a seafaring family.*
story	a description of real or imaginary events	*He especially likes **stories** about animals.*
chronicle	a record of events in the order they happened	*The senator kept a **chronicle** of her years in office.*

LIFT *v.*	to move up to a higher position	*This box is too heavy for me to **lift**.*
raise	to move or lift to a high position	*If you know the answer, **raise** your hand.*
erect	to raise something to an upright position	*We **erected** our tent near the river.*
hoist	to lift up something, especially with ropes and pulleys	*They had to **hoist** the girders to the top of the new skyscraper.*

elevate	to raise or lift up	*She lay in bed with her sprained ankle **elevated** on pillows.*
hold up	to prop up or keep from falling	*He was so tired he could hardly **hold up** his head.*

MAXIMUM *adj.*	the greatest allowed or possible	*This bus carries a **maximum** load of 42 passengers.*
supreme	of the highest rank, power, or importance; most excellent	*Many people have been willing to make the **supreme** sacrifice and die for the freedom of others.*
highest	having the greatest height or importance	*The president holds the **highest** elected office in the country.*
most	greatest in quantity, amount, or degree	*The roller coaster is the **most** exciting ride in the park.*
greatest	largest in number, quantity, degree, intensity, etc.	*The **greatest** gift you can give me is your respect.*
top	of the highest quality, amount, or degree	*The salesman promised me **top** value for my old car.*
largest	greatest in size or quantity; biggest	*The **largest** known volcano is on Mars.*

PLACID *adj.*	having a calm appearance	*The lake was **placid** as we canoed through the mist.*
peaceful	calm and quiet; at peace	*He spent a **peaceful** afternoon reading in the shade.*
quiet	without noise or bustle	*The city grows **quiet** in the middle of the night.*

serene	not disturbed or troubled	*The serene expression on her face helped us to calm down.*
mild	not extreme in any way	*We had a mild winter last year.*
restful	quiet, soothing, and peaceful	*We had a restful vacation at the beach.*
RECIPE *n.*	a list of ingredients and instructions for preparing something, especially a particular food	*I have a wonderful recipe for rhubarb pie.*
formula	a general rule or principle; a set method for doing something	*His formula for success is to get up early, dress neatly, and be polite.*
method	a logical, orderly arrangement of steps for doing something	*She has a very effective teaching method.*
prescription	written directions for preparing or using a medicine	*The doctor gave me a prescription for penicillin.*
SPEED *n.*	rate of movement or action; quickness	*The cart gathered speed as it rolled down the hill.*
velocity	the speed at which an object is traveling	*The train travels at a constant velocity of 70 miles per hour.*
rapidity	a fast rate of motion or occurrence	*The rapidity of her answers showed her great confidence.*
dispatch	promptness; efficient quickness	*Let's finish this job with dispatch.*
pace	rate of movement, or progress	*We climbed the trail at a steady pace.*

tempo	rate of activity; pace	*The **tempo** of city life is too fast for me.*
VALID *adj.*	legally acceptable for use	*You need a **valid** license to drive a car.*
genuine	authentic; not artificial or fake	*This letter bears the **genuine** signature of Abraham Lincoln.*
authentic	not false or imitation	*She has an **authentic** southern accent.*
official	established or made legal by someone in authority	*No one is allowed in here without an **official** pass.*
proper	fit, suitable, or appropriate	*He did not have the **proper** visa for traveling to China.*

Name Synonyms

Even names have synonyms! Many names have different forms in other languages. Some nicknames don't even look or sound like the original names they come from, like *Ted* and *Nell* for *Edward* and *Helen.* Sometimes these nicknames become given names themselves, like *Peggy* and *Robin*, originally nicknames for *Margaret* and *Robert.* For these reasons, many names that we hear around us every day are what we might call "name synonyms." Below is a list of a few common names given in their English forms followed by some of their synonyms. Female names are shown in *italic* type (*Alexandra*); male names are shown in roman type (Alec). A few names that are used for both males and females have been underlined.

Alexander	<u>Alex</u>, Alec, *Alexandra*, *Alexa*, Alexandre, Alejandro, *Alexandrina*
Anthony	Tony, Antonio, *Antonia*, *Toni*, Antony
Arthur	Arturo, Art
Christina	<u>Chris</u>, *Chrissy*, Christian, *Christine*, *Kristen*, *Kirsten*, *Kirstie*, *Tina*, *Christie*
Christopher	<u>Chris</u>, Kit
David	Dave, Davy, Dafydd, Dai, Dewi
Derek	Derrick, Dietrich, Terry
Dorothy	*Dora*, *Dolly*, *Dorothea*, *Dot*, *Dottie*
Edward	Ned, Ted, Eduardo, Edvard, Duarte
Elizabeth	*Eliza*, *Isabel*, *Elsa*, *Lisa*, *Elsie*, *Elspeth*, *Lilian*, *Bessy*, *Betty*, *Libby*, *Liz*, *Lizzy*
Francis	*Frances*, Frank, Francesco, *Francesca*, François, *Françoise*, *Francine*, Franz
Frederick	Fred, Freddie, *Frederica*, Friedrich
George	*Georgia*, Georges, Jorge, Jurgen, Jerzy, *Georgina*, *Georgiana*, *Georgette*
Gerald	Geraldo, Jerry
Helen	*Helena*, *Elena*, *Ellen*, *Nell*

James	Jaime, Jacob, Jacques, Jake, *Jacqueline*, Seamus, Iago, Jim, Jimmy, <u>Jamie</u>
Jane	*Joan, Joanne, Jeanne, Jean, Siobhán, Juana* (*see* **John**)
Jeffrey	Geoffrey, Jeff, Geoff
John	Ian, Sean, Shawn, Jean, Juan, Giovanni, Johann, Johannes, Hans, Ivan, Evan, Jack, *Jackie* (*see* ***Jane***)
Jonathan	Jon, Jonny
Katherine	*Catherine, Kate, Cathy, Katie, Kathleen, Caitlin, Katrine, Catrin, Katya, Katrinka, Kitty, Kit*
Margaret	*Marguerite, Margarita, Margery, Margot, Meg, Greta, Gretchen, Rita, Pearl, Margie, Maggie, Peggy, Peg*
Mark	Marco, Marcos, Marcus
Mary	*Maria, Marie, Miriam, Marion, Marian, Máire, Moira, Mia, Mitzi, May*
Mathilda	*Maud, Tilly, Mattie*
Nicholas	Nicolo, Nikolai, Nick, Klaus
Nicola	*Nicole, Nicolette, Nicky* (*see* **Nicholas**)
Patrick	*Patricia*, <u>*Pat*</u>, *Trisha, Trish, Patsy*, Padraig, Paddy
Paul	*Paula*, Pablo, Paolo, Paulo, *Pauline, Paulette*
Richard	Ricardo, Rick, Dick
Robert	*Roberta*, Roberto, Rupert, <u>Robin</u>, Rob, Bob
Stephen	Steven, Steve, *Stephanie, Steffany*, Stefan, Stefano, Estéban, Étienne, <u>Stevie</u>
Susan	*Sue, Susanna, Suzanne, Shoshana, Suzie, Suzette*
Thomas	Tommaso, Tom, *Thomasina, Tamsin*
William	Will, Bill, Guglielmo, Guillaume, Wilhelm, *Wilhelmina, Wilma, Willa*

Homonyms

Homonyms are words that sound the same but that mean different things. Many homonyms are spelled the same, such as the adjective *faint* (indistinct) and the verb *faint* (to collapse). In your Thesaurus, homonyms that are spelled the same are usually listed as different numbered senses of the entry word, as you will see if you look up **faint**. There are also homonyms that sound the same but are spelled differently. This kind of homonym is listed in small capital letters at the end of the whole entry. Thus, you will see that the entry for **faint** ends with the word FEINT. This means that although *feint* sounds like *faint*, it means something different. Your Thesaurus includes these homonyms in order to help you find the one you are looking for. For example, *choose* and *chews* are homonyms. **Choose** is entered in your Thesaurus, but if you need another word for *chews*, you should look at the entry for **chew**.

Below is a list of many common homonyms. This list will help you to find other spellings of homonyms. Words printed in *italics* are not always homonyms. For example, many people pronounce *ladder* and *latter* the same, with a *d*-like sound; however, some people use a *t* sound in *latter*, making it sound different from *ladder*.

air / heir	bearing / baring
aloud / allowed	beat / beet
alter / altar	beer / bier
aunt / ant	billed / build
awful / offal	birth / berth
bait / bate	bite / byte / bight
band / banned	block / bloc
baron / barren	blue / blew
base / bass	boar / bore
bay / bey	board / bored
beach / beech	bold / bowled
bear / bare	bow / bough

bowl / boll
boy / *buoy*
braid / brayed
brake / break
brood / brewed
bruise / brews
build / billed
buy / by / bye
cash / cache
cast / caste
cause / caws
cell / sell
cellar / seller
censor / censer
cent / sent / scent
chaste / chased
choose / chews
chute / shoot
cite / sight / site
chord / cord / cored
coarse / course
coax / cokes
colonel / kernel
compliment / complement
core / corps
council / counsel
coward / cowered
creak / *creek*
crick / *creek*
cue / queue
current / currant
cymbal / symbol
daze / days
dear / deer
dense / dents

dew / *due* / do
die / dye
dire / dyer
discreet / discrete
earn / urn
faint / feint
fair / fare
fate / *fête*
fawn / faun
faze / phase
feat / feet
file / phial
flair / flare
flee / flea
flow / floe
flower / flour
fold / foaled
for / four / fore
foul / fowl
freeze / frees / frieze
gamble / gambol
gate / gait
gauge / gage
graze / grays
great / grate
guest / guessed
guilt / gilt
guise / guys
hail / hale
hall / haul
handsome / hansom
hear / here
heard / herd
heed / he'd
heir / air

heroine / heroin
hew / hue
hide / hied
high / hie / hi
higher / hire
him / hymn
hoard / horde
hoarse / horse
hold / holed
holy / wholly
hose / hoes
humorous / humerus
idle / idol
instance / instants
intense / intents
jam / jamb
key / quay
knave / nave
knead / need
knight / night
knot / not
know / no
ladder / *latter*
lane / lain
lair / layer
lapse / laps
lax / lacks
lay / lei
layer / lair
leaf / lief
leak / leek
lean / lien
least / leased
lessen / lesson
liable / libel

liar / lyre
lie / lye
load / lode / lowed
loan / lone
loot / lute
low / lo
made / maid
magnet / magnate
mail / male
manner / manor
mantel / mantle
marshal / martial
maze / maize
mean / mien
meat / meet / mete
medal / meddle / *metal* / *mettle*
metal / *mettle*
might / mite
mince / mints
miner / minor
mode / mowed
more / *mower*
morning / mourning
new / knew / gnu
news / gnus
none / nun
oh / owe
one / won
pact / packed
pail / pale
pain / pane
pair / pear / pare
past / passed
patience / patients
pause / paws

peace / piece
peal / peel
pedal / peddle / *petal*
peer / pier
phrase / frays
plain / plane
pour / pore / *poor*
praise / prays / preys
pray / prey
pride / pried
principal / principle
prize / pries
rack / wrack
rain / reign / rein
raise / raze
rancor / ranker
rap / wrap
rapt / rapped / wrapped
read / reed
real / reel
residence / residents
rest / wrest
review / revue
rhyme / rime
right / write / rite / wright
ring / wring
road / rode / rowed
roll / role
rough / ruff
row / roe
rude / rood / rued
rye / wry
sail / sale
see / sea
seem / seam

seen / scene
seize / seas / sees
sense / cents / scents
sew / so / sow
sheer / shear
side / sighed
size / sighs
slay / sleigh
slow / sloe
some / sum
sore / soar
sole / soul
staid / stayed
stake / steak
stare / stair
stationary / stationery
steal / steel
straight / strait
style / stile
surge / serge
sweet / suite
sword / soared
symbol / cymbal
tact / tacked
tale / tail
taper / tapir
taut / taught
tax / tacks
team / teem
tear / tare
tease / teas / tees
tense / tents
throw / throe
time / thyme
to / too / two

tool / tulle
tow / toe
tract / tracked
trust / trussed
turn / tern
unreal / unreel
use / ewes
vain / vein / vane
veil / vale
vile / vial
wade / weighed
wait / weight
waive / wave
wane / wain
war / wore
ward / warred
warn / worn
waste / waist
way / weigh / whey
weak / week
wear / *where* / ware
weather / *whether* / wether
weave / we've
wee / we
weed / we'd
wet / *whet*
wheel / we'll / weal
whine / wine
which / witch
whoa / woe
whole / hole
wild / *whiled*
wind / wined / *whined*
wood / would
worn / warn

wretch / retch
wrote / rote
yoke / yolk
you / ewe
Yule / you'll